ID0757755

URBAN ENVIRONMENTS AND HUMAN BEHAVIOR

An Annotated Bibliography

Community Development Series

SERIES EDITOR: Richard P. Dober

Volumes Published and in Preparation

ENCLOSING BEHAVIOR / Robert Bechtel

URBAN ENVIRONMENTS AND HUMAN BEHAVIOR: An Annotated Bibliography / edited by Gwen Bell, Edwina Randall, and Judith E. R. Roeder

EDUCATIVE ENVIRONMENTS FOR CHILDREN: Implications for Design and Research / edited by Gary Coates

COMPUTER GRAPHICS FOR COMMUNITY DEVELOPMENT / William Fetter

URBAN GRAPHICS / William J. Hannon

EVALUATING THE GEOLOGIC ENVIRONMENT / Roy E. Hunt

DESIGNING FOR HUMAN BEHAVIOR / edited by Jon T. Lang, Charles H. Burnette, and David A. Vachon

APPLYING THE SYSTEMS APPROACH TO URBAN DEVELOPMENT / Jack LaPatra

ENVIRONMENTAL DESIGN: The Role of Preference, Perception and Satisfaction / George L. Peterson

ENVIRONMENTAL DESIGN RESEARCH, VOL. I: Selected Papers / edited by Wolfgang F. E. Preiser

ENVIRONMENTAL DESIGN RESEARCH, VOL. II: Symposia and Workshops / edited by Wolfgang F. E. Preiser

MIXED LAND USES: New Concepts on Old Foundations / Dimitri Procos

ARCHITECTURAL PHOTOGRAPHY: Techniques / Cervin Robinson

TERRAIN ANALYSIS: A Guide to Site Selection Using Aerial Photographic Interpretation / Douglas Way

URBAN ENVIRONMENTS AND HUMAN BEHAVIOR

An Annotated Bibliography

GWEN BELL
Department of Urban Affairs
University of Pittsburgh

with

EDWINA RANDALL
Corapolis, Pennsylvania

and

JUDITH E. R. ROEDER
Pittsburgh Department of City Planning

Dowden, Hutchinson & Ross, Inc.

Stroudsburg, Pennsylvania

Z
5942
.B35

Copyright © 1973 by Dowden, Hutchinson & Ross, Inc.
Library of Congress Catalog Card Number: 72–88982
ISBN: 0–87933–016–3

All rights reserved. No part of this book covered by the copyrights
hereon may be reproduced or transmitted in any form or by any
means—graphic, electronic, or mechanical, including photocopying,
recording, taping or information storage and retrieval systems—without
written permission of the publisher.

Manufactured in the United States of America.

Exclusive distributor outside the United States and Canada:
John Wiley & Sons, Inc.

Series Editor's Preface

These are the critical years for those who believe design can improve the human condition. The idea is as old as Utopian thought. What is new? The melding of observable behavior patterns, and understanding of client aspirations and needs, and the use of the emerging technology to affect the built environment.

Whether this is the basis for a new aesthetic is not yet clear. But no conscionable planner or designer can ignore a growing body of useful information waiting application. How to find it and use it is no easy task. We are fortunate then that Gwen Bell's pathfinding bibliography is now available, advancing the art, the process, and the product.

Richard P. Dober, AIP

53396

Preface and Acknowledgments

This bibliography was started out of frustration. There was no book or set of readings that could provide master's candidates in urban planning an understanding of urban design that would have meaning for them. Picture books on urban form filled with the picturesqueness of European cities and the grossness, if not camp, of U.S. cities abound. Little understanding of the meaning of design can be gained from this path. Thus, a search for the appropriate literature was necessary.

In 1969, each student in an urban form class at the Graduate School of Public and International Affairs, University of Pittsburgh, reviewed five years of one of the major planning or architectural journals bringing back notes on every article that tied together their interests in social planning, human behavior, and urban renewal with urban form. The annotations of each member were reviewed, punched onto cards, and compiled by Paula MacGreevy (Ricci). This was published by the Council of Planning Librarians as *Behavior and Environment,* Exchange Bibliography Number 123. There were about 150 annotations in this document, of which one-third were irrelevant.

The next year, this bibliography served as a working tool for a new class of students, who re-evaluated all citations and updated the search. Marcia Thompson

compiled and edited the annotations which were circulated to a limited number
of people as *Social Activities in Urban Space,* part of the Environmental Planning
Series, a joint publication of the Graduate School of Public and International Affairs
and the Graduate School of Public Health at the University of Pittsburgh.

In the fall of 1971, the third class on urban form continued the development
of this bibliographic tool. A tree search into the source material began, i.e., articles
or books were searched which were referenced in several of the works already
in the bibliography. This led to an appreciation of those social scientists who had
a significant impact and also closed groups that circuitously cited each other.
Since designers as a group tend not to document their ideas, the tree search
did not prove to be a useful method for evaluating conceptual influence. From
this mechanistic method the project moved to a fourth and last stage of comprehensive conceptualization.

Edwina Randall and Judith Roeder joined me in bringing the diverse material
into a holistic format. A framework was developed that tested each document
in terms of its relevance to both behavior and urban form. Then the entries were
divided into three sets: those that approached the problem from a design viewpoint,
from a social science viewpoint, and finally in terms of a synthesis in the urban
framework.

All citations have been read by at least two people, one of the three major
authors as well as one of the members of the classes that worked on it. Each
annotation is signed with the initials of its author:

GB—Gwen Bell	ET—Ed Thomas
ER—Edwina Randall	EW—Eileen Windemere
JR—Judy Roeder	GS—Giselle Stephanopoli
AD—Art Draper	HS—Heidi Shull
AT—Alan Tisdale	JD—Jerry Dettore
AW—Ann Winkelstein	JZ—John Zimmer
BB—Robert Booth	KF—Kim Fellner
BJ—Barbara Jones	LC—Luis Correa
BO—Bea Ornitz	LG—Louis Grumet
DF—David Friedman	LM—Lester Mitchell
DW—Diana Wahl	MK—Margrit Kennedy
EB—Emerson Bryan	MS—Margaret Sperling
ERR—Ed Russel	MT—Marcia Thompson
ES—Elizabeth Stern	NM—Nancy Mason

Preface and
Acknowledgments

NSM—Norma Sue Madden
PM—Paula MacGreevey Ricci
RB—Richard Bickel
RJD—Robert DiAiso
RL—Richard Lyles

SES—Sue Ellen Semple
SS—Susan Stacy
TL—Tish Langord
WP—Walter Plosila

Compilation of the material for the manuscript was made much easier by the help of the librarian of the Graduate School of Public and International Affairs, Mr. Nicholas Caruso. The processing of the manuscript itself was facilitated by Mss. Sue Abegglen and Sandy Haber.

Finally, a special note of thanks must be given to the Carnegie Foundation who have funded Edwina Randall and Judith Roeder under a program for mid-career women in Urban Planning and Administration at the Graduate School of Public and International Affairs.

Gwen Bell
University of Pittsburgh
December 1972

Contents

Series Editor's Preface **v**
Preface and Acknowledgments **vi**
Introduction **xii**

FORETHOUGHT **1**
　　Human Needs **2**
　　Comprehensive Approaches to Human Needs **3**
　　Environment and Health **8**

PART I: DESIGN APPROACHES TO THE URBAN ENVIRONMENT **13**

　Perception Studies **14**
　　Visual Perception **14**
　　Auditory Perception **18**
　　Value Responses to Urban Visual Stimuli **21**
　　The Development of Research Techniques **28**
　　Special Perceptions of the Handicapped and Aged **33**
　　Citizen Participation in the Design Process **34**
　　Citizens in the Planning and Design Process **35**
　　Advocacy Planning **40**

Contents

Examples of Design with User-Participants **42**
Characteristics of Participants **45**
Training for Participation **47**
Community Planning without Professionals **48**
Density and Privacy **51**
Density Measurements **55**
Family Private Space **57**
Personal Space **59**
The Design Process **64**
Perception and the Designer (or, Whither Architectural Determinism?) **73**
Pattern Language **84**

PART II: SOCIAL SCIENCE APPROACHES TO THE URBAN ENVIRONMENT **87**

The Ecological Tradition **88**
The Behavioral Setting **94**
Approaches to the Residential Environment **100**
Social Interaction Studies **105**
Urban Space for Interaction **107**
Neighboring: Who Talks to Whom? and How Does the Researcher Know? **111**
Time and Activity Budgets **121**
Methodologies of Time-Budget Studies **122**
Land Use and Activity Studies **125**
Leisure Time Analysis **128**
Social Science Methodologies **132**

PART III: THE FRAMEWORK OF THE URBAN ENVIRONMENT **137**

The Urban Subcenter **139**
The Central Node **141**
The Shopping Center **143**
New Towns **145**
Spatial Perceptions of the Pedestrian **149**
The Neighborhood **152**
Community Studies **152**
Planning for the Neighborhood **157**
Definitions and Criticism of Neighborhood **158**
The Size of the Neighborhood **165**
Neighborhood Boundaries **168**

Planning for Facilities and Amenities **169**
Population Balance within the Neighborhood **172**
The Small Neighborhood **176**
Childspace in the Small Neighborhood **179**
Emotional Attributes of the Small Neighborhood **186**
The Dwelling Group **192**
High-Density Housing **193**
Health and the High Rise **194**
Managememt of the High Rise **195**
Attitudes to High-Rise Living **200**
Middle Density Housing **206**
Children in the Dwelling Group **209**
The Dwelling Unit **211**
Health Maintenance in the Dwelling Unit **215**
Housing Adjustment to People **217**
Human Adjustment to Housing **220**
People's Movement to Get a House **222**
The Room **225**
Adult Work Space **229**
Childhood Learning Space **232**

Afterthought: Bibliographies and Sets of Readings **235**
Guide to Periodicals **242**
Key Periodicals **243**
Other Journals Utilized **244**
Index of Annotations **247**
Subject Index **261**

Introduction

The remaining years of this century will see new construction to total more than that existing in the world of 1972. There are various projections detailing the extent and characteristics of this development, but only catastrophic events will prevent the occurrence of a vast increase in the *quantity* of construction. This is a fact. But there are no facts, or documented forecasts, concerning the *quality* of the environment that this massive building activity will create.

This guide is addressed first to those who will be responsible for the design of this forthcoming construction bonanza: the architects, urban designers, landscape architects, and planners who should be aware of the requirements of the users of environments.

But the process that ends with the construction of a building, a group of buildings, a park, a neighborhood, or a city begins long before a designer is involved. The important decisions are made by public housing authorities, federal, state, and local urban planning agencies, and financial and corporate institutions. These references should be useful, second, to administrators of these agencies in developing an understanding of the behavioral effects of their decisions which will determine the long range profitability as measured in the development of human potential. The vast sums involved in the construction of housing, schools, community facilities, and even work places for people of differing social and cultural backgrounds have their ultimate payoff not in economic rent but in human development. It is only in rare cases that the people occupying urban space have any real say in its design. These are the super-rich who hire architects and the superpoor, the squatters who design and build their own houses. But the school children, laborers, theatre goers, and office workers as well as those who live in tract houses and apartments, have no control over their environment. Most buildings are designed by a combination of contractors and bureaucratic administrators.

Third, this reference is aimed at social and behavioral scientists who provide the information that is the basis for administrative and design decisions. Studies on human needs and perception, as well as on social characteristics, supply background data for understanding client groups as well as for programming projects of construction and reconstruction. Although social and behavioral scientists are generally more attuned to bibliographical sources than designers and builders, they are generally unaware of the complementary design literature.

The fourth group to whom this guide is addressed are the builders (and their engineers) who are responsible for the construction of most of the man-made environment. The builder uses marketing data and engineering standards to design everything from highways to houses, generally without the aid of an architect or designer, and most definitely without social and behavioral scientists. The literature in this guide is important to contractors as it is directed to impact studies, which are increasingly being required as part of building programs.

Finally, this book is addressed to the educators of designers and social and behavioral scientists, as well as to their students. Faculty, research staffs, and graduate students should be at the frontiers of knowledge regarding the urban environment. Yet the literature is so diffuse and diverse that they too tend to intuitively forge ahead without searching for complementary studies. This guide should provide both a reference to what has been done and a directive to those areas needing research.

It is not the purpose of this publication to be a single source for information relating people and activities to physical space. The chronological arrangement of the annotations allows the reader to determine the sequence of development of data and which original sources should be referred to for primary data to answer a specific need.

The information has been set into a basic category system of three major parts prefaced with a forethought that describes and lists references on the subject of "Human Needs." The first part, "Design Approaches to the Environmental Fit."

examines the literature most closely related to the participants in the formulation of the built environment. It begins with a review of information on perception, from physiological responses to value judgments made by people within individual social and cultural groups, the research techniques that have been developed to do experimental work in perception, and the special problems encountered by the handicapped and the aged in perceiving and using urban space.

The citizen, the user of urban space, as the client for urban buildings, is at last becoming involved increasingly in determining what is built, where it is to be located, whom it should serve, and how it should operate. This necessary input has been included in the design process section.

Although there is a long tradition of studies about density, until recently these have focussed on statistical ratios of people to space rather than social indicators of human welfare. A review of these studies points to the potential for designing satisfactory high density living, where private family space, indoor and outdoor, is provided separately from semi-public, small neighborhood open space, and public open space.

The last section of Part One sets forth the process of design in all its parts and reviews projections and recommendations to improve the design process. The designers' own perceptions of the physical setting follow. The ability to design an environment producing a "behavioral setting" which will encourage the users of urban space to behave in a predetermined manner, "architectural determinism," is discussed in this section.

Many of the concepts in Part One have been developed by social scientists speaking directly to the design process. Those social science approaches less directly related to architecture and planning have been incorporated in Part Two.

The ecological tradition of social scientists concerned with understanding urbanism is traced back to the Chicago School of sociologists and the French human geographers. The contemporary counterparts to these include the environmental psychologists and the social critics of contemporary suburban life styles.

Studying the residential environment has been a tradition among the sociologists who are concerned with human interaction and urbanists looking for alternative measures of evaluation of total impact rather than "cost–benefit–analysis." The major topic of Part Two is social interaction, the patterns that lead from atomistic societies of individuals to community. This has implicit interest for designers as the annotations consider the environment as a variable in nurturing and hindering positive and negative patterns of socialization.

Ecological, socialization, and time and activity studies provide another independent means for the evaluation of community. These provide insight into spatial frictions which cause variations in life style as evidenced in patterns of daily activity. Researchers in the three specializations often use similar techniques. These are listed together in a separate section which covers source material on social science methodologies.

Part Three brings together that literature dealing with particular subsets of the built environment, ranging in scale from the room to the subcenter. Every entry addresses the question of environmental design fit at its level. On the one hand there are no architectural plans included and on the other, no purely behavioral descriptions of such places as "neighborhood." This section is extraordinarily important as such concepts as personal space, social interaction, and behavioral settings, which were discussed in the first two sections are considered in the complexity of the urban framework itself.

Most of the information available to architects, urban designers, and physical planners consists primarily of product information, standard practice manuals, aesthetic urban form historical analyses, and utopian polemics. Very little of this data describes, for the designer, the characteristics that the physical environment should provide to achieve social goals.

Product information is the only body of data used by designers that in any way is adequate. Sweets Catalog, engineering manuals, and Graphic Standards type of information describe, often very colorfully and usually accurately, materials with which the environment is constructed. There is no reference in this literature, however, to people and how they respond to these materials, i.e., how the spaces formed by these materials serve the needs and satisfy the aspirations of the occupants of these spaces. Standard practice manuals give information of space requirements for certain kinds of activities, relationships between functional activities, numbers of facilities for certain population types, and functional data in terms of movement patterns. The empirical information is valid only given the existing environment as the fundamental constant.

There is an extensive collection of books and articles dealing with urban form and aesthetics, which have little reference to behavior. For certain human activities, such as learning, worshipping, shopping, there is information on building types and facilities usually based on functional characteristics of movement patterns extrapolated from empirical data rather than on behavioral characteristics of the users. The literature on urban form tends to analyze the spatial form of urban areas with land use and transportation as variables of location theories. In contrast to a high degree of analytical objectivity in functional urban studies, those on aesthetics tend to be historical and subjective.

There have always been both deliberate and intuitive urban designers and authors of architectural utopias. The Greeks had Utopian thinkers. The idea of Utopia long predates the industrial revolution, which brought about a spate of new Utopian thinkers, many architects who expressed their thoughts in physical constructs.

Ebenezer Howard thought industrial society could be improved by building garden cities. Patrick Geddes also believed that there was a relationship between the physical form of the city and the improvement of the lives of the residents. Camillo Sitte was so convinced of the satisfaction that could be derived from beautiful public spaces that his whole concept of city development was based upon this idea. Frank Lloyd Wright believed that each family should be given its own acre.

Since the beginning of the industrial revolution the rate of social change has far outpaced the rate of physical change in the urban structure. Much of the shape of the built environment in the twentieth century is a reproduction of historically functional forms including the application, as decoration, of no longer meaningful symbols. These forms are being imposed on a society that has a new set of functional, social, and psychological requirements which the replicated forms cannot serve.

Design researchers have recently begun to develop a methodology to produce a vocabulary that considers behavior. Such terminology must relate design, societal goals, and human behavior in a positively reinforcing framework.

The first of many difficulties involved in the new approach is to convince designers that they can only contribute to the creation of environments if they understand the operation of the society and have rid themselves of the romantically enchanting belief that the "city beautiful" is a fit setting for human activities. This idea is as strongly held by most designers as the concept of mass production to solve housing problems. Mass produced or industrialized housing, new cities, either horizontal, vertical, or combined, the city beautiful, all are glamorous ideas that enchant designers and prevent them from facing the realities of designing environments for real people in a real society. Those entrusted with the design of the environment must come to understand that these solutions are too simple to create places in which a socially complex and technologically advanced society can function effectively.

FORETHOUGHT

Human Needs

Architecture, urban design, and urban planning find a common base in the satisfaction of human needs. At the beginning of each project, generally, some hierarchy of needs is proposed that would relate to that particular scheme. Sometimes these are sensible and other times foolish. The need for roots with the past can lead to justifying Greek temples or English cottages in the American southwest. At the same time, the need for modern sanitary equipment may lead to defacing or even tearing down historic buildings which provide communities with roots.

Two problems are apparent: First, there is no societal listing of environmental needs; and second, when such lists are compiled they often lack any operational specifications relating to the building (or conservation) of urban structures. Neither of these is likely to be solved for many years.

This section of the bibliography, then, mainly puts the problems to the builders of the cities and points out some of the literature that will begin to frame operational definitions of human needs and potential environmental responses. Not one of the authors is an architect or planner, but on the one hand they are psychiatrists, psychologists, and philosophers who are deeply concerned with the development of man, and on the other, health professionals who relate the epidemiology of disease to its environment. These two approaches are treated separately.

Comprehensive Approaches to Human Needs

A. H. Maslow's "A Theory of Human Motivation," published in 1943, remains the approach to human needs that is most often cited by others. He has constructed a hierarchical framework in which the lower-level (more basic) needs take precedence over higher-level ones, i.e., the frustration of fulfilling physiological needs reduces the importance of such high level needs as aesthetic pleasure or intellectual curiosity. His specific ordering goes: physiological, safety and security, affection and belonging, esteem, self-actualization, and cognitive and aesthetic. In such an ordering, different standards for different total levels of living can be effectuated, e.g., unless sanitary facilities are sufficient to prevent disease, little emphasis should be placed on special environments for learning or socializing. While there is logic in his order it is relatively difficult to apply in a real situation for a variety of reasons: different castes (or classes) in the same community may be on different levels in the hierarchy; in the middle levels substitutions might occur as people sacrifice in one domain in order to excel in another; and there are those who say affection and belonging bring safety and security, not vice versa, etc. Still Maslow's listing is the most comprehensive and ordered to date.

While many people cite Maslow's listing, very few are aware of the contributions of Simone Weil, whose book *The Need for Roots* was published in 1952, with a fascinating introduction by T. S. Eliot. This lengthy essay was written as policy to be pursued for the rebuilding of France after World War II. Unfortunately, the book was also written during the last year or so of Simon Weil's life, and there is no record that any of her memoranda were translated directly to the rebuilding of her country. Her first paragraph sums up the basis for the development of the needs to be accounted for:

The notion of obligations comes before that of rights, which is subordinate and relative to the former. A right is not effectual by itself, but only in relation to the obligation to which it corresponds, the effective exercise of a right springing not from the individual who possesses it, but from other men who consider themselves as being under a certain obligation toward him. Recognition of an obligation makes it effectual. An obligation which goes unrecognized by anybody loses none of the full force of its existence. A right which goes unrecognized by anybody is not worth very much. (p. 3.)

3

She makes no attempt to order her list of human needs but explains each one in full detail. They are: order, liberty, obedience, responsibility, equality, hierarchism, honor, punishment, freedom of opinion, security, risk, private property, collective property, and truth. These are the dependent variables which only matter if there is the rootedness of people. The middle third of the book deals with uprootedness of towns, countryside, and nationhood (with frequent references to the historic events in Europe since 1789) and the last third with the growing of roots (reconstruction). Direct analogies are possible with any of the major changes that affect the human being in his environment, e.g., freedom from slavery, urban renewal, and forced migration.

None of the other authors deal with the total problem. Each approaches only one facet assuming that many of the basic needs are already met within advanced industrial societies. They then approach the question of quality, with some concepts of how it might be achieved.

All of the authors are looking for noneconomic measures for human development. This noneconomic emphasis continues from this first section all the way through the citations until the very last grouping in the book on the room. The majority of the writings on the room consider it basic space for man to work and to learn. It is hard to imagine that any of the large scale concepts of human needs can be implemented when in the design of the most personal space, efficient human performance is the main consideration. Here is the challenge for the designers!

1943
MASLOW, A. H.
"A Theory of Human Motivation"
Psychological Review, May 1943, **50**, 370–397.

Maslow establishes the existence of basic human needs: physiological, safety, love, esteem, self-actualization, aesthetics. He asserts that man is motivated by "the desire to achieve or maintain the various conditions upon which these basic satisfactions rest and by certain more intellectual desires." Man is thus a perpetually wanting animal and thwarting of any opportunity for need satisfaction results in a threat to his person. A classic theoretical construct in social psychology. (MT)

1952
WEIL, SIMONE
The Need for Roots
New York: G. P. Putnam's Sons, 1952; Harper Colophon Books, 1971.

A philosophic work by a French intellectual who actually worked in an automobile factory and as a field laborer. An examination of rootlessness and a criticism of the spiritual weakness of France prior to World War II. Prepared as a guide for the reconstruction of France. Theoretical guidelines of human needs are included as well as practical suggestions for combatting rootlessness. (ER)

1965
DE JOUVENAL, BERTRAND
"Utopia for Practical Purposes"
Daedalus, Spring 1965, **94** (2), 437–453; *Ekistics,* June 1965, **115,** 325–329.

This French philosopher considers that the happy day for everyman is the utopia for which to strive; vacations then should not be necessary. He also points out that the "problem of work" is an essential problem as this points the way toward happy everyday lives. If this were solved then there would be no problem of leisure time. (GB)

1968
COLES, ROBERT
Children of Crisis: A Study in Courage and Fear
New York: Delta Book, 1968.

The first volume in a series which explores the lives of children in various regional settings. It contains no psychological jargon, just an astonishingly literate view of the total setting in the south in which Black children braved early school integration. Hopeful study of the courage of children and how the civil rights movement gave purpose to their lives. (ER)

DUBOS, RENE
"Man and His Environment: Adaptation and Interaction"
The Fitness of Man's Environment—Smithsonian Annual II, Washington, D.C.:
Smithsonian Institute Press, 1968.

Concise presentation and good sampling of the views of a concerned microbiologist and experimental pathologist. His special emphasis is the evolutionary adaptation and "the child as father of man." His conclusion is that life experience determines what genetic endowments are converted into functional attributes. Darwinian changes may affect mental characteristics. Makes a convincing plea for diversity in surroundings. Sees danger in cultural homogenization, as specialized societies of the past have been vulnerable to collapse when conditions changed. His ecological view is not for a steady-state ecosystem but for all kinds of environment—a biological richness of the human species. (ER)

HALL, EDWARD T.
"Human Needs and Inhuman Cities"
The Fitness of Man's Environment—Smithsonian Annual II, Washington, D.C.:
Smithsonian Press, 1968.

The major fault in our urban environment is that the cultural structure is ignored. Hall calls for housing criteria which balance the sensory input with consistent culturally conditioned needs. He finds that design students can be trained in his philosophy in half the time of liberal arts student. (ER)

1970
FROMM, ERICH
"Humanistic Planning"
The Crisis in Psychoanalysis, New York: Holt, Rinehart & Winston, 1970; *Journal of the American Institute of Planners,* March 1972, **38** (No. 2), 67–71.

This eloquent author makes his point most effectively: "Integrated planning, heretofore, requires integration of the system 'man' into the system 'enterprise –government–society.' It is quite possible that one might find that something which is economically efficient may be humanly, and hence socially, detrimental, and we must be prepared to make choices between our real needs—either the maximal unfolding of man or the maximal growth of production and consumption." (GB)

HAYTHORN, WILLIAM H.
"A Needs by Sources of Satisfaction Analysis of Environmental Habitability"
Habitability Papers. Vol. 2. *Proceedings, 1st National Symposium on Habitability, May 1970*. *Ekistics*, Vol. 30, September 1970, **178**, 200-203.

This is a working paper which reviews the literature and major theories postulated by social philosophers and psychologists as they address themselves to the definition of human needs. Maslow's theory which identified physiological needs, social needs, safety and security and intellectual needs forms the crux of Haythorn's discussion of how social, political, and architectural systems satisfy these needs. Relates easily to Doxiadis' humanistic philosophy of planning. (MT)

PANDE, SHASHI K.
"From Hurried Habitability to Heightened Habitability"
Ekistics September 1970, **178**, 213–217.

Shashi Pande, a well-adapted Indian psychiatrist practicing at Johns Hopkins, questions the current approaches to accounting for the "good life." He argues for the rejuvenation of a modified extended family system so that natural versus professional relationships will be restored, efficiency de-emphasized, a genuinely emotive plane of life developed in the natural habitat of the family, the aged rehabilitated where they belong, teenagers involved, an "emotional security system" rather than the "social" security system instituted, honor for the family reinstituted, the tough exterior of rootless people softened, and conduct regulated by consensual validation. He means to put himself out of business—the cause of any psychiatrist worth his salt. (GB)

1971
FOA, URIEL G.
"Interpersonal and Economic Resources"
Science, January 1971; *Ekistics,* September 1971, **32**, 192–194.

The author constructs a classification of social exchange based on two coordinates of resource characterization: concreteness versus symbolism and particularism versus universalism. He discusses the system as a tool for understanding the effects of urbanization upon human behavior. He notes the move with urbanization toward utilization of universal resources and suggests that solutions may not be in provision of more settings for such phenomena but in the return to the particular. (GB)

SKINNER, B. F.
Beyond Freedom and Dignity
New York: Alfred A. Knopf, 1971.

A mature variation on the theme of *Walden Two*. He makes a strong case for the environment as the instrument for societal change and finds our traditional concept of freedom faulty. The issue of those who disagree is really—who controls those who program? (ER)

Environment and Health

There has been no attempt made to completely cover this field; no material is included that relates to any of the specifics of sanitation, heating, ventilating, sunlight, etc. The related topic of density (which has an epidemiological relation to disease) is discussed separately from health as it is also important to other aspects of programming for the environmental fit.

The set of articles that is selected relate to the first half of this section as they deal primarily with "mental" rather than physical health, thus to the higher-order level needs (according to Maslow).

The listing begins with one of the American Public Health Association's monographs on housing. Others from their series are included in the sections on density and the neighborhood. It also includes one article from Leonard Duhl's book, *The Urban Condition,* which compiled a number of articles that he determined spoke to the question of health in the city.

1941

COMMITTEE ON THE HYGIENE OF HOUSING
Housing for Health
Lancaster, Pennsylvania: American Public Health Association, 1941.

This book contains a collection of written works by such authors as F. Stuart Chapin, Svend H. Riemer, and others. The completed volume contains contributions dealing with family life in home planning, social effects of good housing, planning for recreation, living space, housing surveys, health centers, and the relationship between health and housing. (GB)

1963
WILNER, DANIEL, AND ROSABELLE PRICE WALKELEY
"Effects of Housing on Health and Performance"
Duhl, L. (Ed.) *The Urban Condition*. New York: Basic Books, 1963.

A review of the results of 40 studies which investigated the relationship between housing types and physical and social pathologies. These studies served as the basis for an in-depth Johns Hopkins study, which is described. Results indicated that poor housing conditions were not exclusive determinants of maladjustment. Material and familial considerations also played a major role. (RB & MT)

1964
LIEBERMAN, JAMES E., AND LEONARD J. DUHL
"Physical and Mental Health in the City"
Annals of the American Academy of Political and Social Sciences, March 1964, **352**, 13–24.

The intimate relationship of problems of health and problems of the city forms the basis for a dynamic ecological approach to planning for physical and mental health in the city. Rational coordination is required in order to maximize the contributions of health professionals and city planners. After discussing the scope of the problem and health in the United States, the article offers some goals and ideals. (SS)

1967
MARTIN, A. E.
"Environment, Housing and Health"
Urban Studies, February 1967, **4** (No. 1).

This is an excellent review article from the epidemiological point of view of the interrelations between environment, housing, and health. It has an extensive bibliography and provides a good synthesis arriving at the following conclusions:

"1. During the past century a large number of studies have been undertaken indicating the influence of poor environment and bad housing on health.

2. In spite of the advances in epidemiological techniques there are serious difficulties in methodology and the results must therefore be interpreted with care.

3. The findings of such studies are true only for the social, economic and medical conditions under which they were made.

4. Although many of the effects of bad environment appear to be diminishing there may be isolated groups in the community where the effects may be more serious than may be apparent from community health indices.

5. The evidence shows the clear association of health with socio-economic conditions, overcrowding and air pollution. When these are eliminated the influence of other factors is slight.

6. Advances in medical treatment are having a specific effect in reducing the association between certain medical conditions and poor environment." (GB)

1968
MOLLER, CLIFFORD B.
Architectural Environment and Our Mental Health
New York: Horizon Press, 1968.

The author contends that the goal of architecture, through informed and improved design, must be to guide the inevitable interaction of structured space and man in meaningful and beneficial patterns—to permit an interaction which will contribute to mental health rather than to tension and frustration. He has little understanding of either the basic physical design processes nor health planning. This is a compilation (regurgitation) which is neither complete nor accurate nor very original. (NM & GB)

TIGER, LIONEL
Men In Groups
New York: Random House, 1969.

A sociological-biological study whose central point is that aggressive behavior is an outgrowth of the pattern of corporate male interaction. He traces the evolution of the male bond as a hominoid inheritance from the ecological patterns of primates and finds that it provides a social order and a constructive release of aggression. He further emphasizes that aggression and violence are not individually motivated but directed by the social interaction of males. Behavior "in situ" is not only effected by the physical environment but also by the biological nature of group members. The male bond is the 'spinal cord' which gives location and structure to communities.

He believes that both school and housing plans should make provisions for facilitating the male bond. (ER)

1972

FOX, DAVID J.

"Patterns of Morbidity and Mortality in Mexico City"

The Geographical Review, April 1972, **62** (No. 2), 151–85; *Ekistics,* September 1972, **34**, 166–174.

The author correlates environmental housing conditions and disease and mortality by age. The case study is interesting because the death rate has decreased in Mexico City due to inoculations and vaccinations, and the need is for environmental improvement. There is original data in this paper as well as detailed analysis. (GB)

PART 1: DESIGN APPROACHES TO THE URBAN ENVIRONMENT

The studies described in this section are specifically directed to the design professional responsible for the creation of the built environment. It should be a source of information which will improve his ability to design environments for human activities.

For the behavioral scientist, this information will be valuable in gaining a better understanding of how the designer operates. New areas of research may be discovered by noting what is not here.

The major areas treated in this section are:

1. perception studies that have been conducted by social scientists, psychologists, and urban designers;
2. the effects that density and privacy have on the occupants of the environments;
3. community participation, or methods that can be used to determine the needs and desires of the real clients of the designer;
4. the tools available for predetermining the effect of space on behavior of the user;
5. the methodology of the design process in modern society and the changes in this process needed to make design more effective.

Perception Studies

Visual Perception

It is difficult to believe that so little new research has been conducted in this field, so brilliantly begun by James J. Gibson in the 1940's culminating with the publication, in 1950, of his remarkable *The Perception of the Visual World,* which suggested a vast field for further research that might have been of enormous value to all designers of the physical environment. Gibson's work was based on the theories developed by the late Sir John H. Parsons, published as *An Introduction to the Theory of Perception* by the Cambridge University Press in 1927.

There is an urgent need for additional research of this kind to develop a *Graphic Standards* of the responses and real values of perception of visual stimuli so that designers are made aware of and have the ability to accurately predict the effects of the spaces and settings they are creating, as well as the percepts of the materials selected.

The only work in this area that has been uncovered in this assemblage of reports and books has involved the perception and response of drivers to stimuli based upon an analysis of roadside characteristics. The reason for this may well be the availability of research funds for studies of automobile safety. There is some overlap with studies of pedestrians and drivers relating to the characteristics of perceived patterns of urban space, as defined by edges or boundaries. In the work on the perception of urban form there is not much reference to the visual acuity of the viewer. There is no research, for example, detailing the ability of a viewer to perceive the spacing and texture of edge facilities. This kind of knowledge would permit the development of a vocabulary that would give the designer insight into the kinds of materials and spaces that could be used to provide an environment which would encourage occupants of a space to experience the spatial objectives of the designer rather than having the designer hope that the intended response will occur. Design is an intuitive process and will probably continue to be so. More information about the visual acuity of an observer and about the observers' response to a variety of visual stimuli would take some of the guesswork out of the design process. It is strongly recommended that much more be done in this field because it will allow major progress in the research on environmental determinism as well as on perception itself.

1927
PARSONS, SIR JOHN HERBERT
An Introduction to the Theory of Perception
New York: The Macmillan Company, 1927.

A landmark study of visual perception giving a complete and detailed analysis of the physiology of the eye as well as a comparative anatomy of the visual process. A thorough discussion of all facets of visual perception, including space, movement, dyseritic and epicritic vision, color vision, induction, visual excitation and conduction. (JR)

1950

GIBSON, JAMES J.

The Perception of the Visual World

Boston: Houghton-Mifflin Co., 1950.

Based on work begun to develop a method of training pilots and to study depth perception, a new hypothesis which Gibson calls a "ground theory" is opposed to the "air theory." He believes that there is literally no such things as a perception of space without the perception of a continuous background surface. The main principles of this theory are: (1) The elementary impressions of a visual world are those of surface and edge; (2) there is always some variable in stimulation . . . which corresponds to a property of the spatial world; (3) the stimulus variable within the retinal image to which a property of visual space corresponds need be only a correlate of that property, not a copy of it; (4) the unhomogeneities of the retinal image can be analyzed by the methods of number theory and modern geometry into a set of variables analogous to the variables of physical energy; and, (5) the problem of how we perceive the visual world can be directed into two problems to be considered separately; first, the perception of the substantial or spatial world and, second, the perception of the world of useful and significant things to which we ordinarily attend. This book is required reading for all designers. (JR)

1964

APPLEYARD, DONALD, KEVIN LYNCH, AND J. R. MEYER

The View from the Road

Cambridge: M.I.T. Press, 1964.

In this interesting and profusely illustrated book, the authors provide an outline of techniques which could be used to design highways that would clarify the driver's image of the environment and deepen his understanding of its meaning. Highways could be conscious works of art, making driving a coherent and delightful aesthetic experience. The visual experience of a driver has direct influence on his driving—speed can be regulated, boredom averted and a sense of goal achievement created by properly designed highways, thus improving safety of the driving experience. (HS)

THEIL, PHILIP
"Processional" Architecture
Journal of the American Institute of Architects, February 1964; *Ekistics,* June 1964, **17,** 410–413.

". . . movement forms the context of our spatial experience, and the challenge of the art of architecture lies in the structuring of this time-based pattern of experience so that it will be of value and significance to all those who will perceive in their own time and way."

1967
BECK, ROBERT
"Spatial Meaning and the Property of the Environment"
Research Paper 107, Department of Geography, University of Chicago, 1967; Reprinted by Proshansky, 1970.

Beck performed a study to test symbolic space preferences. His conclusions are weak and one doubts whether his symbols did in fact act as surrogates for space in terms of the following five dimensions: up-down, horizontal-vertical, left-right, dense-diffuse, and open-delineated. (GB)

SPIVACK, MAYER
"Sensory Distortions in Tunnels and Corridors"
Hospitals and Community Psychiatry, January 1967, **18,** 24–30.

"Any new physical environment, whether a bungalow, school, office building or jail, can have significant, immediate and perhaps long range effects upon the behavior of its occupants." Although this article concerns itself with interior hallways of mental hospitals and the effects of visual distortions, glare, and length thereof upon mentally disturbed patients, parallels can be drawn to street and sidewalk design and their effects upon motorists and pedestrians. (AT)

1971
VARMING, MICHAEL
"The Planning of Motorroads in the Landscape"
Ekistics, March 1971, **31,** 247–250.

A plea and a system for including driver performance and response in highway design to enhance the experience of traveling and to reduce accidents. Roads should be designed with the knowledge that driving quality results from the development of a visual rhythm in a time sequence. The visual analysis of the course of the route with photographs and interpretation of the response of drivers is a necessary step in the process of highway design (in addition to the usual political, economic, and engineering processes). (JR)

Auditory Perception

Noise pollution is easily recognized. There is factual, physical evidence that relates declining hearing ability in humans to intense levels of noise. Many communities have adopted standards of permissible emissions of noise. This is partly if not entirely a result of the measurability of noise. The recent national interest in pollution has concentrated on air, water, and noise. However, the national interest has only been focused on visual pollution that has been caused by billboards in open countrysides and uninhabited areas.

Because auditory perception is more easily measured than visual perception, and because modern technology has contributed disturbing amounts of noise-producing elements, some fine research has been conducted on the damage—physical and emotional—caused by noise pollution. Another contributing factor, of course, is the lowering of construction standards that results in buildings with much higher levels of sound transmission. Because of that, environmental noise impinges on the privacy of residents in almost all new housing.

The entries in this section include a basic study by Bolt, Beranek, and Newman, Inc., one of the foremost acoustical design firms in the country. This study was prepared for the Federal Housing Authority to identify noise sources, to determine the response of residents to levels of noise inside dwellings, and to recommend acceptable standards of tolerable sound levels for satisfactory human occupancy. Those standards have not yet been adopted, although the F.H.A. has adopted sound transmission levels for construction of buildings under federal programs. There is, however, a clear difference between acceptable sound transmission levels in walls, floors, and roofs and an acceptable level of sound inside a building, these are not necessarily related phenomena. The acceptable F.H.A. transmission levels do not consider the variety of sounds emitted in different neighborhoods, nor do they consider the sounds emitted from air conditioners and other mechanical gadgets that are installed in every new dwelling.

Henry Still in his book *In Quest of Quiet* discussed the effect of various forms of noise pollution on the lives of people and hypothesized about the effects of noise on their equilibrium. The acceptable level of noise varies from one culture to another. People in some other cultures would be disturbed without high levels of noise.

Warren Brodey and Michael Southworth have done work with the blind to measure the perceptual aspects of sound as a source of information about "place" paralleling the work of the group who have done similar research using mapping techniques for visual stimuli.

1964
BRODEY, WARREN
"Sound and Space"
American Institute of Architects Journal, July 1964, **29,** 58–60.

A description of the auditory perception of the blind and their sensitivity to space. (GB)

1967
BOLT, BERANEK, AND NEWMAN, INC.
Noise in Urban and Suburban Areas: Results of Field Studies
Los Angeles: Bolt, Beranek and Newman, Inc., 1967.

The Federal Housing Administration sponsored a research project to find better methods of design for comfort and privacy within the household. This study identified all significant noise sources, other than aircraft, known to create disturbances within the home; it analyzed the results to determine the response of residents to noisy situations. The objective of this research was to provide the F.H.A. information on the noise environment so that design for controlling noise could be improved. (GS)

1969
BRODEY, WARREN
"The Other Than Visual World of the Blind"
Ekistics, August 1969, **28,** 100–103; *Architectural Design,* January 1969, **39,** 9–10.

A report of a "perception study group" in which Brodey, a psychiatrist, attempted to formulate questions and search for answers to the problem of how we perceive. The blind students of the group described ways of perceiving their environment by their other senses. Several examples of sound, smell, and tactile ways of perceiving environment are discussed.

SOUTHWORTH, MICHAEL
"The Sonic Environment of Cities"
Environment and Behavior, June 1969.

Southworth builds on the work of W. Brodey with the blind to build up an auditory survey of Boston. He carries the work further by identifying visual–auditory correlations. Finally he proposes methods of sonic design. He concludes "our first actions toward escaping the visual bondage of the contemporary city would be twofold: (a) to reduce and control noise and (b) to increase the informativeness of the soundscape. These steps toward the sonic city would not only enhance city life by helping to overcome the stress and anonymity of today's visual city, but would be one measure for developing the sensory awareness of city residents and would provide an environment more responsive to human action and purpose."

1970
STILL, HENRY
In Quest of Quiet
Harrisburg, Pa.: Stackpole Books, 1970.

This book is divided into four sections: (1) the sounds of civilization; (2) the cost of high speed travel; (3) the case for tranquility; and (4) the nature of sound. It analyzes the extent that noise damages men's physical, emotional, and mental equilibrium. He introduces the concept of acoustic privacy regarding the dwelling unit, noise-producing situations, and man's life.

Value Responses to Urban Visual Stimuli

There is one master in the study of how people perceive spaces and identify with them. Kevin Lynch is the master, and the book cited so often is *The Image of the City*. This book is an analysis of the degree to which people can find the city and its different neighborhoods identifiable through their physical forms. The process of identification of "place" is a series of interconnected visual experiences for the residents. The technique used to determine the components that constitute imageability of a city was a survey asking residents to map the city and present the visual clues they use to know where they are. Lynch developed a vocabulary of five symbols—path, edge, node, district, and landmark—to define "place." Paths are described as routes with various characteristics that are identifiable by the user; primarily the continuity of the route. Although a route will often continue, it tends not to be identified as a path if its character changes by variations in land use, architectural forms, or directional changes. The edge is a barrier between two different kinds of areas which may be, but do not have to be, paths. The Charles River in Boston is given as an example of an edge that is not a path. Nodes are defined as the "strategic foci into which the observer can enter, typically either junctions of paths or concentrations of some characteristic." Districts are internally recognizable areas, "which the observer can mentally go inside of, and which have some common character." The definition of a district is not wholly visual, but also includes social clues, primarily indicating either class or ethnic composition of the residents or special land uses such as major commercial or entertainment and cultural centers. Landmarks are visually distinguishable buildings or spaces that tend to be unique to their location, i.e., either by contrasting with their surroundings or by being visible from far off areas.

Lynch believes that these elements are the building blocks in the design process, and that designers must make use of these to reinforce the imageability of the city. In designing paths, or buildings or spaces on paths, an analysis of the factors contributing to the special definition of the path should be made by measuring the visual clues of scale, orientation, shape, grain and texture of surfaces, setbacks, signage, etc. This process of visual analysis has been extended by several additional studies that can aid the designer in becoming aware of the existing visual qualities of a place, and in creating new visual scenarios which can provide a resident with a sense of identification.

The original work by Kevin Lynch has had a significant effect on designers only because of the usefulness of his analytical methods as a tool of description. Because Lynch has been required reading for every design student for a decade, and because of the value of his work in creating a framework into which personal observations can be placed, he has been successful. This is a tool for visual awareness, but not a design methodology. Some primary schools have developed methods for teaching visual awareness in very young children using the Lynch analysis. This is excellent. A visually aware generation will demand higher design standards in the built environment. However, it is very disheartening to note that there has been no effort made to use Lynch's work as a basis for the development of a design methodology, for the definition of the perceptive qualities of "grain and texture" or form, massing, landscaping, and scale. It can only be suggested that Lynch be read as the seminal and only work to which no exciting contributions have been made. What is really needed is an in-depth study of visual perception and acuity combined with the value perceptions that Lynch recognized.

LEE TERENCE
"Perceived Distance as a Function of Direction in the City"
Environment and Behavior, June 1970, **2,** 40–52

The decision to make a journey is compounded of many influences. The paper is concerned with one of the cost variables, distance. It proceeds on the assumption that there is lawfulness in the relationship between physical and perceived distance in cities. The author's hypothesis was that the residents' ideas of the city are characterized by focal orientation built up by the satisfaction of the city center and resulting in a foreshortening of distance in the downtown direction. This study which measured perceived distance for 22 varied destinations, located inward and outward from a single inception point, confirmed the hypothesis. (LC)

The graphical mapping technique that Lynch developed has been applied by some researchers while a verbal form of mapping to gather data about respondents, imagery of their cities has been used by others. The information developed in these studies confirms Lynch's findings. George Rand suggests that modern man is adapting to a changed time–distance scale. Based on interviews with both airplane pilots and taxi drivers, he found that the imagery of cities known to each of the two groups was markedly different. The results of his work demonstrate that time–movement scale strongly alters the perceived nature of the environment. Designers, however, seem to still operate as if man were confined to his two feet.

Comparative studies have also been carried out to determine the differences in response to the visual environment and to determine the kinds of visual cues recognized by people in different cultures. Very pronounced differences have been found, indicating that design rules will vary from one country to another and from one subculture to another.

1966
SEGALL, MARSHALL H., DONALD T. CAMPBELL, AND MELVILLE J. JESKOVITS
The Influence of Culture on Visual Perception
Indianapolis: Bobb Merrill Co., 1966.

A worldwide interdisciplinary study by anthropologists and psychologists which systematically measures the interrelationship between culture and individual perception. Reveals differences across culture in susceptibility to geometric or optical illusions. The report stresses that these differences are not racial. Major conclusions: We learn to perceive; in spite of the phenomenological absoluteness of perception, it is determined by habits of inference. These habits vary from society to society. A theoretical study of a technical nature. (ER)

1967

DART, FRANCIS E., AND PANNA LAL PRADHAN
"Cross Cultural Teaching of Science"
Science, Feb. 10, 1967, **155**, 3763, 649–656; *Ekistics,* March 1967, **23**, 174–176.

Asian and Hawaiian children are compared in terms of their visual representation of their environment. The survey showed the differences in perception and representation of space. Inferences are made regarding the importance of these differences. (GB)

1969

RAND, GEORGE
"Pre-Copernican Views of the City"
Architectural Forum, September 1969, **131,** 76–81.

The rapid rate of technological change makes Euclidian concepts of time and distance less valid as place indices. Man adapts by personalizing his image of the environment. He views spatially separate places as if they were an extension of the home realm. Taxi drivers and airplane pilots in Worcester, Massachusetts, were tested to determine their actual comprehension of the environment. The taxi drivers' image of the city was based on the known sequence of places and streets rather than comprehension of the topographical relationship of places to each other. The implication for new urban forms organized in terms of sequence of places and hierarchy of routes is discussed. (AW)

SINTON, DAVID
"Attitudes, A Source of the Housing Problem"
Urban Housing Issues and Problems, *Connection*, **6,** 1 and 2, 50–57
Cambridge: Harvard Graduate School of Design, 1969.

A survey of periodicals was used to examine the image of housing in the United States, the United Kingdom, and France. Image building in the United States and the United Kingdom is found to be reinforcing the single unit dwelling. In

France, periodicals showed no major emphasis on either single or multiple units. Land was intensively used as part of the house in the English ads. American ads projected the house as part of the land. Author believes that the poor could be better housed if land ownership could be discouraged as an American practice in home ownership. Suggests marketing techniques and leadership could alter housing attitudes. (ER)

1972
ROZELLE, RICHARD M., AND JAMES C. BAZER
"Meaning and Value in Conceptualizing the City"
Journal of the American Institute of Planners, March 1972, **38** (No. 2), 116–122.

Fifty-two residents of Houston, Texas, were interviewed to determine how they assigned meaning and value to elements of their city; specifically how they saw the city, how they remembered it, and what they regarded as important about it. Distinctively different patterns of responses were produced by each of the three approaches. The overall findings suggest that verbal tasks utilizing carefully chosen questions may be capable of eliciting information similar to the visual imagery produced by sketch maps . . . and it has greater flexibility. In addition, verbal procedures appear to elicit a more complete range of responses with regard to meaning and value than the sketch maps. (GB)

Another set of studies has sought to determine the values attributed to the environment and its buildings by using photographs as artificial stimuli for evaluating the response of subjects tested in controlled experiments. The photographs themselves must be seen for these studies to be of value to the designer. Unfortunately, many of the reports published did not reproduce the visual material used as the basis of the tests described.

These studies, when looked at as a group, seem random because they are uncodified, are contradictory, and do not indicate how they fit together or where the direction for future work lies. They almost uniformly suggest that additional study is needed, but until the people working in this area can begin to put it all together it is not likely to be of much use to the designer.

1967

PETERSON, GEORGE
"Measuring Visual Preferences of Residential Neighborhoods"
Ekistics, March 1967, **23,** 169–173.

Peterson extracts information from his Ph.D. dissertation on setting up a taxonomic system for visual appearance of residential areas by simulating the visual environment photographically. He hypothesizes that the perception of residential desirability depends on nine variables: greenery, open space, age, expensiveness, safety, privacy, beauty, closeness to nature, quality of the photographs. These criteria are analyzed and recorded in multidimensional models (taxonomic trees) according to frequency cited by his sample group. (RJD & MT)

1969

SANOFF, HENRY
Visual Attributes of the Physical Environment
Research Report, Design Research Laboratory, School of Design, North Carolina State University, 1969.

An experiment which focused on the visual attributes of the environment used photographs and a semantic differential test to assess the relation between visual satisfaction, complexity, ambiguity, and novelty. Thirty design experts and 30 planning students were used as subjects. Factor analysis and analysis of variance were used. It is suggested that the results should be used to effect a greater visual impact of designed environments. (GB)

1970

STEA, DAVID, & ROGER W. DOWNS
"From the Outside Looking in at the Inside Looking Out"
Environment and Behavior, June 1970, **2** (1), 3–12.

It has become customary to refer to the image as being the product of the process of collecting, coding, and evaluating information about the spatial environment. According to the authors, very little general theory has been developed to deal with modern concepts of image mapping and none has satisfactorily dealt with all its conceptual difficulties. The rationale for the study of image maps is to provide the additional constructs for the explanation and prediction of human behavior. The article discusses the research strategies employed and evaluates five studies in these areas. (LC)

MARKMAN, ROBERT
"Sensation-Seeking and Environmental Preference"
EDRA 2, Environmental Design Research Association, Pittsburgh, October 1970.

This study measured the relationship between sensation seeking and environmental preference using three sample populations: Freshman design, upper class design, and non-design students at North Carolina State University. Upper class design students tested highest on the sensation-seeking scale. Silhouette drawings were used as visual stimuli and questionnaires were developed which encompassed the dimensions of simplicity–complexity and commonness–novelty. (MT)

1971

DIAISO, R., D. M. FRIEDMAN, L. MITCHELL, AND E. SCHWEITZER
Perception of the Housing Environment
Urban and Environmental Health Planning Paper 2, University of Pittsburgh, 1971.

Their research tested the type of housing preferred by black and white racial groups by using photographs as stimulae: Three sets of photographs depicting low, medium, and high density housing were shown to approximately 380 respondents. A questionnaire utilizing semantic differential was used in conjunction with factor analysis to interpret the results. The respondents' perception of neighborhood quality, convenience to facilities, usable open space, density, safety, attractiveness, and segregation was analyzed. Additionally, preference for housing type was correlated with stage in life cycles. Although there was a great similarity in environmental disposition between blacks and whites, there were significant differences with respect to perception of specific neighborhood variables. (RJD)

1972

HONIKMAN, BASIL
"An Investigation of the Relationship between Construing of the Environment and Its Physical Form"
Environmental Design: Research and Practice, EDRA 3/AR 8, Los Angeles, 1972.

Photographs were shown to a group of subjects to determine the relationship between a qualitative evaluation and physical characteristics. The measurement techniques are very specialized and not widely used, including laddering to identify subordinate and superordinate relationships and then the making of several grids. This research requires extensive follow up to determine its ultimate usefulness. (JR)

KAPLAN, STEPHEN, & JOHN S. WENDT
"Preference and the Visual Environment: Complexity and Some Alternatives"
Environmental Design: Research and Practice, EDRA 3/AR 8, Los Angeles, 1972.

Environmental preference, including the preference for natural scenes, as a function of the complexity of stimulus was tested by having 88 subjects rate 56 color slides. Conclusions were that (1) natural scenes were preferred to urban scenes; (2) within both the natural and urban scenes, those with greater complexity were preferred; and (3) complexity did not account for the preference for natural over urban scenes. An interesting finding was that natural and urban scenes were each preferred over all suburban scenes, with complexity being the preference scale within each of the three groups. (JR)

The Development of Research Techniques

One of the more interesting reports discovered in the preparation of this project was an evaluation of the method of testing for value judgments of spaces and buildings by the use of photographs, as some of the above studies have done. This investigation, by R. W. Seaton and J. B. Collins, tested real buildings, color slides, and black and white photographs of a few selected buildings. Preference for the buildings on a comparative basis was consistent, but the range of values was greater for real buildings than for any simulation. The study leads to serious questioning of this technique for trying to establish more subtle gradations of judgments than simply which building is preferred from a group of buildings. One tends to wonder what the real value is of research to determine the preference of the design of buildings without research to determine the reasons for the preference.

1972

HOWARD, ROGER B., F. GERNAN MLYNARSKI, AND G. C. SAUER, JR.
"A Comparative Analysis of Affective Responses to Real and Represented Environments"
Environmental Design: Research and Practice, EDRA 3/AR 8, Los Angeles, 1972.

An experiment to determine the relative value of the use of actual environments, color slides, and black and white slides, with a second variable being previous familiarity with the environment being tested. The same buildings were used by each subject. It was demonstrated that the response to photographs was not the same as to the actual structures. This experiment suggests caution in evaluating research using pictures to elicit environmental responses. (JR)

SEATON, R. W., AND J. B. COLLINS
"Validity and Reliability of Ratings of Simulated Buildings"
Environmental Design: Research and Practice, EDRA 3/AR 8, Los Angeles, 1972.

An experiment to determine the relative value of the use of actual environments, photographs to determine the ratings subjects would give based upon the media shown in evaluating buildings. The conclusion was that the preference for the buildings being compared was consistent, but the range of values was greater for real buildings than for any simulation and color slides were closer to the real building than black and white photographs or architectural models. (JR)

It seems likely that anyone considering the development of a research methodology will be interested in most of the following citations, to which they should refer for a complete reading.

1964

BYERS, PAUL

"Still Photography in the Systematic Recording and Analysis of Behavioral Data"
Human Organization, Spring 1964, **23**, 78–85.

This article discusses the problem of the lack of systematic training concerning the proper use of cameras in the field of behavioral sciences. The camera can be used to support prior ideas or to find out what we may not know. In many instances the use of photography will enable us to see more than our eye alone will. Training in photography for behavioral science use should include a broad range of information including: technical methods, interaction of subject—photographer–viewer, and learning to "read" photographs for new information. The author states some of the methods he has used in a graduate course to teach these needed skills. A very interesting article for anyone interested in using photography in the social sciences. (DF)

1968

SANOFF, HENRY

Techniques of Evaluation for Designers
Design Research Laboratory, School of Design, North Carolina State University, Raleigh, May 1968.

A series of methods of data collection, together with a series of techniques for massing data to evaluate the effectiveness of built spaces after construction. This kind of user analysis would be equally helpful if it occurred before the buildings were constructed to develop a strong program upon which the design can be based. (JR)

1970

SCOTT, JAMES

"Testing a Housing Design Reference: A Pilot Study"
Architectural Association Quarterly, January 1970, **2**, 23–31.

A pilot study on housing in London performed to ascertain qualities that can be itemized and relevant criteria in assessing the success of a housing area. Tests features of designed environment against range of social criteria. Valuable because reliability tests confirm expected relationship between grouping of dwellings and social contact which affirms sense of belonging to specific aspects of environment. (SES)

GOLLEDGE, REGINALD, AND GEORGIA ZANNARAS
"The Perception of Urban Structure: An Experimental Approach"
EDRA 2, Environmental Design Research Association, October 1970.

The authors outline the procedures for investigating the perceptual structure of cities. Controlled laboratory experiments were developed which isolated relevant behavioral concepts for examination under laboratory conditions. These were then verified by field studies. Methodologies for all phases of the research were explained. (MT & NM)

MCKECHNIE, GEORGE
"Measuring Environmental Dispositions with the Environmental Response Inventory"
EDRA 2, Environmental Design Research Association, 1970.

This paper describes a survey carried out to assess environmental dispositions (attitudes, sentiments, beliefs, and values) which cut across demographic variables (intensity of vegetation) and get at individual preference configurations ("Personological scales"). The instrument used is the environmental response inventory (ERI) which traces environmental disposition to personality characteristics. "Environmental types" were distinguished by their identification with headings in the typology: pastoralism, urbanism, modernism, abstract conservationism, etc. Participants in the survey were a group of 800 subjects (400 male and 400 female) from several U.S. colleges. Separate analyses were registered for males and females. (MT)

1971
HOINVILLE, G.
"Evaluating Community Preference"
Environment and Planning, 1971, **3** (No. 1), 33–50.

G. Hoinville described a new method of research. It is a "priority evaluation approach"—a communication process with the public that allows one to understand the nature of the behavior attitudes and possible "trade-off." The objective of the research is to determine measurements of community preferences so that priority values can be identified and quantified for future use in community and social planning. (EB)

1972
BLASDEL, HUGO G.
"Multidimensional Scaling for Architectural Environments"
Environmental Design: Research and Practice, EDRA 3/AR 8, Los Angeles, 1972.

A method of environmental evaluation based on respondents scaling visual attributes. Factor analysis is used to group the rating scales indicative of a common variable. The technique does not depend on the assumption of a common interpretation of the rating scales but assumes multiple and interrelated meanings among the scales. According to the author, "Perhaps the major implication for research and the profession is that there exists a way of saying, 'This environment is better than that because a large number of observers see a quality difference relative to some attribute.'" (JR & GB)

ESTES, MARK D.
"Data Management Techniques Applied to People/Activity Relationships within the Built Environment"
Environmental Design: Research and Practice, EDRA 3/AR 8, Los Angeles, 1972.

A method of analysis for designers in determining functional relationships of spaces based on users' input. Detail is brought forth on how to manage and analyze the data generated for such a purpose—more than on the structuring of the questionnaire or techniques for gathering the data or than on putting the data to use. (JR & GB)

HERSHBERGER, ROBERT G.
"Toward a Set of Semantic Scales to Measure the Meaning of Architectural Environments"
Environmental Design: Research and Practice, EDRA 3/AR 8, Los Angeles, 1972.

A clear statement of the needs of the designer for information about the relationships between the formal properties and attributes of what he designed and the thoughts, feelings, attitudes, and behaviors which they tend to involve. An evaluation of scales recommended by other researchers is presented together with a set of 20 semantic scales to measure the meaning of architectural environments. (JR)

Special Perceptions of the Handicapped and Aged

The feelings stimulated by contact with other people and the reactions generated by being enclosed in space vary among individuals but they are primarily culturally conditioned responses. As a group, the handicapped have special problems in adapting to the built environment because of limitations in their ability to perceive or because of their restricted mobility. It is precisely that group which needs its environment to reinforce its security. Yet it is the handicapped that are most often ignored by designers.

1960
FRIEDEN, ELAINE
"Social Differences and Their Consequences for Housing and Aged"
Journal of the American Institute of Planners, May 1960, **26**, 119–124.

Housing for older people must embody consideration of the social needs of its occupants if it is to be satisfactory. These needs vary according to background and living habits. For example, the two groups studied, single elderly women and elderly ethnic couples, had some similar needs and other needs which were dissimilar. Both groups opposed public housing, although for different reasons. Both confronted a loss of a formal role of life and a loss of physical agility. Yet, their methods of providing themselves with security and some form of meaningful activity differed. Article suggests useful methodology for delineating housing needs of the elderly. (MT & SS)

1970

DUOSKIN, STEPHEN

"The Disabled's Encounter with the Environment"

Design and Environment, Vol. 1, No. 2, Summer 1970, pp. 60–63.

The author, confined to a wheel chair and crutches, gives suggestions to planners for making life easier for the disabled by modifying simple things like curbs, stairs, floor surfaces, seating, etc. (NM)

1971

PLANNING RESEARCH UNIT, UNIVERSITY OF EDINBURGH

Planning for Disabled in the Urban Environment

London: Central Council for the Disabled, 1971.

A basic description of interface properties between the disabled, or the elderly, and the environment. A well-illustrated and put together "how to" report. (GB)

1972

VASH, CAROLYN L.

"Discrimination by Design: Mobility Barriers"

Environmental Design Research and Practice, EDRA 3/AR 8, Los Angeles, 1972.

The physical characteristics of the built environment do not adequately consider the needs of the physically handicapped; this is caused by neglect and thoughtlessness on the part of designers. The legal neglect is documented by the real neglect —no concern by designers is specified and a plea or design of buildings and neighborhoods in which the physically disadvantaged can cope is strongly articulated. (JR)

Citizen Participation in the Design Process

Throughout history the individual has participated in the design process. Christopher Alexander in *Notes on a Synthesis of Form* describes the excellent fit between traditional peasant housing and the way of living. At the other extreme, castles, cathedrals, and palaces were under the control of kings, priests, and noblemen who directed the designers. Only in the twentieth century has building been taken out of the hand of the user and the responsibility transferred almost fully to the technologist and designer.

Zoning ordinances, building codes, and complex construction systems have pushed the client aside. The poor cannot build their own houses (except in the most rural areas) as the codes and specifications could not be met; and the wealthy are hemmed in for the same reasons. However, the rich can hire "the best architects" and are led into playing games which give them a sense of power over the design process. The poor, however, have not been incorporated into the design phase but are moved in to inhabit the buildings after the designers go away, never again to cast their shadow across the site.

It is fitting in democracies that after one of the traditional means of self-expression is taken away from people, they will demand reinstatement of that freedom. Comprehension and understanding of this need has taken more than half a century, and only since the 1960's have the people begun to demand that they be considered in the design process.

Approaches for developing methodologies so that nontechnicians can have significant inputs into the design process take on different forms. The literature is divided into six sections:

Citizens in the Planning Design Process
Advocacy Planning
Examples of Design with User-Participants
Characteristics of Participants
Training for Participation
Community Planning without Professionals

Citizens in the Planning and Design Process

After the first urban renewal projects of the 1950's, it became painfully evident to politicians, planners, and the population, that redevelopment was a dangerous weapon of the technocrats which could spoil the face of the city. The whole series of articles on Boston's West End, by Gans, Hartman, and Fried, underlined the necessity for participation. But even before the after-effects were reported, in 1953 William Slayton suggested that participation should be incorporated into the design of renewal areas. Then in the 1960's, after the outcry of the social planners, James Wilson published his reader on public participation in the renewal process.

A theme that runs throughout these writings is the conflicting values of citizens versus planners which reflects their respective emphasis on community versus metropolis, short range versus long range goals, intuitiveness versus trained judgments, and inability to articulate versus the command of a wide variety of tools from drawings to words to express their point of view. Because of these conflicts, in part, the concept developed that planners should be trained to advocate for the user.

1953
SLAYTON, WILLIAM L., AND R. DEWEY
"Urban Redevelopment and the Urbanite"
Coleman Woodbury (Ed.), *The Future of Cities and Urban Redevelopment,* Chicago: University of Chicago Press, 1953.

This article deals with an examination of the needs and desires of participants in an urban redevelopment program. The relationships among external space, attitudes, and community organization are explored. The authors suggest that physical planning has failed to distinguish between planning for services and that which will influence social relations of the environment. Community organizations can help planning by bringing forth resident needs in terms of kinds of housing, space relations, community facilities, and other public works. Examples of community organizations are given for three cities. Both forms and functions of organizations are covered in the article. (WP)

1959

KAUFMAN, HAROLD

"Toward an Interactional Conception of Community"

Social Forces, October 1959, **38**; Reprinted in Warren, 1966.

An early view of the community as an arena for participation. He states that, "by definition the ends of the community development programs are entirely oriented toward improving and increasing identification with the locality." He is concerned with the role of the sociologist whom he thinks should be working with and making explicit various alternative designs for "the good community and suggesting conditions under which these goals may be realized." He makes an early attempt at conceptualizing the relationships between homogeneous and cosmopolitan types of communities and community participation in design. (GB & WP)

1963

WILSON, JAMES Q.

"Planning and Politics: Citizen Participation in Urban Renewal"

Journal of the American Institute of Planners, November 1963, **29**, 242–249. Reprinted in Warren, 1966, and Wilson, 1966.

Wilson attempts to place citizen participation (planning with people) in perspective. The view of neighborhood residents toward urban renewal is a product of class composition. This means that in low-income renewal areas collective action serves as a bargaining device for increased community services but not for the definition of positive goals for renewal. The lower class neighborhoods, in contrast to more affluent areas, oppose extensive physical changes. Renewal, in such cases, cannot serve to attract the suburbanite to the central city. Urban renewal plans will differ radically according to the class composition of the citizens. (WP)

1966

DAVIES, J. CLARENCE

Neighborhood Groups and Urban Renewal

New York: Columbia University Press, 1966.

This book examines neighborhood groups in the urban renewal process through three case studies in New York City. The author rejects Wilson's thesis that the class bias of city planners affects the type of plan that develops. He claims it is difficult to determine how the area could have been redeveloped had citizens not participated in the way that they did. The author finds that the goals pursued through neighborhood participation tend to be primarily status quo in nature, tend to always oppose whatever is proposed, and make long-range planning difficult. Is this surprising for New York City? (WP)

1969

BURNS, MARY
"Planning for People"
Town and Country Planning, Jan.–Feb. 1969, **37**, (No. 1–2), 74–80.

Review of the Town and Country Planning Association 1968 National Conference (England) discussing planning the environment by public participation to get away from setting the family car higher in priority than the family's needs. (BB)

HYMAN, HERBERT H.
"Planning with Citizens: Two Styles"
Journal of the American Institute of Planners, March 1969, **35**, 105–112.

This was an original field study of Boston's South End Renewal Project. The interaction between planner and citizen was studied and differing planner–participant roles discovered and related to two different plans that resulted. Two factors were found most important in differentiation: (1) the planner's orientation; (2) varying values of citizen groups that dominated the planning process. When planners identified with elite groups and designed a more aesthetic plan there was less citizen influence in modifying the plan, there was more radical change in land use, and more streets were closed off. When planners identified with pluralistic models several discrete plans for various sub-areas were developed and consolidated through citizen bodies. In this case there was less change made in the land use, fewer streets were closed off, there was less land clearance and more scattered site low income housing. Excellent study which provides feedback on the effects of participation for physical design. (WP)

REYNOLDS, JOSEPHINE P.
"Public Participation in Planning"
Town Planning Review, July 1969, **40**, 131–148.

This article discusses the aims of public participation and how far the present activities of government succeed in achieving them. Given the present status of mass education in Britain, any increase in participation will result in nonrepresentative, self-interest pressure groups. She also concludes that the priorities and goals of the public will always reflect some degree of self-interest and thus be at variance with those of the professionals. Unstructured article with unclear intent. (WP)

1970
RICHARDSON, N. H.
"Participatory Democracy and Planning"
Town Planning Institute Journal, Feb. 1970, **56**, (No. 2), 52–56.

The article asserts that participatory democracy in planning is essential. The citizens and the planner must work together if urban change and renewal are to be responsive to local social and domestic needs. The professional planner can lose sight of the citizen he is planning for. It discusses two case studies in urban planning in Canada: Alexander Park and Kensington, and shows how effective citizen participation can be. Suggests neighborhood councils as a means of bringing citizens and planners together. (NSM)

1971
WALKER, GEOFFREY, AND ALAN G. RIGBY
"Public Participation in the Rhonda Valleys"
Journal of the Town Planning Institute, April 1971, **57**, 161-160.

This case study of public participation in South Wales found that citizens had trouble grasping the concept of the regional plan as an overall strategy and not a detailed document. The citizens were mostly concerned about issues such as housing renewal. Their input to the physical plan dealt with such issues as hillside recreation space and the location of woods. This article provides additional case study information on the issues and concerns of citizens in designing their environment. (WP)

SIMMIE, J. M.
"Public Participation: A Case Study from Oxfordshire"
Journal of the Town Planning Institute, April 1971, **57**, 161–162.

This is a study of the effects of citizen participation in Great Britain. The author found three types of participants in the development of a plan in an English city—leaders, actives, and passives. It was discovered that participation was disproportionately a matter for social minorities at opposite ends of the class spectrum. The result therefore is conflict instead of cooperation. The author concludes that citizen participation means government by minorities. Excellent feedback as to how citizen participation is structured and operationalized. (WP)

JORGENSON, LISA
"New York's Squatters: Vanguard of Community Control?"
City, Fall 1971, **5**, (No. 5), 35–39.

The new phase of citizen input into New York City's housing program is squatting in condemned buildings in an organized fashion. The squatters demand rights to stay and point out that the impending renewal will move them out and away from their livelihood. A question to grapple with. (GB)

Advocacy Planning

In 1965, Paul Davidoff made "advocacy planning" a popular term to connote the new generation of "social planners" who became involved in the political process on the part of minority groups, the poor, and even the forgotten middle-classes. He gave this approach credibility and professional respectability. Yet, it must be remembered that it is but one way to involve citizens in the process of designing their own communities and in practice, it has shown to demand a unique planner as well as a unique group of citizens. Furthermore, in changing physical designs (rather than social programs or political structures) some of the techniques discussed later probably are needed to supplement the trained advocate, especially the training and gaming techniques for participation in the process.

From the 1965 proposal by Davidoff, to Peattie's and Hatch's essays of 1968 and Blecher's book of 1971, the evaluations focus on new ways for planning social and physical design simultaneously, and not on the resulting physical structure.

1965

DAVIDOFF, PAUL

"Advocacy and Pluralism in Planning"

Journal of the American Institute of Planners, Nov. 1965, **31**, 331–337.

This was the first major article on advocacy planning. The author suggests that planners should engage in the political process as advocates of the interests of government and other groups. Thus, plural physical and redevelopment plans that reflect different political, social, and economic interests can result. Presently in urban design most citizens are reacting to agency programs rather than proposing their concepts of appropriate goals and future action. Advocacy planners can begin to provide the means by which physical relations and conditions can be related to the way they serve their users. Such planning can assure that participation by low-income persons can lead to solutions which are cost–beneficial to themselves. (WP)

1968

SPIEGEL, HANS B. C.

Neighborhood Power and Control: Implications for Urban Planning

Institute of Urban Environment, Columbia University, November 1968.

As a result of conferences and a review of literature, this study summarizes the potential of citizen participation in planning and urban redevelopment. Federal programs have introduced class oriented machinery and planning for social and physical development. The lower class is both a principal beneficiary and participant. In this context, planning becomes more concerned with the micro-environment of the neighborhood, with human needs, and less with the designation of land for the placement of physical objects. Advocacy planning then expands the options open to the client group in dealing with their environment. Participation means more "immediate" planning and greater concern with environmental management adapted to needs satisfaction corresponding to unique life styles of communities. (WP)

PEATTIE, LISA R.

"Reflections on Advocacy Planning"

Journal of the American Institute of Planners, March 1968, **34**, 80–88.

This article discusses the experiences of being advocate planners in one city. It is an excellent summary of problems and opportunities. She notes that advocacy plans tend to be more reaction plans than enactment; reflects sources of support; and that in some cases the values and technical interests of the advocate become more important than those of the clients supposedly represented. (WP)

HATCH, RICHARD C.
"Some Thoughts on Advocacy Planning"
Architectural Forum, 1968, **128,** 72–73, 103, 109.

The founder of one of the first advocacy planning centers discusses his experiences. He doubts whether advocate planners are more competent to plan than the average slum dweller but they are better prepared to deal with public agencies. He admits that even advocate planners fail to involve the poor in an important way in conventional physical planning which he says is too remote an activity for most poor people. And because of advocate planners' backgrounds in many cases they end up supporting those plans which reflect middle-class needs and aspirations. Article provides informative discussion of advocacy planning as a method for increased citizen participation in decision making. (WP)

1971
BLECHER, EARL M.
Advocacy Planning for Urban Development
New York: Praeger, 1971.

Excellent summary of advocacy planning in practice in six demonstration programs including a design center. The author notes that advocacy planning in contrast to other methods of city planning shifts the emphasis to include processes that will help produce tangible environmental products. A number of examples of client interests, influencing physical plans through the intervention of the advocate planner, are provided. (WP)

Examples of Design with User-Participants
These examples include case studies of advocacy planning, surveys of design changes which citizens made after the architects left, and the creation of workbooks

for developing in the users some of the tools of the designers. The importance of these approaches cannot fully be evaluated until more analysis of the input from the people versus the professional has been made.

1968
EDITORS, *Progressive Architecture*
"Advocacy Planning—What It Is, How It Works"
Progressive Architecture, Sept. 1968, **XLIX** (9), 102–115.

This article summarizes the activities and experiences of four advocate planning centers involving students, architects, and planners. Each center varies in its operations and its concerns. ARCH, for example, is redesigning an area to keep more of what is already there, to develop "checkerboard" housing. The article provides some indicators of what architectural advocate planners do to help citizens participate more effectively in planning the design of their neighborhoods. (WP)

1969
SIEVERTS, THOMAS
"Spontaneous Architecture"
Architectural Association Quarterly, July 1969, **1,** No. 3.

These are observations on the degree to which people have changed their built environment made by a number of German architectural students. They sought to identify environments which provoke "encrustment" or invite nesting. They assumed that these activities, which lead to a kind of self-expression, even if ugly or at least not in a neat order, are necessary for full human development. (GB)

BERKELEY, ELLEN PERRY
"Woodlawn Gardens"
Architectural Forum, July/August 1969, **131,** 72–77.

The importance of process in determining product is emphasized in this report on a low income housing project in Chicago. The process of on-going communication, interaction, and feedback among neighborhood residents, the architect, and the contractor is described in detail and presented as a means of assuring a satisfactory urban environment for its users. (AW)

KAUFMAN, EDGAR, JR.
"2001 B.C. to 2001 Centre Avenue"
Architectural Forum, October 1969, **131,** 54–58.

The built environment of a people reflects, preserves and exalts their values. Thus today's elaborate bathrooms and shopping centers reflect our values as did the temples and public architecture of former generations. Within this frame of reference, the community project undertaken by the residents of the Pittsburgh Hill district along with faculty and students of Carnegie–Mellon University assumes both artistic and philosophical importance. (AW)

DIXON, JOHN MORRIS
"Planning Workbook for the Community"
Architectural Forum, December 1969, **131,** 32–40.

A description of a workbook designed to help community residents decide what changes they may want in their neighborhood and housing and to prepare concrete proposals to implement these desired changes. The contents of the four-part workbook are outlined in detail and illustrated with sample pages. Some criticisms of the workbook are given. (AW)

1972
ANDREW, PAUL, MALCOLM CRISTIE AND RICHARD MARTIN
"Squatter Manifesto"
Ekistics, August 1972, **34,** 108–113.

The authors report on a squatter settlement in Lusaka, Zambia, describing its organization from doorstep to community both in words and plans. They propose a strategy of further community development based on citizen participation. (GB)

Characteristics of Participants

When the citizens are brought into the design process, especially in large-scale renewal or community planning, then the question is, which ones and how are they chosen. There is a vast literature on citizen participation in local government which has not been drawn on here. Several articles are selected which illustrate some of the ways citizens may be involved and some of the shortcomings of various techniques for gaining participation.

1964

NEW, PETER KONG MING, AND J. THOMAS MAY
"Alienation and Communication among Urban Renovators"
Human Organization, Winter 1966, **25,** 352–358.

The various relevant, though heterogeneous, parties concerned with the immediate action programs in urban planning lack a common dialogue. A study of local ward politicians, urban planners, the clergy, and social workers and their response to the question: "What will be the outcome of this particular neighborhood and how do you fit into the future planning of the area." (RB)

1968

BABCOCK, RICHARD F., AND FRED P. BOSSELMAN
"C.P.: A Suburban Suggestion for the Central City"
Land Use Controls, 1968, ASPO **2,** 21–32.

The authors propose alternative methods of participation based on experiences with homogeneous suburbs. A neighborhood board would be established to provide residents with opportunities to participate in decisions about zoning, density, housing, and open space. Residents would also control the architectural design of housing. The authors' analysis suggests that low-income central city residents should have the same participation opportunities as suburbanites.

CLAVEL, PIERRE
"Planners and Citizen Boards: Some Applications of Social Theory to the Problem of Plan Implementation"
Journal of the American Institute of Planners, May 1968, **34,** 130–139.

This article is based on a study of planning where expert advice was provided to nonpartisan citizen boards. A state of inequality was found between experts and board that limits the extent to which experts can be used. The study notes the problems and obstacles involved in expecting rural citizens to understand experts and technical issues (site locations, balanced development, etc.). Citizens' major defense is to reject the expert and reaffirm the status quo. Thus planners should pay greater attention to the type of environment and the values of the citizens in designing solutions. This is limited as it is a single study. (WP)

1969
MARANS, ROBERT W., AND JOHN B. LANSING
"Evaluation of Neighborhood Quality"
Journal of the American Institute of Planners, May 1969, **35,** 195–199.

By conducting an attitude survey, the authors have been able to determine how a cross section of residents perceive the quality of their environment. It is the authors' opinion that this type of study is of more value than the articulation of the vocal elite who present themselves under the guise of citizen participation in the planning process. (RM)

1970
GILBERT, NEIL, AND JOSEPH W. EATON
"Who Speaks for the Poor"
Journal of the American Institute of Planners, 1970, **36,** 411–416.

This is a study of resident assessments of conditions in anti-poverty neighborhoods. It indicates that active planners and citizens were highly critical of existing neighborhood conditions but a large survey of all residents showed apparent contentment with the physical conditions of their neighborhood. The study raises questions of whether the judgments of professionals and self-selected citizen spokesmen are actually the imposition of middle class values: Or is it that the residents simply reflect an adaptation to the personal realities of a life of limited alternatives? And does citizen participation mean representation? (WP)

1971
FELLMAN, GORDON, AND BARBARA BRANDT
"Working Class Protest against an Urban Highway"
Environment and Behavior, March 1971, **3** (No. 1), 61–79.

The authors examine reactions in a neighborhood endangered by the prospect of the dissolution of their area. It was observed that residents perceived themselves as politically impotent in the face of governmental and institutional pressure. Data was gathered on the kinds of people who actively protested and those who didn't: the functions, latent and manifest, sociological and psychological were analyzed. The contradiction between widely accepted pluralist democratic theory and political reality was pointed out with the recommendation that new forms of representation and influence effective for all segments of the society be devised. However, many questions were left unanswered. (BJ)

Training for Participation
One of the many problems of creating an environment for participation in the design process is that most of today's citizens do not have any design training—even at the grade school level—coupled with a tradition of bowing to authority and technology. A hope is to provide means for the citizens to learn now and to educate youngsters to respond to visual stimuli from the very beginning. A monograph and an article describing experiments along these lines are annotated below.

1969

BERKELEY, ELLEN PERRY

"Environmental Education from Kindergarten On Up"

Forum, June 1969, **130,** 46–53.

Environmental studies is a new field of formal education for our children designed to make them more aware of the visual, social, and political aspects of their environment and their place within it. This is a survey article describing many of the programs in terms of their goals, media and methods used, and introducing many persons actively engaged in this work. The author deplores our present urban environment and hopes the programs will educate a public that "knows enough to see other possibilities and cares enough to demand them." (AW)

1970

GROUP FOR ENVIRONMENTAL EDUCATION, INC.

Our Man-Made Environment Book Seven

Cambridge: M.I.T. Press, 1970.

An environmental "workbook" for children. The educational form of the text is designed to improve environmental sensitivity and three-dimensional comprehension. Factual information is concise and the cut out graphics reinforce learning in a visual–spatial way. The explanation of urban form has adult application potential. Could be used to present physical design to the nonvisual. (ER)

Community Planning without Professionals

Three examples of citizens self-help that have strong physical design aspects are provided. These examples are from groups of people in India, Greece, and Japan who have no opportunity to obtain professional help. Interestingly each of these is probably more hopeful of the future of the environment and progress of the citizens than some of the sophisticated case studies in the U.S., where the professionals and people have grated against each others values using their efforts to wriggle money from federal coffers rather than to plan and to build, which is, after all, the goal of urban design.

1966

CLINARD, MARSHALL B.
Slums and Community Development
New York: The Free Press, 1966.

   This is a long, exhaustive, extensively researched examination of slums and slum dwellers, worldwide, and community development as an answer to the problems of the slum. The author's greatest contribution is to show with special reference to the slums of underdeveloped and developing countries, the enormity of the problem and its imperviousness to attack by traditional methods of slum clearance, social services, and economic development. A case study of a community development project in a Delhi slum shows the part that self-help can and must play to initiate change. (ES)

MALTBY, JAMES, CECILY MARTIN, DIMITRI PHILIPPEDES, AND BJORN ROE
"Ilisses, A Village Community in Athens"
Ekistics, September, 1966, **22**, 188–195.

   A study of a small community in the center of Athens. The authors first develop the physical features of the community and its historical development. They then review the government of the community and what it has done for the residents. The second major step of the study is the social survey. In this they attempt to find out the following: (1) household characteristics, (2) income, (3) dwelling characteristics, (4) shopping patterns and leisure time activities, the functions of the community government, attitudes of residents toward their local problems and toward the community. (ES)

1969

TAIRA, KOJI

"Urban Poverty, Ragpickers, and the Ants' Villa in Tokyo"

Economic Development and Cultural Change, 1969, **17** (2), 163–168. *Ekistics*
166, 1969. Reprinted in McQuade, 1971, Bell, 1972.

To quote from Walter McQuade's introduction: "The setting may sound exotic,
but the comparisons are there. Certainly the average American ghetto dweller
in all his misfortune has nothing on the despised and impoverished ragpickers
of Tokyo. And certainly anyone familiar with the planning profession in America
can only be fascinated by the Dostoevskian cast of characters who helped the
ragpickers to better their lives. A ruined businessman; a wandering monk; a tubercular young lady of good family; and a somewhat mysterious pro-
motor–intellectual—these four nonprofessionals performed for the ragpickers a
function that in this country would probably be called advocacy. The story of
their success is instructive, and also, in a modest way, heartening."

Certainly there are two important aspects of this essay: the integration of work
into family life and child raising within a small neighborhood and also the role
of the advocates in finding a living environment within Tokyo, a modernizing urban
setting. (GB)

Density and Privacy

The basic studies in density tolerance levels were conducted, using rats as subjects, by John B. Calhoun. Observing rats live, reproduce, and interact with one another under different sets of density conditions, Calhoun developed inferences regarding environmental stimuli and social responses to density within a human society. There are clearly differences in the way a society operates under the stresses engendered by high density living—according to Calhoun. The statistics among human subjects are not nearly so clear, although Galle *et al.* have attempted a direct correlation using Calhoun's hypotheses.

In lieu of statistical facts, standard planning rule-of-thumb ratios do exist and are accepted as (if nothing else) reasonable. After the basic citations, short lists on privacy and traditional density measurements have been added.

William C. Loring, in an interesting study of social disorganization in households, found no correlation using the usual measures of deterioration in housing, but found definite effects with density. Loring did not, however, distinguish between dwelling space, outdoor space (public and private), and total space. The elements missing from these kinds of surveys and statistical analyses are those factors allowing high-income families to live satisfactorily in the upper east side in New

York while other families whose most distinguishing mark is low income live in lesser density without satisfaction, and with, in fact, social distress. The more recent research done in the United States leads to the conclusion that "density" is a factor in the various kinds of social malaise to a far greater degree than any dilapidation. But "density" in its narrowest definition of people per square foot of living space does not necessarily correlate unless it is measured as a ratio of usable interior space within a household per person. This is a very different kind of measurement than that commonly used by planners.

Robert C. Schmitt has presented a fascinating statistical analysis of Hong Kong where these correlations are not valid; on the contrary, with ten times the density of the densest block in Manhattan, murders are almost unheard of and crime rates are very low. The obvious conclusion is that different cultures acclimate to densities in different ways (which is just as well if one reads any of the projections for world-wide population increases). There are several additional studies that tend to confirm the hypothesis that it is overcrowding within living units, not lot area density, that has socially negative correlations in the United States, among them studies by J. M. Miller and Gerhardt Rosenberg.

The general conclusion made by Jane Jacobs in *The Death and Life of Great American Cities* is that if families have enough living space for themselves, then overall density is not relevant for a successful urban environment. This re-enforces the conclusion of the planners who diverge from standard planning theory and admit that high density is not all bad. No one disputes the fact that dismal, depressed, dilapidated housing is bad, nor does anyone really dispute the fact that there is more comfort in more interior space per family.

1956
LORING, WILLIAM C.
"Housing Characteristics and Social Disorganization"
Social Problems, January 1956, **3**, 167.

The author analyzes data from a study by the housing association of metropolitan Boston comparing normal with disorganized households and attempting to determine which, if any, of several physical characteristics of housing and neighborhood are related to social disorganization. Items such as lack of private bath, poor maintenance of dwelling units, deterioration, etc. (the usual measures of substandard housing) do not seem to have a marked effect on the incidence of disorganization within households. On the other hand, those elements related to neighborhood and household density (e.g., space in dwelling, number of rooms dividing it, total space used in common) appear to be the most significant items. He further hypothesizes that density is most relevant to social disorganization in terms of social or cultural roles acting in a given physical space. Over-density can aggravate or accelerate any tendency to disorganization but not cause or motivate it. (NM)

1961

MILLER, J. M.
"Residential Density: Relating People to Space Rather than to Ground Area"
Journal of the American Institute of Planners, February 1961.

A brief to divorce the concept of density from its traditional land-surface connotation; density comparisons among rural, suburban, and urban areas are meaningless since each area involves a different way of life, and therefore, will have different standards and needs. The relationship of people to their residential dwelling is, therefore, not to two-dimensional land coverage, but to three-dimensional interior space. Livability is determined by proper design of this space in terms of its convenience, privacy, efficiency, attractiveness, and suitability for the activities to be pursued therein. A thought-provoking article. (AW)

1963

SCHMITT, ROBERT C.
"Implications of Density in Hong Kong"
Journal of the American Institute of Planners, August 1963, **29**, 210–217.

A clear and lucid statistical analysis of the differences in characteristics between the effects of density, measured both in terms of acreage per family and square feet per family, in Hong Kong and the United States. This analysis demonstrates that culture is part of the adaptability of man, that high density living does not necessarily engender crime or social dysfunction in a society. (JR)

1966

CALHOUN, JOHN B.

"The Role of Space in Animal Sociology"

Journal of Social Issues, October 1966, **22**, 46–59.

This article is concerned with the interaction of animals with their environment in terms of space. The study concludes that this interaction and the response of the animal to environmental stimuli are major determinants of social behavior. Inferences are made regarding tolerable human densities from the laboratory research on animals. Important for anyone studying density. (LM & GB)

SCHMITT, ROBERT C.

"Density, Health, and Social Disorganization"

Journal of the American Institute of Planners, January 1966, **32**, 38–40.

The study asks, "which measure is more closely identified with social disorganization, population per net acre (density) or persons per room (overcrowding)?" Data analysis from Honolulu emphasizes that, in that area, density is the more significant variable. Author contrasts his findings with those of Jane Jacobs. (AW)

1968

ROSENBERG, GERHARDT

"High Population Density in Relation to Social Behavior"

Ekistics, June 1968, **25**, 425–428.

Distinction should be made between crowding of buildings on land and crowding of people into buildings. High density of buildings and fairly high densities of population can result from competition for favorable residential locations caused by urbanization forces of a free market economy which lowers cost of labor generally without regard to the human condition. Often effects of high density are loneliness rather than crowding. But lack of stimulation and adaptation to change can be as harmful as stressful crowding. (SES)

1971

CANTER, DAVID, AND SANDRA CANTER

"Close Together in Tokyo"

Design and Environment, 1971, **2**, 60–63.

The authors carefully describe many details which are the source of the success of the very dense environment of Tokyo—privacy, garden design, attention to details, etc. (GS)

1972
GALLE, OMER R., WALTER R. GOVE, AND J. MILLER McPHERSON
"Population Density and Pathology: What Are the Relations for Man?"
Science, April 7, 1972, **176**, 23–30.

The authors assume the hypotheses of Calhoun regarding the various pathologies of rats when they are overcrowded and test for similar pathologies on a community level in the city of Chicago. First using a simple measure of number of people per area in the community, the authors found no correlation. Then using people per room as the density indicator correlations were found with the pathological indices of mortality, fertility, ineffectual parental care (measured by public assistance), and juvenile delinquency. However, the authors still deny that they might have found any "casual links." While the findings are truly fascinating one must wade through the jargon of social scientism to get at them. (GB)

BIRD, CAROLINE
The Crowding Syndrome: Learning to Live with Too Much and Too Many
New York: David McKay Co., Inc., 1972.

A very bad book: badly written, presented, documented and filled with errors. There is no original research, and she misconstrues many of the main points of those who have studied the problems of density and crowding. (GB)

Density Measurements

There are some almost classic studies that have been done recently by planners about density and land use as a reflection of standard density patterns. These are evaluations and projections of land uses from a metropolitan scale to a world-wide, ecumenopolis scale.

1961
STEVENS, P. H. M.
"Densities in Housing Areas"
Tropical Building Studies, No. 1, London; *Ekistics,* August 1961, **70,** 131–139.

A very useful set of tables has been constructed to provide some indices for selecting suitable densities for various sites. The criteria are (1) health factors; (2) living space within the dwelling; (3) social factors including characteristics of private and public open space, provision of amenities, and attitudes towards privacy; (4) technical factors; and (5) economic factors. (GB)

1966
BLUMENFELD, HANS, M. BOGDANOU, G. BURGEL, A. CHRISTAKIS, P. A. EMERY, R. L. MEIER, B. E. NEWLING, G. A. PAPAGEORGIOU, J. G. PAPAIOANNOU, AND P. PAPPAS
"Population Densities in Human Settlements"
Ekistics, December 1966, **22** (133), 411–417.

This is a report of a working group on densities with background papers on special topics. They discuss setting standards for international density counts—as well as upper and lower thresholds of desirable densities. They include both developing and developed countries in their concepts, and the relationship of the income variable to densities. (GB)

DOXIADIS, C. A.
"Densities of Human Settlements"
Ekistics, July 1966, **22** (128), 77–101.

Doxiadis has provided a written introduction as well as defined the scope of research on density which is undertaken at the Athens Center of Ekistics. Density is approached from the scale of the megalopolis, the metropolis, and the neighborhood. At each scale there is a large quantity of comparative data for the major world cities at a gross level and for Athens, Greece, at a micro level. This provides a good overview for looking at the density problem. (GB)

1970
KILBRIDGE, MAURICE, ROBERT O'BLOCK, AND PAUL TEPLITZ
"Population Density Concepts and Measures"
Urban Analysis, Division of Research, Graduate School of Business Administration,
Harvard University, Cambridge, Massachusetts.

This essay is found in a book analyzing urban models. The authors describe and rate the different methodologies to measure density at the urban and metropolitan scales. They suggest that density measures, as presently used, are too imprecise to achieve operational usefulness for modeling the urban environment. This is an excellent summary with a good bibliography. (GB)

Family Private Space

A factor that tends to correlate, both physically and in social terms with density, is the amount of private space a family has been allocated. Complementary articles on this subject are found in the section on the dwelling unit.

Both privacy and land use density differ greatly between cultural groups. Nancy J. Marshall has developed a privacy preference scale to measure intimacy, the ability to neighbor or not to neighbor, seclusion, solitude, anonymity, and reserve.

1962
WILLMOTT, PETER
"Housing Density and Town Design"
Town Planning Review, July 1962, **33**, 115–128.

This study of Stevenage sought to determine inhabitant attitudes toward density, privacy, and services. Secondarily, it examined the effects of the neighborhood unit in the town. Given a density of 55 habitable rooms per acre, only 1% of the respondents felt that the density was too low, whereas 40% felt this was too high. These feelings were in direct opposition to those of the architects and planners. Forty-six percent of the residents were concerned about the perceived lack of privacy whereas 25% felt open space was reduced by high density. (BJ)

1964
WILLIS, MARGARET
"Designing for Privacy"
Ekistics, January 1964, **17**, 47–52.

A report of an interview survey made in London to determine how people define privacy. Responses relate to internal privacy, being overlooked, privacy in relationship to neighbors, window location, and design. Conclusions suggest that privacy is more important in times and areas of social change. The article does not draw conclusions related to designs. (SMS)

1970
MARSHALL, NANCY J.
"Environmental Components of Orientations toward Privacy"
EDRA 2, Environmental Design Research Association, October 1970.

Using the privacy preference scale, six orientations toward privacy were identified; intimacy, not neighboring, seclusion, solitude, anonymity, reserve. Individual differences in orientation were assessed. Samples included junior college students and adults. The study also examined the relation between environmental density and privacy preference and some environmental and behavioral correlates of privacy preferences. This research reveals important value data for designing compatible environments. (MT & NM)

SMITH, RICHARD ALAN
"Crowding in the City: The Japanese Solution"
Landscape, Winter 1970, **18**, 3–10.

The author believes that American cities could benefit from the application of various design principles found in Japanese cities. These include: (1) an integrated system of standardized, modular housing which makes it possible for the working class to live as well as the upper class. Since all housing is virtually the same, "If architecture contributes to the well-being of the emperor, so it does also to the well-being of the barber"; (2) flexibility—allowing structures to serve a wide range of functions; (3) utilization of various principles of order and composition including: (a) process designing (saobi), (b) activity space (kaiwai), (c) forced line or curved street (hizumi), (d) borrowing space (ikedore); (e) great diversity and intensity of land use; (f) neighborhood centers in which the greater the variety of businesses, services, and institutions, the better is the center; (g) use of store roofs for creation of elaborate children's amusement parks, outdoor restaurants, etc.; (h) extensive use of subterranean space. (JZ)

Personal Space

Edward T. Hall calls "personal space" proxemics, defined as the interrelated observations and theories of man's use of space as a specialized elaboration of culture. In his first two books, *The Silent Language* and *The Hidden Dimension,* Hall explores nonverbal forms of communication as functions of culture, showing that there are strong but subtle forces in all cultures that determine sensory perceptions and relationships of people to the built environment. These characteristics vary widely from one society to another and can cause discomfort and misunderstanding between people from different backgrounds. This applies to both communication and the kind of space in which people find themselves. Hall believes designers should be more aware of the cultural requirements of their clients and the study of cultures should be part of the training of designers.

Another view of personal space taken in a more evolutionary perspective is Robert Ardrey's *The Territorial Imperative* in which animal behavior is viewed as background for the analysis of the development of human needs for personal space. The thought here is that the need for a boundary of space is not a phenomena unique to humans but that the need also occurs in the animal kingdom and, therefore, is an innate biological requirement.

Robert Sommer has developed techniques for the study of territorial and proxemic demands to be used by designers in determining the limits of territoriality and the relation to the adjacent environment. *Personal Space* (1969) presents a summary of the basic ideas and *The New Evaluator Cookbook* (1972) translates the ideas to design.

Personal space is clearly related to questions of density and the article by Daniel Stokols makes this bridge.

1965

STEA, DAVID

"Territoriality, the Interior Aspect: Space, Territory, and Human Movement"
Landscape, Autumn 1965, **15**, 13–17.

Changes in designed interiors affect human conceptions of space, territory, and orientation. Stea supports his hypothesis by describing some empirical research which attempted to measure the extent to which office workers manipulate individual and collective territories with various kinds of furniture. Interior topography relates clearly to the social systems of clusters of workers—expressing status and privacy values and ultimately affecting productivity and broader territorial orientation when changed. (MT)

1966
SOMMER, ROBERT
"Man's Proximate Environment"
Journal of Social Issues, October 1966, **22**, 59–71.

Most high density and pathology studies have been done on animals. Man's behavior is just becoming known. Even though man's territory (plot of land or area of free movement) is important, it appears that his territory may be reduced to 6 to 12 sq. ft. (defense shelter) if the proximate environment is well arranged. Experiments that show a wide range of pathology with high density populations have not yet effectively separated high density from low socioeconomic groups. Sommer provides convincing argument for the value of psycho-architectural analysis in urban design. (LM & MT)

HALL, EDWARD T.
The Hidden Dimension
Garden City, New York: Anchor Books, 1966.

Hall deals with the structure of experience as it is molded by culture, in his words with "the deep, common, unstated experiences which members of a given culture share, communicate without knowing, and which form the backdrop against which all other events are judged." Hall believes that communication constitutes the core of culture, of life itself, that language is the major element in the formation of both thought and perception, and that people from different cultures, because they speak different languages, inhabit different sensory worlds . . . proxemics is the term he has coined for the interrelated observations and theories of man's use of space as a specialized elaboration of culture. An excellent study. (MS)

1967
SOMMER, ROBERT
"Can Behavior Studies Be Useful as Well as Ornamental?"
Transactions of the Bartlett Society, 1966–1967, **5**, 47–66.

Psychologist's conclusions in regard to physical space and behavior. He cites studies which show that environmental change elicits behavioral changes which are judged as beneficial by society. Suggests that industrial relations techniques for users of the built environment be developed to provide feedback to designers. His generalizations relate most specifically to the scale of his own research on personal space. (ER & GB)

1969
SOMMER, ROBERT
Personal Space, the Behavioral Basis of Design
Englewood Cliffs, New Jersey: Prentice-Hall, 1969.

   The title, "Personal Space" implies two usages with which the book is concerned: (1) the "emotionally charged zone around each person which helps regulate the spacing of individuals and (2) the processes by which people mark out and personalize the spaces they inhabit." The book is especially concerned with the spatial arrangements implied in these two usages. It is also an attempt to elucidate some of the questions of value in the design process in which matters of physical form arise only after one has decided what he wants to do. The book is divided into two parts: first, an introduction to spatial behavior and, second, an application of these concepts to particular settings. It explores (1) various mechanisms for controlling distributions and density of people; (2) methods evolved to keep people out of each other's way; (3) the intimate connection between space and status; (4) and what is meant by privacy. In the second half of the book, he explores man-made environment systems. (PM)

1970
KENNEDY, DONALD
"Indoor Territoriality: An Anthropological Perspective"
Proceedings of the Interprofessional Council on Environmental Design, May 18–20, 1970, American Society of Civil Engineers.

   Kennedy relates an example of using concepts of territoriality in the design of a pediatric hospital. He suggests six ways in which territoriality helps man to work in his environment. A short paper, but it has some ideas. (GB)

1971
HALL, EDWARD T.
"Proxemics and Design"
Design and Environment, Winter 1971, **8**, 24–25, 58.

   Hall spells out how his approach—proxemics—varies from that of Barker, Sommer, Ittelson, and Gibson. He reviews himself. Biased but valid. (GB)

SOMMER, ROBERT
"The New Evaluator Cookbook"
Design Awareness, New York: Rinehart Press, 1971; Reprinted in *Design and Environment,* Winter 1971, **8**, 35–37, 59.

Sommer evaluates techniques and results of eight user feedback studies within buildings, and in one case a park. These studies fit with his own research on personal space but also relate to the wider human activity feedback appropriate for evaluating and suggesting design changes. A concise, readable document that should help anyone wanting to do this kind of research. (GB)

1972

RAPPOPORT, AMOS
"Australian Aborigines and the Definition of Place"
Environmental Design: Research and Practice, EDRA 3/AR 8, Los Angeles, 1972.

A case study of the Australian aborigines, a culture in which the building of structures and boundaries are unimportant in determining their concept of place and how it is defined. The aborigines utilize the physical structure of the landscape in finding a sense of place. (JR)

STOKOLS, DANIEL
"A Social-Psychological Model of Human Crowding Phenomena"
Journal of the American Institute of Planners, March 1972, **38** (2), 72–83.

Stokols differentiates between spatial considerations in terms of the physical conditions of crowding (density) and crowding as a psychological experience. Although the limitation of space remains as the essential ingredient of crowding the proposed model introduces personal and social variables which have a direct bearing on a person's perception of spatial restriction as well as on his attempts to cope with the constraint. His experimental hypotheses all relate to relatively small scaled settings. These are: (1) Limitation of space will engender an experience of crowding to the extent that it introduces noxious physical effects or places constraints on personal or social activities; (2) under conditions of spatial limitation: (a) a noisy situation will be perceived as more crowded than a quiet one; (b) a cluttered area will appear more crowded; (c) situations involving social interference will appear more crowded; (d) time will increase a feeling of crowding; (e) persons who are by nature aggressive or impatient will experience stronger crowding sensations. (GB)

The Design Process

The creation of a built environment that truly serves all of human society is an extraordinarily complex process which involves many professional disciplines and diverse, special-interest groups. A process must be formulated by which a designer can effectively produce a physical setting for the conduct of a satisfactory life for each member of a community. Such a process requires a more holistically structured basis for decision than now exists. The crisis-oriented method of for mulating programs to solve urban problems has contributed to the creation of far more problems than it has resolved. All policy decisions have implications that are reflected in the entire social, economic, and physical structure of the society. It should be abundantly clear by now that uncoordinated efforts to solve any single problem will result only in the creation of new problems. A serious effort must be made to develop new methods of coordinating urban policy decisions and the design of the built environment.

Robert Goodman calls planners tools of the status quo even though they may be engaged in advocacy planning. He calls for planners to become active in working for change instead of reinforcing the present. Gerald M. McCue points out in *Creating the Human Environment* that the public will be forced to look to other groups to give it the kind of environment it seeks if the design professions do not soon take responsibility for creating a more viable environment than is now being built.

Christopher Alexander has been one of the significant innovators in the design process. In their book *Community and Privacy*, Chermayeff and Alexander articulated the viewpoint that there is a balance between the private needs and the community needs of urban residents. Then in his doctoral dissertation *Notes on the Synthesis of Form,* he lashed out at the simplistic approach to cities, thinking in terms of hierarchical tree structures and suggested, instead, that cities are complex lattices. While he does not deny that discrete subcenters and neighborhoods exist, he believes that they are interlocked with a variety of other places and functions. This reflects the point of view of the Team 10 group which was to look at each design problem in terms of its connectedness with spaces. While Team 10 makes the statement poetically, Alexander does it mathematically. His latest work is treated separately as it presents a new vocabulary of design, "pattern language."

As most of the articles described below indicate, the essence of the problem is not of design, but of programming for the built environment and being able to predict the results of each piece we build on the total environment; the social and economic results as well as the physical results. Only when the real requirements of society are known and only when the behavior of people in a physical setting can be predicted will it be possible to develop programs that can serve as the basis for design of a satisfactory environment.

1960

DOBUSH, PETER, JOHN C. PARKIN, AND C. E. PRAFF
"Report of the Committee of Inquiry into the Design of Residential Environment of the Royal Architectural Institute of Canada, 1960"
Royal Architectural Institute of Canada Journal, May 1960, 175–229. *Ekistics,* September 1960, **59**, 166–172.

This report emphasizes the importance of behavioral science research in creating viable residential environments for Canada's future. They urge that architects study the behavioral sciences and that courses and experts in these fields be brought into the architectural schools. They also call for a richer mix of housing environments that fit a richer mix of life styles in the society as a whole. In their words they want "freedom by design." This is an outstanding report of its kind. (GB)

1961
KEPES, GYORGY
"Notes on Expression in the Cityscape"
Daedalus, Winter 1961; *Ekistics,* March 1961, **11**, 208–215.

Author views city as a mobile "collage." The city is a sequence of well-defined units, with boundaries to separate and distinguish units from the whole and links to connect units into the whole. Thus, individual neighborhoods viewed together, define the personality of the entire city while the city, in turn, defines the neighborhoods. Kepes also discusses the symbolism inherent in the use of space, structure, light, texture, and rhythm in cities, with culture as the decoder of the implicit messages. (KF)

1962
TEAM 10
"Team 10 Primer"
Architectural Design, December 1962, **32**, 559–602.

The authors state that all planning, regardless of scale, should be based on mobility stems, whether rapid transit, vehicular or pedestrian. The architect, when designing for anonymous clients must interpret their needs in terms of community structure. It is the responsibility of the planner to supply the social information necessary to translate "constant human qualities into space."

Ideal urban infrastructure can be accomplished by (1) developing road and communication systems as the urban infrastructure; (2) working with dispersal, not forcing accepted density concepts, but keeping places of maximum intensity; (3) using "throw away" technology; (4) developing a "mechanized aesthetic"; (5) developing twentieth century mass housing; and (6) establishing conditions good for mental health and well being. The high rise structure with multilevel mobility paths creating clusters would be stressed to create the optimum habitat. The traditional dichotomy of urbanism and architecture must be done away with before any effective planning can occur. The article is worth looking at, especially for the illustrations and the text, if you accept the premise that mobility patterns are the planner's core. (TL)

1965
CHERMAYEFF, S., AND CHRISTOPHER ALEXANDER
Community and Privacy, Towards a New Architecture of Humanism
Garden City, New York: Anchor Books, 1965.

The authors advocate a science for environmental design based on the premise that every activity must have its own physical zone and that there is a hierarchy of relationships between man and his environment. They define basic requirements for urban dwellings as having a maximum of privacy while still relating to the community and analyze some housing plans and types of housing in relation to these requirements. A very interesting and thought-provoking book. (NSM)

ALEXANDER, CHRISTOPHER
"A City Is Not a Tree"
Architectural Forum, May 1965, **122**, 58–61.

A lovely, semi-philosophical discussion of the form cities take. The article compares the natural, or spontaneous, city with the artificial, or planned city. The natural city has a semi-lattice pattern, with many overlapping sets or units, while the planned city is created in a tree pattern, with sets either totally inclusive or totally disjoint. In a tree, no piece within a unit is connected to another unit except through the entire unit; this is unlike the neighborhood, where various institutions (schools, clubs, post offices) serve overlapping areas and constituencies. The author contends that we have traded the richness of semi-latticing for the simplicity of tree structure. (KF)

1966
ALEXANDER, CHRISTOPHER
Notes on the Synthesis of Form
Cambridge: Harvard University Press, 1966.

An innovative analytical approach to design. Developed in a way to represent design problems to make them easier to solve. Design is viewed as an effort to achieve "fit" between the form and its context. The process of achieving good fit is viewed as the process of neutralizing misfits between the form and the context. In unself-conscious cultures (primitive) the process of fitting is adaptive. In self-conscious cultures (Western Civilization) adaptation cannot keep pace with the changing culture so that the complexity and interaction of problems becomes unmanageable. Design solutions lie in forming a formal picture of the designer's mental picture which is based on subjective concepts.

The new analytical approach alleviates the dependence on vocabulary and semantics and brings the design process out in the open where it can be controlled through the use of "sets." Set M is the set of all misfits that can be named and set L is the set of links between the misfits. The decomposition of set M into its independent subsets allows the designer to develop a more manageable system. The process is one of analysis and synthesis in reaching the final form. An example of the process is presented. The author quantifies some ideas of the Smithsons. He overstates the semantic problem of designers. (JD)

1967
CARR, STEPHEN
"The City of the Mind"
W. R. Ewald, Jr. (Ed.), *Environment for Man: The Next Fifty Years.* Bloomington: Indiana University Press, 1967.

Carr discusses each step of the planning process and its significance to environmental design. He articulates the notion of behavioral settings. He poses the problems of whether the environmental form provides the required settings to support the desired behavior. He proposes nine criteria for environmental form: (1) increasing environmental settings and potential interactions; (2) stimulating environmental exploration; (3) increasing the perceptual accessibility of urban form; (4) structuring city form in congruence with mental structures; (5) enhancing unique qualities of environmental settings; (6) increasing exposure to settings of highest common significance; (7) increasing the plasticity of city form to action of small groups; (8) facilitating a rhythm of behavioral and perceptual constraint and release; and (9) adapting environmental settings to facilitate plans being executed within them. (GB)

SOMMER, ROBERT
"Can Behavior Studies be Useful as Well as Ornamental?"
Transactions of the Bartlett Society, **5**, 1966–1967, 47–66.

Psychologist's conclusions in regard to the physical world and behavior. The problem is seen as having no simple connection. Studies are cited showing benefits of environmental change on behavior. A coordinator–planner–sociologist is call on to translate theories into fact. Major suggestion is that industrial relations techniques for users of the built environment be adapted to provide feedback to the designers. (ER)

SMITHSON, ALLISON, AND PETER SMITHSON
Urban Structuring
New York: A Studio Vista/Reinhold Art Paperback, 1967.

Presentation of a set of ideas about architecture and urban design developed from the general theory of modern architecture modified by economic and social trends. Ideas fall into five groups. (1) Association—human patterns of association and their hierarchy necessarily influence the physical structure of a community. Each different community defines a different structure. (2) Identity—human identification with a dwelling unit or environment depends on the associational patterns with the physical structure. (3) Patterns of Growth—a "loose" plan for urban growth is advocated depending on a new "ease of communications" for social cohesion. This plan would include an integrated transportation system from pedestrian ways and sewers to superhighways. (4) Mobility—a network of equal value roads which can easily be changed or rearranged, so as to break down the urban pyramid into a loose cluster. (5) Cluster—any coming together. In conclusion, their ideal urban structure equals a net of freeways enclosing superblocks which are internally oriented. They advocate a concentrated urban sprawl and seem to disregard the sense of "downtown" or "city" or "happening." Jane Jacobs would despise their ideas. (JD)

1968

TURNER, JOHN

"Architecture That Works"

Architectural Design, August 1968, **38**, 355–360. *Ekistics* January 1959, **58**, 40–44.

This is a report of the process of building a barriada. It describes the input and organization of people in providing their own built environment. Turner puts it over as the solution to housing problems in developing countries. (GB)

1969

HALPRIN, LAWRENCE

The RSVP Cycle—Creative Processes in the Human Environment

New York: George Braziller, 1969.

Halprin sees the creation of an environment and planning for its effectuation as a process. He seeks to "free the creative process" by making the process visible. The process he calls RSVP cycles for Resource, Score, Valuation, and Performance. Fundamental to the process is scoring (as in musical score), a system of symbols which can convey or guide the interactions between elements —space, time rhythm, sequences, people, etc. Human experience is an essential ingredient in the score and Halprin sees people involvement as a means of breaking down the modern dichotomy of artist versus people. (JD)

MCCUE, GERALD M., WILLIAM R. EWALD, JR., AND THE MIDWEST RESEARCH INSTITUTE

Creating the Human Environment

Urbana, Illinois: University of Illinois Press, 1970.

A report prepared for the American Institute of Architects to foresee the future of the architectural profession. Part One, by William R. Ewald, Jr., is a predictive view of the future looking to the year 2000. Part Two, by the Midwest Research Institute, is a detailed analysis of the future of the building industry, including construction, financing, land use and land values, marketing, and technology. Part three, by Gerald M. McCue, is a study of the future of the architectural profession and its role in the creation of a better environment for human life. This section is appropriate not only for architects, but also for planners and all those concerned with human society and its physical environment. It is a plea for architects to accept the responsibility to become agents of social change, with the implied threat that if professional designers do not accept this challenge some other group will. (JR)

1971
GOODMAN, ROBERT
After the Planners
New York: Simon and Schuster, 1971.

"Planners want 'social change' . . . . But the kind of 'social change' they usually find themselves dealing with, whether or not they recognize it, is organizing the oppressed into a system incapable of providing them with a humane existence, pacifying them with the meager welfare offering that helps maintain the status quo. At best we help ameliorate the condition produced by the status quo; at worst we engage in outright destruction." Goodman calls for "community socialism" in which all the members of a community will have equal financial resources and will, therefore, be able to freely choose a way of life and a humane society. (JR)

PORTEOUS, J. DOUGLAS
"Design with People: The Quality of the Urban Environment"
Environment and Behavior, 1971, **3**, 155.

All urban problems have an environmental quality component. Urban environmental quality research has been discouraged until recently by the complexity of the urban scene. In view of the latter, three behavioral concepts are discussed at three scales: at the city scale, cognitive representations of the urban environment (mental maps); at the neighborhood scale, concepts of territoriality and activity systems; and at the micro-scale, the determination of behavior by the built environment. In each case the relationships between environment and behavior are explored. In particular, the substantial differences between the perceptions, attitudes, and actions of urban designers and their user-client, the public, are emphasized. In this context the evolution of the planning process is considered as a developmental model. The present state of the art indicates a need for future investigation of the public's use of designed space, the belief-systems of both planners and the public, and means by which the public may be incorporated as participants into the planning, designing, and policy-making processes. (JR)

1972

GOLDSTEEN, JOEL
"Group Composition in Urban Planning"
Environmental Design: Research and Practice, EDRA 3/AR 2, Department of
Architecture, UCLA, 1972.

A research project to evaluate the quality of the product of multidisciplinary
groups such as those operating in most urban planning projects with the composition of the group as the variable. The groups analyzed were characterized as
homogeneous and heterogeneous. The conclusion sheds doubt on the prevailing
theories about the efficacy of a multidisciplinary approach to problem solving.
(JR)

MARKUS, THOMAS A.
"A Doughnut Model of the Environment and Its Design"
Environmental Design: Research and Practice, EDRA 3/AR 2, Department of
Architecture, UCLA, 1972.

A systematic model, at any scale from room to region, considered to consist
of people and environment. The parts of the system are objectives, activities,
environment, building, and resources. (JR)

POLLOWY, ANNE-MARIE, AND MICHEL BEZMAN
"Design-Oriented Approach to Developmental Needs: An Operational Framework
Relating Activity Patterns to Environmental Requirements through the Performance
Approach"
Environmental Design: Research and Practice, EDRA 3/AR 8, Los Angeles, 1972.

A methodology for setting performance specifications for designers. The programming process described includes goal statement, attainable objectives, performance requirements according to activity patterns and needs, performance criteria,
and, finally, feedback. (JR)

Perception and the Designer
(or, Whither Architectural
Determinism?)

The design of a building, a street, a group of buildings, or a neighborhood, even a city is the cumulative response of a great many people to what they believe the environment, or at least the part they control, ought to be, both functionally and visually. How things are done, how they should operate, and what they should look like are influenced by both the surroundings and our heritage, in the form of a tradition of design. The designer is not often an innovator, but usually a follower of tradition.

The design of streets and squares is part of a long history of urban design and has special spatial qualities. Francoise Vigier correlates these spatial qualities and the responses they elicit. The response to an environment is learned, and the designer encourages the response he desires by using traditional architectural elements that are perceived by the user and responded to automatically. Vigier suggests further research which can test more accurately simulations of urban situations to aid the designer in predicting responses of users to spatial characteristics.

The term "architectural determinism" is the designer's version of the work that has been done by Park, Barker, and others in developing the theory of behavioral settings. Architectural determinism, whose most lucid spokesman is Terence Lee, is a concept that accepts the physical environment as a strong influence on behavior, and, by implication, tends to blame social problems on the physical environment. There is certainly no significant disagreement that the physical setting can influence behavior, or that people do respond to their surroundings, but there is divergence of opinion as to the degree of influence.

Patrick Geddes was certainly one of the first people to wed the form of the built environment with the culture of the people. And Patrick Geddes came from the more neutral turf of botany. Geddes not only combined the two approaches but did so on a cross-cultural basis, applying his ideas in India as well as in Northern Europe. His matrix in which the trilogy of the environment (place, work, and folk) is crossed by the four parts of a process (conceptualizing, designing, building, and recording) encompasses all that is covered in this bibliography. But Geddes has been little recognized outside of a planning elite. Lewis Mumford's ideas were directly influenced by Geddes and the two stand out as pioneers in environmental determinism.

Many of the approaches to design including the cognitive values of the user have resulted in the development of new vocabularies, models, and notation systems.

Isador Chein has presented a theoretical model that looks at the environment from the point of view of understanding behavior. From the analysis of a setting, the model predicts behavior and thus (in his view) increases understanding.

Philip Thiel developed a notation scheme so that the behavioral path could be programmed and schematically followed. The language of Maki and Goldberg addresses itself to the experiential meanings of the users and is close to Thiel's in looking at linkages and is certainly similar to the ideas of Steinetz.

Carl Steinetz has examined the relationship between physical form and activity organization. He concludes that by the design of the environment itself, and through the establishment of congruent and expressive systems of form, designers can significantly influence the achievement of a more meaningful environment. Chein, Thiel, Maki, Goldberg, and Steinetz may have made sense to themselves but it is not clear that they have developed general enough schemes to be useful to others.

In two papers, A. E. Parr discusses the need for visual diversity. He recognizes the need that people have for visual and auditory stimulation in order to best use their environment. His thesis is that man has a sensory appetite that is not satisfied by most modern architecture and urban design especially in the lack of decoration. His articles are based on intuition and it is clear that additional research is needed to test the validity of these concepts, such as that of Fiske and Maddi.

Architectural psychology is the study of the perception and response to the physical environment from a specific architectural viewpoint. The suggestion is made by Murray A. Milne that the responses to be evaluated are not just visual, but also sound, touch, temperature, force, gravity, odor, and taste. It is not accidental that his article, the most recent one cited, is entitled "The Beginnings of a Theory of Architectural Control." His early books and writings, in contrast, are less scientific but interesting. In 1956, Gyorgy Kepes, an artist wrote the most beautiful book on the subject of visual perception and design. The book itself is a perceptual and design experience.

1917
GEDDES, PATRICK
Cities in Evolution
Rov. Ed., London: Williamo & Norgatc, 1040.

Geddes was one of the first people to relate urban forms to behavioral patterns. His diagrams trace the interactive feedback process between place, work, and folk and the process facts, memories, plans, and acts—the two processes of concern in this directory. (GB)

1938
MUMFORD, LEWIS
The Culture of Cities
New York: Harcourt, Brace & Co., 1938.

A beautifully written evaluation of the urban balance of the medieval town, the development of the baroque city, and the "mis-urbanization" and havoc created by the rise of industrialism. Fascinating early insights into the development of the concept of privacy. His total discussion reflects his overriding concern with human behavior as evidenced in culture and its interactive deterministic force in the shape of cities. (ER)

1954
CHEIN, ISIDOR
"The Environment as a Determinant of Behavior"
Journal of Social Psychology, 1954, **39**, 115–127.

This is a comprehensive theoretical model for looking at the "geo-behavioral" environment, i.e., the geographic environment from the point of view of understanding behavior. The author discusses and defines the nature of such features as stimuli, goals, objects and noxiants, supports and constraints, discriminants, manipulants, means-end and pseudomeans, etc., which he hopes will be useful in predicting as well as understanding behavior. (ES)

1956
KEPES, GYORGY
The New Landscape in Art and Science
Chicago: Paul Theobald and Co., 1956.

In our modern era of specialization there exists both poet and artist, scientist and engineer. However, the natural world is the common basis for all. The senses of the poet and artist have been expanded and stimulated by the scientist and engineer. There are new sights, sounds, tastes, and textures—this is the new landscape. Kepes feels that "through ordering their sensory experiences humans can establish a working harmony with their physical surroundings." As a book on perception, it is more to be seen than read. (HS)

1961
FISKE, DONALD W., AND SALVATORE R. MADDI
Functions of Varied Experience
Homewood, Illinois: Dorsey Press, 1961.

This book is about varied experiences, their effect on organisms, and the functions they serve. Variation in experience comes from the changes occurring from moment to moment in the environment, both external and internal. The most applicable chapter is No. 14 by John R. Platt which links the physiological and psychological elements of aesthetic appreciation. Long lasting aesthetic satisfaction is produced not by one pattern but only by a pattern developing into patterns continuously full of new information. (JD)

THIEL, PHILIP
"Notes on the Description, Scaling, Notation and Scoring on Some Perceptual and Cognitive Attributes of the Physical Environment"
H. Proshansky (ed.), *Environmental Psychology*, New York: Holt, Rinehart, and Winston, 1970
An extremely detailed notation device for following the path of an individual in his environment. The notation is complex and its utilization to provide more appropriate environments is unclear. (GB & BS)

1962
BAKEMA, J.B.
"Some Thought about Relationships between Buildings and Cities"
Ekistics, August–September 1962, **82**, 96–99.
Bakema addresses the question of guiding people from the slow scale to the fast scale, and from the small scale to the large scale. It is an approach to integrating house, neighborhood, and city. "The scale of living in one world on earth confronts the scale of table and bed." (GB)

MAKI, FUMIHIKO, AND JERRY GOLDBERG
"Linkage in Collective Form"
Ekistics, August–September 1962, **82**, 100–104.
Four design functions are defined in making parts of the city "imageable": to mediate, to define, to repeat, and to mark sequential. They give examples of each. They note that once any element is used as a link it takes on a complicated set of secondary (experiential) meanings to the users. While this is a design tool of its own, it relates to perception. (GB)

1963

GUTHEIM, FREDERICK

"Urban Space and Urban Design"

In Wingo, Lowden, Jr. (Ed.), *Cities and Space: The Future Use of Urban Land,*
Baltimore: Johns Hopkins Paperbacks, 1963.

This is a short synoptic essay. Urban design is related first to its background in art and architecture, then to perception and suiting the social fabric of the city, and on to its relation to new technology. He creates a synthesis around the point of integrating the past into the future as a city reflects the continuum of man's life in its broadest sense. (GB)

1964

PARR, A. E.

"Environmental Design and Psychology"

Landscape, Winter 1964–1965, **14**, 15–18.

A discussion of the idea that we need visual diversity in our environment as a matter of mental health. Parr suggests that twentieth century architecture, which repudiates decoration, starves the sensory appetite and helps account for juvenile delinquency and adult boredom. Concludes with suggestions for research. (SMS)

1965

VIGIER, FRANCOISE

"Experimental Approach to Urban Design"

Journal of the American Institute of Planners, Feb. 1965, **30**, 21–31.

This paper attempts to clarify the role of urban design in relation to other environmental design disciplines, through an examination of the applicability of standard cognitive texting techniques to an urban situation. Drawing from the theory of perception as well as from recent experiment, the author demonstrates what appears to be a close correlation between the spatial qualities of streets and squares and the responses they elicit. Some doubt is cast upon the perceptual strength of traditional architectural elements and a strategy for further plans is suggested: (1) understand ambiguity, (2) improved research techniques such as more accurate simulation of urban situations. (WL)

IZUMI, KIYOSHI
"Psychosocial Phenomena and Building Design"
Building Research, 1965, **2**, 9–12.
Reprinted in Proshansky, 1970.

Stressing the need for serious consideration of psychological and social implications of building design, Izumi cites examples of ambiguous design, achieving privacy through design, and facilitating social relationships by design.

He views architecture as an imposing art. Because its influence is so total on an individual, its effect should be more seriously considered in the design and program stage. (JD)

FITCH, JAMES MARSTON
"Experiential Bases for Aesthetic Decision"
Annals of the New York Academy of Sciences, 1965, **128**, 706–714. Reprinted in Proshansky, 1970.

The author's major point of view is that there is a failure to relate aesthetics to experiential reality. Modern man has come to isolate aesthetics as if it were based only on visual perception. Actually, auditory perception, sensory perception, and the other components of experience are impinging on the individual as he makes his judgments so that they too influence him. Aesthetic enjoyment of a building can only be a matter of total sensory perception. He uses a hospital as a case study. He identifies modifications of the environment for different stress levels and develops a feel for the point aesthetics comes into play. (JD)

1966

GUTMAN, ROBERT
"Site Planning and Social Behavior"
Journal of Social Issues, October 1966, **22**, 103–115.

This article deals with the site plan or spatial arrangement of dwelling units summarizing the answers of existing research to the following questions: (1) What is the general nature of the phenomenon, (2) what is meant by the site plan, (3) what is the process through which site plans influence behavior, and (4) what kinds of behavior conceivable can be influenced by a site plan. Although Gutman claims that this research has given "excessive attention to the site plan as communication network," the reader may be rather surprised at the variety of approaches that have been utilized. Gutman leaves open the question of whether differences in site plan features result in corresponding differences in behavior. He is only willing to conclude that surely there must be better and worse methods of planning a site, so that it remains for us to "learn how to translate architectural theories into terms which can be tested with empirical techniques." This is a preliminary report relating to concepts of architectural determinism. (EW & GB)

KATES, ROBERT W.
"Stimulus and Symbol, the View from the Bridge"
Journal of Social Issues, October 1966, **22**, 21–29.

The central task of the social and behavioral sciences in the study of the environment is to relate the stimulus properties of the environment to their symbolic human manifestation and in turn to define the stimulus properties of the symbolic environment that men create. In so doing they will bridge the gap between environmental scientists who tend to study only literal physical and chemical impacts of the environment and the environmental designers who tend to ignore the behavioral consequences of their work. (PM)

PARR, A. E.
"Psychological Aspects of Urbanology"
Journal of Social Issues, October 1966, **22**, 30–39.

He considered here the idea that the most neglected aspect of urbanology is the direct impact upon human psychology of the sensory perception of man-made designs that are rapidly replacing the natural forms of our surroundings. Parr identifies the new landscape as a replacement of the unending variety of nature with a small selection of rigorously repetitive forms reduced to even greater uniformity by explicit architectural directives, and an enclosure of space (entombment) becoming absolute. Parr proposes a study of the psychological effects of visual monotony and enclosure in various forms to be attacked from two different directions: (1) psychological study of the mental and emotional needs that the environmental design should attempt to satisfy; (2) behavioral responses to the actual surroundings. (RJD)

SONNENFELD, JOSEPH
"Variable Values in Space and Landscape, An Inquiry into the Nature of Environmental Necessity"
Journal of Social Issues, October 1966, **22,** 71–83.

A basic distinction is made between space (a conceptual abstract) and landscape (the visually particular). The author analyzes their perception by native and nonnative populations. He concludes that a nonnative group (the typical planner's group) is difficult to type (but that generally space rather than landscape is more important). By utilizing the great human capacity to adapt to given conditions the planner can gradually force acceptance of architecturally created landscape and space, rather than attempting to accommodate the latter to individual or group tastes. (Crass, but realistic.) Emphasis should be placed on safe, not satisfying environments. The article for all its elaborate analysis, draws such general conclusions, that it is of no real value beyond the above. (TL)

1967

RAPPOPORT, AMOS, AND ROBERT KANTOR
"Complexity and Ambiguity in Environmental Design"
Journal of the American Institute of Planners, July 1967, **33,** 210–222.

A discussion of the idea that we need complexity and ambiguity in our visual environment. Refers to work by other writers, empirical psychological studies, and current literature. Authors suggest an "optimal perceptual rate" which bears on design at the scale of a street or facade. Article relates easily to those by Parr and Peterson as well as to Lynch's *The Image of the City.* (SMS)

REICHEK, JESSE
"Additional Remarks on the Design of Our Cities"
Transactions of the Bartlett Society, 1966–1967, **5,** 67–80.

Artists reaction to urban environment. Knowledge explosion caused us to think and act self-consciously. Art is in this author's opinion self-consciously lacking in emotion. Planners are deficient in physical-visual systemization and architects in nonphysical order. Trouble in defining urban order because it cannot be defined as the tradition of order in the city. The city is moving toward ambiguous forms. Asks if structure should be self-regulating. Defends freeway, automobile, and cities such as Los Angeles. Recognizes that this is a new urban form which is in conflict with sexual morality and the work ethic, but it is not chaos. (ER)

1968
STEINETZ, CARL
"Meaning and Congruence of Urban Form and Activity"
Journal of the American Institute of Planners, July 1968, **34**, 233–248.

Steinetz examines the relationship between physical form and activity organization and concludes that by the design of the environment itself and through establishment of a congruent and expressive system of forms, city designers can significantly influence achievement of a more meaningful environment. Study uses survey of form and activity characteristics and measures similarities among spatial distributions of various survey and interview variables. (PM)

1969
GANS, H. J.
"Planning for People not Buildings"
Environment and Planning, 1969, **1**, (1), 33–46.

Gans devotes his paper to the proposition that planners should help people solve their problems and realize their goals by planning for their social and personal needs in lieu of planning for the physical environment. Gans suggests that the planner should be a servant of the people, who proposes a variety of programs to solve problems and achieve goals so that people can have a choice of ideas or solutions. The main theme of the entire article is "the planner should devote himself first to people, and only secondarily to buildings." (EB)

LEE, TERENCE
"The Psychology of Spatial Orientation"
Architectural Asociation Quarterly, July 1969, **1**, 11–15.

This article is a plea for the systematic study of human behavior as an integral part of the modern design process. "If this person's effort after meaning is followed by a closely related 'effort after using,' and if both these active processes are found rewarding because the new experiences interlock with and extend the old ones, then the design has surely passed its first test. If, in addition, the physical construction has the effect of bridging some hitherto interrelated areas of human experience, if it makes connections between previously independent socio-spatial schemata to form new orders of whereness and whatness, exciting new patterns of meaning and use, then it will be design above the ordinary run."

PARR, A. E.
"Problems of Reason, Feeling and Habitat"
Architectural Association Quarterly, July 1969, **1**, 5–11.

Parr's essay confronts the question: To what extent does human sensitivity to the visual and auditory components of the environment contribute to comfort, well-being, and mental vigor? He includes in his discussion an evaluation of contemporary architecture—megastructures, malls—and the psychological benefits of human scale in the built environment. He concludes that our perception of time and space and changes are closely linked with stimuli from the environment and that nostalgia and sentimentality for the past are legitimate human mechanisms by which our lives achieve continuity and meaning. (MT)

1970
CANTER, DAVID V.
"The Place of Architectural Psychology: A Consideration of Some Findings"
EDRA 2. Environmental Design Research Association, October 1970.

Canter attempts an explanation of the theoretical dimensions of architectural psychology, indicating its imperfections to date and reviewing the literature concerned with this field. Article also appraises the role of coding systems and the value and appropriateness and complexity in the environment. Provides good introduction to the current theory and research. (MT)

1971
LEE, TERENCE
"The Effect of the Built Environment on Human Behavior"
International Journal of Environmental Studies, May 1971.

Strong case for architectural determinism. Theoretical article but laced with factual measurements from various studies which relate the social to the spatial and vice versa. Author is of the opinion that "human actions do not come in random streams but in matching bundles." This is selective simplifying of the input by the human organism for manageable patterns from sources of satisfaction and lawful regularity to genetic or cultural characteristics. A new scientific theory of human behavior in the city is emerging and the author believes there is enough consensus for social good to make explicit goals for planning. (ER)

GARDINER, STEPHEN
"Cruel Aesthetics"
The Architect, June 1971. 1, 35–39.

Ignoring the user of a building for the sake either of some blanket solution to universal problems of vast housing plans or of the architect's aesthetic is deemed cruel. The use of glass is, for example, in cases where it denies privacy or refuses to open to admit fresh air, an example of the self-indulgent architect's fantasy at the expense of the resident. (ES)

1972
MILNE, MURRAY A.
"The Beginnings of a Theory of Environmental Control"
Environmental Design: Research and Practice EDRA 3/AR 8, Department of Architecture, UCLA 1972.

A suggestion that designers look at the physical environment not as space but as generators of stimulation to the senses. Each source of the energy to which humans respond (light, infrared, sound, temperature, force, gravity, odor, and taste) is analyzed with a list of attributes of architectural materials. (JR)

Pattern Language

Christopher Alexander has invented a vocabulary to identify the psychological, cultural, and social requirements of the environment. This vocabulary is a pattern language which describes behavior in design terms. The patterns are design components which are defined analytically and which are combined and arranged into forms that "fit." The vocabulary can be used to describe all possible designs for the environment. The concept is fascinating; however, its usefulness to the designer has yet to be demonstrated.

1969
ALEXANDER, CHRISTOPHER
"Major Changes in Environment Form Required by Social and Psychological Demands"
Ekistics, August 1969, **28**, 78–86.

Careful consideration of psychological problems and social demands, which have previously been ignored by planners, can and should influence the shape of our cities to come. The author proposes 20 new form patterns (based on observations by three social psychologists: Leighton, Maslow, and Erikson) and describes the problem which each solves, offering hypotheses to test each pattern. An excellent study. (MS)

1970
ALEXANDER, CHRISTOPHER, SANFORD HIRSHEN, SARA ISHIKAWA, CHRISTIE COFFIN, AND SHLOMO ANGEL
Houses Generated by Patterns
Berkeley, Calif.: Center for Environmental Structure, 1970.

This is a competition entry for low-cost housing in Peru. The concept for relating behavioral patterns to design is clearly indicated. The variations in the housing area are much greater than in usual site designs. It also shows that the concept of behavioral setting needs to be augmented with participation by residents in the design process.

ALEXANDER, CHRISTOPHER
"Changes in Form"
Architectural Design, March 1970, **40**, 122–125.

An effort to define cultural patterns which we need and do not have, and which satisfy human needs. The cultural patterns have design implications. Combines psychological hypothesis. Twenty examples. (SMS)

MONTGOMERY, ROGERS
"Pattern Language"
Architectural Forum, January/February 1970, **132**, 52–59.

A new concept, called pattern language, intended to impart a rational basis to design has been created by Christopher Alexander at the Center for Environmental Structure, Berkeley, California. Pattern language is a three-dimensional application of the concept of work plus grammar equals a written product. When patterns, devined as reusable design components, are arranged in accordance with the rules for their combination, an infinite variety of man-made environments becomes possible. Analysis of the three part structure of each pattern reveals the concern with a behavior-oriented user needs concept.

Three projects utilizing this language are discussed and ample illustrations of the patterns and the designs planned from their use are presented. An exciting article for planners. (AW)

PART 2: SOCIAL SCIENCE APPROACHES TO THE URBAN ENVIRONMENT

Sociologists, geographers, and anthropologists have traditions for viewing man's interaction with his environment. This has, in the past, been in a separate stream from the designers; but they have considered the environment as an operational framework.

The first section, on the ecological tradition, traces the sociologists' early concern with the local environment up to the present-day conceptualization of behavioral settings and the residential environment.

Social interaction studies, considering space as the independent variable, make up the second section.

Time and activity studies catalog both where and what. These have been used to complement land use studies of designers as well as to obtain a grasp on the patterns of everyday life.

Social science methodologies of use to the designer are cited in the final section.

The Ecological Tradition

The social ecologists began writing in the 1920's with Jean Brunhes in France and the Chicago School in the United States. The tradition has been kept alive to this day by Paul Chombart de Lauwe and Anne Buttimer.

Although the beginnings of such theory delt with "the natural development" of urban areas, the focus has changed to deal with planned areas in order to guide environmental designers. The more general references are included below, while those that relate to behavioral settings and the residential environment follow.

1916

PARK, ROBERT EZRA

Human Communities: The City and Human Ecology

Glencoe, Illinois: The Free Press, 1952.

This book reprints a series of Park's essays, including:

"A City as a Natural Phenomenon" in which he refutes a general index for rating the environment. His major point is that "high grade" communities fail to be either self-reproducing or self-sufficient and must depend on "low grade" communities for survival.

"Community Organization and Juvenile Delinquency," written in 1925, in which he points to the child as the real neighbor in the local community and emphasizes play as the format for finding and establishing social associations.

"The City: Suggestions for the Investigation of Human Behavior in the Urban Environment," a 1916 essay with prophetic insights into social/urban order.

"Symbiosis and Socialization: A Frame of Reference for the Study of Society," in which he analyzes institutions and collective behavior in the city. (ER)

1920

BRUNHES, JEAN

Human Geography

New York: Rand McNally, 1920.

An early overview of the terrestrial whole by a French geographer. The chief aim of the book was to show the connection between physical environment and human activity. Examples overdrawn to the point of environmental determinism. Nomadism and the concept of private property are also explored in some depth. Early insights into the rootlessness of the industrial city and the resultant nomadism as a way of life. (ER)

1926

MCKENZIE, R. D.

"The Scope of Human Ecology"

Journal of Applied Sociology, March 1926, **10,** 316–323.

Reprinted in Theodorsen, 1961.

This essay which precedes Park's by ten years discusses urban ecological processes without drawing the direct analogies. He hypothesized that behavioral choice increases with progress of civilization. Less interesting to read than Park. (GB)

1936
PARK, ROBERT EZRA
"Human Ecology"
American Journal of Sociology, July 1936, **42**, 1–15.
Reprinted in Theodorsen, 1961; Warren, 1966.

Park takes an ecological approach to the human community in which "human beings occupying the same habitat come into competing but reciprocally meaningful relationships to each other and the natural environment" and those relationships constitute a "community in that their activities become intertwined in a natural economy." Park sees the forces of competition, dominance, and succession as operating to determine the shape and form a human community takes. "Human ecology" is defined as "an attempt to investigate the processes by which the biotic balance and the social equilibrium (1) are maintained once achieved and (2) the equilibrium are disturbed, the transition is made from one relatively stable order to another." (PM)

1938
WIRTH, LOUIS
"Urbanism as a Way of Life"
American Journal of Sociology, July 1938, **44**, 1–24.
Reprinted in Hatt, 1957; Gutman, 1970.

In formulating his theories of urbanism, behaviorism played a central role. The issues of health, loneliness, and anonymity, as well as their consequences are treated. This well-written essay continues to ring true. (GB)

1945

WIRTH, LOUIS

"Human Ecology"

American Journal of Sociology, May 1945, 483–488.

Reprinted in Theodorsen, 1961; Warren, 1966.

An articulate essay expressing the notion that the physical structure sets the stage for man's social life and psychological disposition. He also defines "ecology" as a tie between planning and the social sciences. (GB)

1947

FIREY, WALTER

Land Use in Central Boston

Cambridge: Harvard University Press, 1947.

Critical evaluation of ecological theory in terms of factual data. Attempts to construct an alternative ecological theory which considers the cultural and social systems in determining land use, as opposed to the three groupings of ecological theories—idealized descriptive themes; empirically rationalistic theories; and methodologically rationalistic theories. He sets forth two hypotheses: (1) values (volitional adaptation) comprise one of the criteria by which certain systems choose locations, and (2) that interests (rational adaptations) dominate the spatial adaptation of certain social systems with these interests coming indirectly from broader and larger cultural systems. Discusses the role of social values and nonrational adaptations to space and the cultural context of rational adaptation to space. Findings show the cultural component missing from each of the general theories. The author suggests that the best approach to integrating the cultural components is through a theory of proportionality in land use. (ER)

1950

HAWLEY, AMOS H.

Human Ecology: A Theory of Community Structure

New York: Ronald Press, 1950.

Hawley's human ecology social theory of community development is circuitous but condenses sociological, economic, and anthropological contributions of mobility, settlement patterns, caste systems, and urbanization. (AD)

1956

THOMAS, WILLIAM L., JR.
Man's Role in Changing the Face of the Earth
Chicago: University of Chicago Press, 1956.

 A geographer's anthropological and theoretical account of man's capacity to alter natural environment, the manner in which this is done, and validity of these actions (historical, physical, and biological effects man initiates, inhibits, or deflects as opposed to differences in cultural conduct). Useful as frame of reference for detailed study. (AD)

1965

CHOMBART DE LAUWE, PAUL HENRY
Des Hommes et des Villes
Paris: Payot, 1965.

 Chombart de Lauwe discusses in general terms what has changed in modern city life compared to that in the preindustrial city. He suggests that interdisciplinary planning should come closer to providing for needs of all age groups, ethnic groups, male and female, all classes and professions. He proposes studies of the kind Herbert Gans reports on in his book *The Levittowners* and gives some specific examples that are applicable to France and Paris but not always to American conditions. (MK)

1967

WEBBER, MELVIN M., AND CAROLYN C. WEBBER
"Culture, Territoriality and the Elastic Mile"
H. Wentworth Eldredge (Ed)., *Taming Megalopolis,* Vol. 1, 1967.

 The Webbers discuss the fact that sociologists are now concerned with social-cultural variants in perceptions of space and in social meanings as affected by space. Especially significant are the investigations into the culture of the working class ethnic groups, indicating striking variations in responses to space among population subgroups. They speculate about space related behavior of intellectual elites and then summarize some of the more relevant inquiries into working class behavior. The results of these investigations suggest some policy guidelines for city building programs. (PM)

1969

BUTTIMER, ANNE

"Social Space in Interdisciplinary Perspective"

The Geographical Review, July 1969, **59**, 417–426.

The author is mainly concerned with the development of the social space concept as manifested in the writings of Emile Durkheim, Chombart de Lauwe, and Sorre. She attempts to trace the dialogue between geographer and sociologist in France and discusses application of this concept in urban research today. She asserts that the usefulness of this concept is in "connections postulated between the internal subjective order (attitudes, traditions, and aspirations) and the external spatial order within an urban milieu." For example the relationship between a lack of sensory stimulation in routine urban occupations and the quest for sensory stimulation in outdoor recreational activity can be studied through the concept of social space. She stresses practical application of the social space concept by making value connections between internal subjective order (attitudes, traditions, aspirations) and external spatial order, within urban milieu. This is an excellent background article that is complementary to Michelson's book. (PM & SES)

1970

HARVEY, DAVID

"Social Process and Spatial Form: An Analysis of the Conceptual Problems of Urban Planning"

Regional Science Asociation Papers, 1970, **25**, 47–70.

A theoretical article in which the author defends the thesis that the languages of social behavioral and spatial concepts are completely different. He selects polar examples of "spatial environmental determinists" which he sets against "social process determinists." He discusses the research problems of developing projects that bridge the two languages, but also underlines the necessity of doing so if one is to construct a genuine theory of the city. (GB)

1971

BUTTIMER, ANNE

"Sociology and Planning"

Town Planning Review, April 1971, **42** (2), 145–180.

This paper is concerned with the communications gap between the academic community and the planners. It illustrates the traditional view of planners regarding sociology and the sociologist on planning. It also explains some of the traditional tasks assigned to the sociologist by planners and illustrates the area of consensus among sociologists relevant to planning. Last, it treats the potential avenues of dialogue between planners and sociologists. (ET)

The Behavioral Setting

The first theorist of ecological behaviorism was Robert A. Park, the inventor of the term "environmental psychology." In 1916, Park suggested that psychologists begin to think in terms of the environment as a stimulus for behavior and to measure the effects of environment upon the behavior of man. It has not been until very recently that this way of looking at human behavior has been pursued as a systematic method of evaluating activity patterns. The influence of the physical setting on the behavior of people has been best understood and studied by Roger G. Barker whose description of the concept of ecological psychology, published in 1968, has been the basis for extensive recent research.

The observation of "setting" and the behavior of its occupants clearly demonstrates the fact that place does influence behavior. This indicates that the designer, if he is aware of the kinds of spaces and setting he is creating, can reinforce the conduct of the users of space either negatively or positively. The characteristics of behavior-environment congruence that have been reported are supported by several theorists, including (1) operant learning, (2) observational and instructional learning, (3) behavior setting theory, and (4) social exchange theory. All these theories support the idea that there is a strong correlation between setting and behavior which is little understood as yet, but significant enough to recommend intensive additional research. The ability of a design to influence the behavior of the occupants of space is very complex, because the interactions of people and physical settings are difficult to measure. The research methods and measurement techniques used in this kind of research are extremely complex, but the pursuit of these studies will be valuable both in understanding behavior and as a tool for environmental designers.

1961

PARK, ROBERT EZRA

Human Communities, The City and Human Ecology

Glencoe, Illinois: The Free Press, 1952.

A collection of ecological essays written between 1916 and 1936 by one of America's most creative urbanists and influential teachers. His early insights, his questions, and his abstract systematic way of describing cities and their moral order has and can contribute much to the comprehension of our urban environment and its inhabitants. Important original source. Extremely readable style of a journalist without technical jargon. (ER)

1960

BARKER, ROGER G.

"Ecology and Motivation"

Nebraska Symposium in Motivation, 1960, **8,** 1–49.

Based on a comparative study of a midwestern United States town and one in Yorkshire, England, with regard to the relationship between the number of behavior settings and the number of people available to take responsible positions within these settings in each town. This article draws some significant conclusions about differences in participation, responsibility, sense of importance, and breadth of social contacts depending upon overpopulated versus underpopulated ecological environments. Backed by data regarding industrial absenteeism, Rotary Club attendance, Sunday School enrollment, and school music festival participation in large versus small establishments respectively, the conclusion that under-populated settings always elicit greater response has far-reaching implications for educators, town planners, architects, and sociologists, to name a few. (ES)

1961

BARKER, ROGER G., AND LOUISE S. BARKER

"The Psychological Ecology of Old People in Midwest, Kansas, and Yoredale, Yorkshire"

Journal of Gerontology, 1961, **16,** 144–160.

This article describes a study undertaken in 1954 to evaluate and compare the place of old people in two different community systems. The authors offer a definition of "behavior settings" and a classification system for measuring the involvement of individuals in public, non-family (outdoor) behavior settings. The involvement criteria are: (1) territorial range, (2) occupancy time, (3) exposure time, (4) zones of penetration. The uses of ten behavior settings in each town were compared according to these criteria; conclusions indicated that the psychological ecology of both elderly populations were not dissimilar, despite different physical environments and that the "environments of old people in both towns 'regress' (differ from the community at large and from settings of adults) in the same way that environments of children differ." (MT)

1966
STUDER, RAYMOND G., AND DAVID STEA
"Architectural Programming, Environmental Design, and Human Behavior"
Journal of Social Issues, October 1966, **22,** 127–131.

Paper attempts to define environment design and to provide a context for a new language of description. The claim is made that behavioral needs provide the only reasonable basis for design, and that problems in design are meaningful only when formulated in behavioral terms. A program for synthesis and the act of transforming a symbolically represented system of behavioral requirements into a formal system is illustrated with several examples. This related directly to the establishment of behavior settings and the later work of Alexander and Barker. (PM & GB)

1968
BARKER, ROGER G.
Ecological Psychology, Concepts and Methods for Studying the Environment of Human Behavior
Stanford University Press, 1968.

Concerned with methods and concepts for dealing with the ecological environment of human behavior. Describes in detail "behavior settings" and how to test for them, by extensive surveys within a small town. This is an excellent book on which many studies have been based. (BO & GB)

STUDER, RAYMOND G.
"Behavior Manipulation"
Ekistics, June 1968, **25,** 409–413.

The basic premise is that environment design is the manipulation of behaviors. He builds a construct whereby parts of the environment are treated as stimuli. The basic implications of the utilization of behavioral settings in design are outlined. (GB)

1969

STUDER, RAYMOND G.

"The Dynamics of Behavior-Contingent Physical Systems"

Ekistics, March 1969, **27** (160), 185–197.

He proposes a methodology for designing environments which are both conceptualized and realized as dynamic systems capable of moving toward more appropriate states. He outlines an iterative process for design which includes an information and control system as integral components. (GB)

RUSCH, CHARLES W.

"On the Relation of Form to Behavior"

Design Methods Group Newsletter, October 1969, **3** (No. 10).

He considers three different aspects of the design problem: (1) the relation of structure and mechanics; (2) the study of the behavior settings; and (3) what the perception of designed environment means in terms of the emotions it evokes, while he emphasizes that vested interests and administrative controls for the environment provide the greatest limiting elements. (GB)

1970

KUNZE, DONALD

"Observation of Residential Behavior Settings"

Design and Community, School of Design, North Carolina State University, 1970.

Kunze describes a weekend study of nine similar behavior settings in each of four rural towns in North Carolina with populations below 2,000. Age, sex/race, site, activities, and physical implements used in the settings were classified for participant groups in each setting. An index which would describe parts of the physical environment in terms of their ability to support various physical and social activities is the expected utility of this research. (MT)

KASMAR, J.

"Development of a Usable Lexicon of Environmental Descriptors"

Environment and Behavior, September 1970, **2,** 153–170.

Kasmar constructs a glossary of architectural descriptors which are relevant to physical elements in a designed space. Four stages of research were conducted, using four different sample groups for each stage. Pairs of adjectives were thus evolved to characterize conditions in a number of room types. Some of those sets of key descriptors related to: adequacy of size, acoustics, pleasantness, scale, cleanliness, and usualness in design. (MT)

BECHTEL, ROBERT B.
"A Behavioral Comparison of Urban and Small Town Environments"
EDRA 2, Environmental Design Research Association, October 1970.

An adaptation, with modifications, of Barker's behavior setting survey technique to the urban area. Behavior settings available to urban block residents are compared with those available to small town residents. City block residents have more behavioral settings available to them, yet they do not participate as actively in controlling their settings as town residents do. City dwellers are swept into "service" and functional-type activities; small town residents are more involved with residential social life. The author suggests that urban residential environments should be designed to promote a more socially demanding setting. (MT & NM)

1971
GUMP, PAUL V.
"Milieu, Environment, and Behavior"
Environment and Behavior, Winter 1971, **8,** 49–50, 60.

"The functioning environment consists of milieu and standing patterns of behavior in a synomorphic relation. This conception provides an environmental unit which includes the target of designers' efforts and also provides some bridge from that target to the behaviors and experiences of milieu inhabitants. Of course, a more comprehensive understanding is necessary regarding how milieu can be shaped to "pull" the desired synomorph programs: fuller description of the ecological idea is available. But much more understanding awaits collaborative research efforts of designers and behavioral scientists." (Last paragraph of article.)

1972
ELLIS, WILLIAM R., JR.
"Planning Design and Black Community Style: The Problem of Occasion-Adequate Space"
Environmental Design: Research and Practice, EDRA 3/AR 8, Los Angeles, 1972.

An excellent discussion in the introduction of the problems facing physical and social-behavioral researchers. An analysis of Goffman's social occasion with a comparison with Barker's behavioral settings is applied to adult and adolescent gatherings in poor black urban neighborhoods to suggest approaches to designing spaces in which these social occasions occur. (JR)

PREISER, WOLFGANG F. E.
"The Use of Ethological Methods in Environmental Analysis"
Environmental Design: Research and Practice, EDRA 3/AR 8, Los Angeles, 1972.

A case study to observe and analyze how people react to and interact in a specific space. Observations included data on time, frequency, and duration; location of stationary and moving subjects; and body posture, types, etc. The case study took place in a plaza and the author concluded that this space did not facilitate a diversity of behavior categories which would be desirable and then made a few suggestions that would be useful to designers. (JR & GB)

WICKER, ALLAN W.
"Mediating Behavior-Environment Congruence"
Behavioral Science, May 1972, **17**, 265–278.

A lucid review of the literature of behavioral-setting theory and research, perhaps the best summary of this field published. The theories of operant learning, behavior setting theory, observational learning, and social exchange theory are discussed. For each theory research problems are recommended. (ER)

OLSON, JR., LEONARD
"Optimization of Choice in a Semi Structured Physical Environment: A Model of Environmental Design"
Preiser, W. F. E. (ed.) *Environmental Design Perspectives, Viewpoints on the Profession, Education and Research*
Orangeburg, N.Y.: Man–Environment Systems: Focus Series, **1**, 112–121.

The author develops a classification matrix for environment and human reactions. On one dimension, environments are classified on a scale from structured to unstructured. The human reactions are classified as either behavioral or perceptual/aesthetic. User choice is assumed to take the form, in settings, of a range of structured behavior and opportunities for unstructured behavior and aesthetic experience, and the provision of linking behaviors between settings. This essay provided insights into the application of Barker's ideas to environmental design. (GB)

LEWIS AND CLARK COLLEGE LIBRARY
PORTLAND, OREGON 97219

Approaches to the Residential Environment

With the coming of age of residential redevelopment in the 1960's and the general discontent with patterns of suburban development, it was clear that ecological research could be applied directly for the development of better housing environments.

The triggers for this were a number of exposes on renewal and suburban life such as those of Gans, *The Urban Villagers* and *The Levittowners;* Spectorsky, *The Exurbanites;* and Whyte, *The Organization Man;* as well as the revelations on the interactive effect of environment on social life, which are outlined in the section on "Interaction."

Beginning with the article in 1961 by Rosow and culminating with Perin's book of 1971, the social scientists have been crying for the designers to listen to their findings. No matter how it is written the message is the same: planners, architects, and urban designers can build better environments if they pay attention to the feedback from the social scientists or if they incorporate the social scientists and their methodologies into the design process.

Has their message come across?

The evidence is varied. Two groups have been created which mix designers who want to listen to social scientists and social scientists who want to talk to designers. One is the Environmental Design Research Association which has existed since 1969 in order to have an annual get together. Over one-half of the papers from their conferences have been selected for this bibliography. The other is the Design Methods Group which exists via a newsletter. In both, the theme is research and methodology. In addition, two new journals have come into existence on the same premise: *Design and Environment* and *Environment and Behavior*.

The evidence is less clear in terms of actual building. Although more and more design firms are hiring tame sociologists, design schools are including such people as Suzanne Keller and John Zeisel on their faculties, and the public agencies are requiring that the social dimension should be evident in the design program, our cities and buildings themselves have changed little. This is partially due to the great inertia existing both in the process and in urban structure. The building practices of today will have their ultimate impact on the future.

Of the following listing, it is probably most important for the designer to read the Michelson and Perin books (both available in paperback editions). Michelson is easiest to read. He summarizes many sociological studies and includes a wide variety of plans, diagrams, cartoons, and other visual material. His major message is the importance of and need for research in order to build better residential environments. In contrast, Perin prescribes design based on prose interpretation of environmental research of social scientists. She believes that other human needs are so much more important than clarity of image and beauty of design that these will give way in order to achieve an environmental fit. This book is imperative for the designer to read because it represents the logical extreme of the social scientists let loose to plan cities.

All of the authors on this subject agree with Herbert Gans that "people are more important than buildings." However, cities must accommodate the needs of both, and for this it is necessary to temper one approach with the other—to match these readings with the design approaches, and both with the various scales of settlement from the dwelling to the large city.

1961
ROSOW, I.
"The Social Effects of the Physical Environment"
Journal of the American Institute of Planners, May 1961, **27,** 127–134.

Highly readable article full of ideas to consider, although superceded by Michelson. Questions the theory that creation of certain housing conditions can change social relationships. He does believe that where social pathological conditions exist, "slum clearance pays dividends in terms of social welfare and hard cash." He notes nonconforming uses, instances where people did not use specific features or spaces in the ways intended. (EW)

1963

SCHORR, ALVIN L.

"Housing and Its Effects"

Slums and Social Insecurity, Washington, D.C.: United States Government Printing Office, 1963.

This is a review of literature in which Schorr asserts that the impact of physical housing on human behavior is understated. He calls for research. A general overview. (GB)

1965

MICHELSON, WILLIAM

Value Orientation and Urban Form

Ph.D. Dissertation, Harvard University, 1965.

Michelson's dissertation, which formed a conceptual basis for some of his later work, analyzes the relationship between urban form and value orientation. (MT)

1966

VAPNARSKY, C. A.

"An Approach to the Sociology of Housing"

Ekistics, Aug. 1966, **22,** 127.

He reviews and summarizes a wide variety of literature, some of which is not in English, according to three categories of the sociology of housing: (1) analysis of social processes relating to housing policy; (2) relations between housing and family life; and (3) relations between housing and community. (GB)

GUTMAN, ROBERT

"Site Planning and Social Behavior"

Journal of Social Issues, October 1966, **22,** 103–116.

This article deals with the site plan or spatial arrangement of dwelling units summarizing the answers of existing research to the following questions: (1) what is the general nature of the phenomenon? (2) what is meant by the site plan? (3) what is the process through which site plans influence behavior? (4) what kinds of behavior conceivably can be influenced by a site plan? Although Gutman claims that this research has given "excessive attention to the site plan as communication network," the reader may be rather surprised at the variety of approaches that have been utilized. Gutman leaves open the question of whether differences in site plan features result in corresponding differences in behavior. He is only willing to conclude that surely there must be better and worse methods of planning a site, so that it remains for us to "learn how to translate architectural theories into terms which can be tested with empirical techniques." This is a preliminary report leading to such concepts as environmental behavioral setting. (EW & GB)

MICHELSON, WILLIAM
"An Empirical Analysis of Urban Environmental Preferences"
AIP Journal, November 1966, **32,** 355–360.

Describes an investigation (75 extensive interviews) into how social variables affect the physical environment. Urges that planners reduce the urban physical environment to the most basic level, the view of each individual. Enumerates the various results of his study and then makes appropriate conclusions, of which the call for diversity is paramount.

1970

MICHELSON, WILLIAM
Man and His Urban Environment: A Sociological Approach
Reading, Mass.: Addison-Wesley Publishing Co., 1970.

Michelson presents evidence concerning the relationship of housing and neighborhoods to particular life styles and stages of the life cycle. He collated 24 specific findings. From these he goes on to suggest appropriate formats for further research. This is a very readable paperback, and anyone using this bibliography should probably read it. The bibliography includes about a third of the citations in Michelson's book.

COATES, GARY
"Residential Behavior Patterns"
Design and Community, School of Design, North Carolina State University, Raleigh, 1970.

Coates' paper proposes a codification scheme which applies social research to designing the residential environment. His scheme emphasizes the ecological dimensions of human activity in the residential setting. "Environment" includes boundary conditions, spatial proximity, form and paths; "behavior" pertains to life style (social class, stage of life cycle, and environmental disposition). A well organized and useful statement.

1971
PERIN, CONSTANCE
With Man in Mind
Cambridge, Mass: MIT Press, 1971

Constance Perin argues for the institutionalization of behavioral research in both a lively and well documented approach. She not only thinks planners must have "Man in Mind" but believes that man has a mind. In one sense, this book can be considered as an argument for participatory design and against significance for environmental designers. Her description of the responsive environments are behavioral: "The quality and livability of the physical design is one that can preserve and affirm good will and harmony." While the book should be required reading for designers, it could become a dangerous tool for non-designers for advocating do-it-yourself communities. (GB)

SONNENFELD, J.
"Monadic and Dyadic Approaches to the Study of Behavior in Environment"
Proceedings of the Asociation of American Geographers, 1971, **3**, 165–169.

The psychologists's concept of the dyad, man and the environment, has suggested the addition of "otherman," who intervenes in the actor/reactor relationship. This philosophic article suggests approaches to the formulation of these relationships. (GB)

RAVETZ, ALISON
"The Use of Surveys in the Assessment of Residential Design"
Architectural Research and Teaching, April 1971, **1** (No. 3), 23–32.

The value of the survey as a research technique in the design of residential buildings is examined with particular reference to the Quarrey Hill Flat's surveys made in 1969. This paper points out possible misinterpretations of data and mistakes which may be made when the person who prepares a survey insinuates his own ideas concerning the source of the problem. (GS)

Social Interaction Studies

From the time of the cave man, structures have been molded to maximize human interactions. At the same time the first structures were often fortified to fend off outsiders, undesirables, and, of course, "the barbarians." The original hearth did both: it frightened off the wild beasts and drew the family into a circle of warmth and sociability.

Present interrelations are much more complex. The circle of family and friends may range around the globe while the enemy may live next door. Contemporary urban structures have developed a number of specific units for maximizing specialized contacts. The office building, the university, the resort, and the convention center are all designed to bring people together by planned chance to meet potential clients, marriage partners, or intellectual peers. Middle class residential areas such as those found in the contemporary new towns are also designed for children to find someone to play with, mothers to meet over shared interests, shared tasks, and gossip, and families to develop a web of supportive friendships which render services that "money cannot buy." The ghettos of deteriorating slums and public housing may evolve such social arrangements in spite of structural barriers.

At various times during an individual's life or even various times during the same day, movements are made through the urban network to find just the right contact in the right place. Teenage hangouts, gay bars, country clubs, and park benches reflect some of these needs.

Communications technology has only increased the number of face to face transactions. The most frequent use of the phone is to make a date for a meeting often on a neutral turf which serves the special purpose—at a restaurant, a hotel, the park, or an office. Communications have also brought knowledge about specialized places for certain kinds of encounters. The yellow pages, the TV, the radio, and the newspaper constantly bombard one with notices of "where its at" from the time a celebrity group will arrive at the airport to the location of hearings on pending congressional bills or even women's club meetings. More people are attracted to move out from the home neighborhood and into the wider context of the city and worldly affairs with greater frequency. This leaves the home itself unguarded, resulting in opportunity for robberies. In this case, a strong small neighborhood is needed more than ever—a web of people who bother when a stranger appears, who stop a stray moving van at a house, and who care if they see the newspapers or milk piling up outside the door. Without neighborhood support, professional services are drawn on for surveillance. As one moves through the city and similar situations repeat themselves, fear and a withdrawal from events replace spontaneous interaction, and result in such phenomena as noninvolvement in the witness of human tragedy.

Awareness of the spread of fear has brought people to search for a strong supportive living group situation. With small family sizes, greater participation of everyone in the work and educational forces, the strength must come from an extra-familial sized group—a small association of friends.

The commune movement has been one response.

Other examples of the special living group arrangements include the swinging singles apartments where mingling is the thing; retirement colonies in which boredom is replaced by bingo; and the very specialized intellectual retreats such as the Salk Center in California, Woods Hole in Massachusetts, and Taliesen, East and West. Each of these that are successful are similar in scope to communes, being large enough for supportive services but small enough for first name contact with the entire community. When these colonies grow to become towns and universities, they lose this special function.

However, all of these living arrangements only serve a minority of the population. Few people have the convictions needed to live in a commune, the money to afford specialized quarters for the swingers and elderly, or the intense interest to isolate themselves with intellectuals even if they were qualified. In all these cases, individuality is lost for group identity, and anonimity is sacrificed for sociability. These sacrifices are not necessary in the search for security. Living within an area where people are "good neighbors" however, does not create such significant pressures. The solution for most people is to find a "neighborhood" within the urban framework whether it is an apartment building, or along a street, or in a cluster of town houses. This unit is not necessarily significant for the planning of facilities, such as grade schools, nor may it be important for the formation of friendship, but it is imperative for the safety and security of the individual or family group.

Gans, Whyte, and Festinger have investigated the residential grouping as a setting for interaction, while Mel Webber and R. L. Meier have continually stressed that the whole city must be built for sustaining human contact. The importance lies in the integration of the two. The framework within which the small unit can operate is as important as detailed design of dwelling groups and the two must operate to allow individuals to move throughout the city, interacting at various special places. Since these points have been written about separately, first the large scale and then the small scale are discussed.

Urban Space for Interaction

R. L. Meier's *Communication Theory of Urban Growth* (1962) stimulated the development of conceptualizing the city as the focus of transactions which are measured in information bits rather than space. Following from this, an argument was developed primarily by Mel Webber (1903 and 1904), that the city need not be necessarily a spatial phenomena and that city planners could discard all such concepts as the neighborhood, the community, the central business district, etc. His writing was an academic complement to science fiction writers who have emphasized the atomistic communication-interlocked self-sufficient space-capsule type living on earth. While Webber's followers discarded the old-worn-out spatial generalizations (which in many cases were hackneyed in everyday professional use), communications technology did not magically fill the void. If anything, information has placed a greater burden on the specialized facilities of cities which have direct spatial expressions.

The rethinking of communications effects on the city in the second half of the sixties, particularly by R. L. Meier (1968) and Gottmann (1970), brought out new spatial potentials for communication maximizing centers. Each of these authors is an academician and not a design-oriented planner. And each stopped short of physical expressions of their ideas.

Christopher Alexander in his essay on "The City as a Mechanism for Sustaining Human Contact" (1967) and C. A. Doxiadis on "Man's Movement and His Settlements" (1970), who are both trained in architecture, take a theoretical approach and then add its design dimensions. Alexander goes down to the scale of the dwelling unit, while Doxiadis stops at that subunit in which most daily urban systems operate. These authors provide some hope for bridging the gap to the next section of writings which present the social scientists findings on neighboring.

1962

MEIER, R. L.
A Communications Theory of Urban Growth
Cambridge: M.I.T. Press, 1962.

Meier theorizes that urban development can be measured in terms of transactions, each of which is made up of a finite number of "bits." This theory is derived from Shannon's more general information theory. Meier relates his theory both to the utilization of time and space in the metropolis, and then to the technological transaction capacity. He notes the significance of overload and describes the different outcomes resulting from stress in both human and mechanized systems. It is truly a general theory, relating to all sizes of urban places and both developed and underdeveloped areas. As yet, it is not operational as a methodology because of a number of problems involving really counting "information bits" and transactions. It remains an excellent, thought-provoking monograph. (GB)

1963

WEBBER, MELVIN M.

"Order in Diversity: Community without Propinquity"
Lowdon Wingo, Ed., *Cities and Space,* Baltimore: Johns Hopkins Press, 1963.
Reprinted in Proshansky, 1970; Gutman, 1970.

Webber contends that the essential qualities of the city are cultural and not territorial. He then argues for planning for a pluralistic environment in which there are no elements resembling "neighborhood" or "communities." His case is stated with a great deal of articulateness. (GB)

1964

WEBBER, MELVIN M.

"The Urban Place and the Nonplace Realm"
Explorations into Urban Structure
Philadelphia: University of Pennsylvania Press, 1964.

This essay deals with processes and forms simultaneously and seeks a clearer conception of the urban community. He suggests that planners must see the city as a culturally conditioned system of dynamic interrelationships between individuals and groups as modified by locational distributions. He discusses social interaction in terms of role identification in the educated classes and neighborhood identification for others. (PM & GB)

1967

ALEXANDER, CHRISTOPHER

"The City as a Mechanism for Sustaining Human Contact"
William Ewald, Ed., *Environment for Man,* Bloomington: Indiana University Press, 1967.

A remarkable synthesis of urban form for dwelling units. An example of social engineering. Alexander hypothesizes that an individual requires three to four intimate contacts to sustain mental health. Cities tend to increase the number of secondary contacts. From this requirement for sustaining intimate contacts, Alexander develops 12 geometric features which should be required in the development of a dwelling unit. On the basis of these geometric requirements he synthesizes a new form for high density living. (RJD)

1968
MEIER, R. L.
"The Metropolis as a Transaction-Maximizing System"
Daedalus, Fall 1968, **97** (No. 4), 1292–1313.

The planner's self-imposed directive: the design of a city must promote the harmonious interaction of a population. Measures of vitality are the aggregate of transactions per unit of time. Suggests a variety of transactional measures (policies) to bring all parts of society into the mainstream. Well written with ideas that continue to be stimulating. (GB)

1970
DOXIADIS, C. A.
"Man's Movement and His Settlements"
Ekistics, May 1970, Vol. 29, **174,** 296–321.

The framework of settlements should minimize man's effort for contacts with a maximum number of people. Understanding the behavior suggests the division of daily, weekly, monthly, and yearly movement systems. The frequency and related energy consumption (cost) provide a framework relating to urban structure that has order. (GB)

GOTTMANN, JEAN
"Urban Centrality and the Interweaving of Quaternary Activities"
Ekistics, May 1970, **174,** 322-331.
Reprinted in Bell, 1972.

Transactional activities are likely to occur in the cultural centers of megalopolises rather than the traditional central areas because they have many of the nine important factors for the future: (1) accessibility; (2) information flows; (3) transactional performance; (4) sophisticated labor markets; (5) amenities and entertainment; (6) expert consultation services; (7) markets for money and credit; (8) specialized shopping; and (9) quality educational facilities. This provides almost a personal behavioral view of big cities, especially for taste-making individuals. (GB)

1972

PACKARD, VANCE

A Nation of Strangers

New York: David McKay Co., Inc., 1972.

The argument in the book is the need to recreate the neighborhood and replace the values of change and mobility with constancy and continuity. On the one hand, his data attests to the correlation of mobility and disruption of traditional patterns with various pathologies, including divorce (not assuming the value of getting out of a bad relationship), but on the other he lets himself also state the conditions and personality types who swing with the changing scene. Thus, his data and his conclusion almost stand as separate essays. Interestingly, his prescription for neighborhood is much the same as his predecessors of the first half of the century: to meet the needs of children within walking distance, and to establish a diverse and stable community of young and old and rich and poor. His conclusion reads almost as a super-reaction to his data, and the first half is worth reading on its own for an analysis of effects of mobility on patterns of social interaction. (GB)

Neighboring: Who Talks to Whom? and How Does the Researcher Know?

In 1950, when Leon Festinger, Kurt Back, and Stanley Schacter wrote down their findings on friendship formation as determined by the structure of married students' housing at M.I.T., they opened up a flourishing area of research of interest to the designers of housing. They suggested that "neighboring" and even "friendship formation" could be engineered. (What an appropriate finding for the M.I.T. campus!)

In putting the findings of Festinger *et al.* into perspective, it is worth looking not only at the subsequent case study and methodological research, but also at a parallel line of study by the family sociologists concerned with the extension of the family and kin network into the wider mesh of society. Elizabeth Bott (1957, 1971) provided the basic research by relating various aspects of family life-styles to their extension into friendship networks. This transition is from the primitive tribe where territory, kinship, and friendship boundaries are the same to the megalopolis where few territories overlap, but loosely woven interacting networks of nonadjacent spatially defined nodes provide extensive diversity. Between the two archtypes, there are a variety of more closely integrated patterns which are most predominant today among the majority of the population.

The writings in this section are all by nondesigners, primarily sociologists who discuss the spatial setting for interaction—and thus provide the planners and architects with data for planning housing and apartment groupings. In the third part where material is organized on the housing group, the small neighborhood, and the traditional neighborhood unit, there are references which tie these kinds of data together in ways more appropriate to designers. For the designer, who does not want to get involved in the details of the sociological arguments, it would be appropriate to skip this next section and move directly to the discussion in the third part of this book—on the spatial dimensions themselves. However, the meat is here for chewing, particularly in cookbooks describing the process of studying human interaction.

Unfortunately, the sociologists themselves still have not reached any kind of consensus on patterns of interaction. Suzanne Keller in her 1968 book on the neighborhood (discussed in detail in the section on "neighborhood") distinguishes between neighbor, neighboring, and neighborhood. Many of the writers confuse all three, but especially the first two. One reason that they do this is that many write without reading. Five of the 19 scholars did not show any evidence of reading works by others writing on this same subject. The network of cross referencing points out the importance of the research of Festinger, Gans, and Bott, and the synthesis of Keller.

1950

FESTINGER, LEON, STANLEY SCHACTER, AND KURT BACK
Social Pressures in Informal Groups: A Study of Human Factors in Housing
New York: Harper, 1950.

A study of housing projects in Boston, inhabited by M.I.T. students and their families. Basis for study was the orientation to the way the small face-to-face group functions in the lives of people and the conditions under which this function produces one result or another. Reveals the dependence of friendship formation on the physical formation of houses. Also studies how membership in groups affected people's attitudes and behavior. Found a high level of uniformity in regard to attitudes towards and activity in tenant organization within each of the social groups in the project. Of special interest is the appendix on the methodology of the field study. (PM)

CAPLOW, T., AND R. FOREMAN
"Neighborhood Interaction in a Homogeneous Community"
American Sociological Review, 1950, **50,** 357–366.

This article discusses a study done on an extremely homogeneous group of students living in a university village to determine neighborhood interaction. Each family was asked to rate its relationship with every other family on the block. A high rate of sociability was found within this block of 50 families. Accessibility was a factor, but the great similarity of interest and background was primary. (NSM)

1951

FESTINGER, LEON
"Architecture and Group Membership"
Journal of Social Issues, 1951, **7,** 152–164.

Festinger describes the value of group membership and individual cross-group mobility, highlighting involuntary group membership (family, ethnic identity).

Architectural design has a decided effect on formation of friendships among residents of projects; cases of satisfying and dissatisfying involuntary group membership are cited as they related to architectural features and group social standards. (MT)

1953

FESTINGER, LEON, AND DANIEL KATZ
"Observation of Group Behavior"
Research Methods in the Behavioral Sciences, Chapters 8 and 9, New York: Dryden Press, 1953.

Written primarily for social psychologists, this volume and most of the problems discussed are from the field of social psychology. Describes approaches and methods of research applicable in all areas of social science research. Book includes research settings, sampling procedures, methods of collecting data, analysis, and application of findings. (PM & MT)

WHYTE, WILLIAM H., JR.
"How the New Suburbia Socializes"
Fortune, August 1953, **49,** 120–122, 186–198.
Included in Whyte's *The Organization Man,* New York: Simon and Schuster, 1956.

Though written when suburbia was in its genesis, this article provides remarkable insights into social implications of this new man-made environment.

The author believes that a community's design has a powerful effect on social interaction. As a case study he focuses on Park Forest, Illinois, where he studied 105 rental courts. The result: each court developed its own unique character and behavior patterns. Furthermore, the uniqueness is maintained although new people move into the units. He reaches the following conclusions: "(1) Individuals tend to become most friendly with neighbors whose driveways adjoin theirs; (2) people in most central positions make the greatest number of social contacts; (3) street width and traffic determine friendship patterns that cross streets; (4) people make friends with those in back of them only where some physical feature allows for contact."

In spite of his strong convictions on what design can do, he is cautious about extreme applications and does not suggest "imprisoned brotherhood." (JZ)

WALLIN, PAUL
"A Guttman Scale for Measuring Women's Neighborliness"
American Journal of Sociology, November 1953, **59,** 244–246.

In the process of describing a research tool, this article defines neighborhood and neighbor. The instrument, a Guttman scale, can be used to measure neighborliness among women under sixty in large or small urban areas. It is suggested that this method might be used in testing intra-community and inter-community differences in neighborliness. (BJ)

1954

MANN, PETER H.
"The Concept of Neighborliness"
American Journal of Sociology, September 1954, 163–168.

Neighborhood unit planning is intended to promote fuller social relationships between neighbors. However, neighborliness may be latent as well as manifest and the latter is not sufficient to assess the integration of a neighborhood group. There is no single type of neighborhood that is right for all groups. In modern cities, there are neighborhoods with different degrees of neighborliness. (BJ)

1957

BOTT, ELIZABETH
Family and Social Network
London: Tavistock Publication, 1957; reprinted 1971.

Elizabeth Bott's book is an excellent analysis of the social and psychological organization of some English urban families with primary emphasis on variation in conjugal role relationships and their influence on the connectedness in the total family network and social environment. Data were gathered through extensive interviews with families in similar phases of familial development but from different socioeconomic strata. An expert study. (MT)

ARGYLE, MICHAEL
The Scientific Study of Human Behavior
London: Methuen and Co., 1957.

Argyle examines one aspect of social psychology, that of social interaction (socialization and personality concepts are excluded). Research is described which validates the basic theories of social interaction, especially those dealing with person to person contact and small group behavior. (MT)

1958
FAVA, SYLVIA FLEIS
"Contrasts in Neighboring: New York City and a Suburban Community"
W. M. Dobriner, Ed., *The Suburban Community,* 1958.
New York: Putnam.

This study contrasted differing behavior patterns among residents of (1) a central city borough of Manhattan; (2) an outer city area in the borough of Queens; and (3) a suburban area in Nassau County. About 200 residents were interviewed among white, middle class homeowners. The suburban residents have significantly higher neighboring scores. The author agrees with Walter Martin that people are drawn to suburbs partly because they share a strong desire for more "neighboring" and increased community participation. (JZ)

1959
HOLE, VERE
"Social Effects of Planned Rehousing"
Town Planning Review, July 1959, **30,** 161–173.

Deals with social problems raised by transfer of families from central areas of cities to housing estates in Scotland. Selection of tenants produced a far more homogeneous population on new housing estate yet no sense of community. Instead a host of small internally interacting groups developed between which there were no connecting links. Social impoverishment through no clearly defined means for establishing contact. The only culturally approved pattern was that of reserved withdrawal. Emphasis in rehousing should be on estate as well as dwelling if genuine communities are to be created. (MK)

1960
WILLMOTT, PETER, AND MICHAEL YOUNG
Family and Class in a London Suburb
London: Routledge and Kegan Paul, 1960.

Young and Willmott compare two communities in the suburban east end of London: Woodford and Bethnal Green, with attention to several sociological features of the populations: old people and their relationship to the community system,

116

mother–daughter relationships and marriage patterns, friendliness toward outsiders, kinship relationships and social mobility, and class membership and stratification. A thorough description of survey techniques and methodology is included. (MT)

USEEM, RUTH HILL, AND DUANE L. GIBSON
"The Function of Neighboring for the Middle Class Male"
Human Organization, Summer 1960, **19,** 68–76.

Anthropologically oriented study of 75 mid-western, middle management men and their attempts to maintain their individual equilibriums by selecting neighborhoods reflective of their self-imagined status. (AT)

1961
GANS, HERBERT J.
"Planning and Social Life, Friendship and Neighbor Relations in Suburban Communities"
American Institute of Planning Journal, May 1961, **27,** 134–141.
Reprinted in Gutman 1970; Bell, 1972.

In new and existing communities, propinquity brings neighbors into visual or social contact. The intensity and/or quality of friendships are based on homogeneity of interests, e.g., similar political beliefs, child rearing methods, etc. While site planning may to some degree encourage or discourage social patterns it should not be the ultimate goal of the planner to produce a specific pattern, but to provide for the maximum possibility of choice. If and when sufficient studies indicate that some locations in a site plan will inevitably result in greater social contact than others, potential occupants should be informed, so that they may take this into consideration when choosing a home. (RM)

1962
HARE, A. PAUL
Small Group Research
New York: The Free Press of Glencoe, 1962.

The book is divided into three sections: Part one, group process and structure, part two, six variables that affect the interaction process, and part three, performance characteristics. In the three parts, the same material is organized in three different ways. The first part considers the central tendencies of the interaction process and group structure. The second part emphasizes the deviations from typical patterns which may result from variables such as group size, leadership and personality. The third part reviews the differences in productivity due to variation in group processes and structures. The author has included a bibliography of 1385 items for further psychological or sociological research. (AD)

GULICK, JOHN, C. E. BOWERMAN, AND KURT BACK
"Newcomer Enculturation in the City: Attitudes and Participation"
Chapin, F. S. and Weiss, S., Eds., *Urban Growth Dynamics,* New York: John Wiley, 1962.

A variety of data was collected on social enculturation through neighboring and participation in social groups. The authors conclude that relative satisfaction is related to two phenomena: that the majority of the newcomers are from the region and thus there is no serious social readjustment and that newcomers from outside are often professionals and readily adjust to new places. In this case and other similar ones, the planner need not make special compensations, particularly in the design of new middle class communities. (GB)

1964
PITT, GILLIAN M.
"The Problem of Loneliness"
Town and Country Planning, January 1964, **32,** 30–31.

Women, bored and lonely, average age 33, two or more preschool children . . . where . . . suburbs, New Towns, and estates near London, so reports the National Council of Social Service in a 1957 study. Women have a greater task of readjustment after moving to a new location. A high proportion of the people who move come from settled communities surrounded by friends and relatives. After the move, the husband has the continuity of work-oriented relationships; women do not have the same continuity of companionship. To further aggravate the situation, in the rush to get the new home into a pleasing condition, more money in the family budget is allotted to household needs at the expense of the entertainment budget. As a result, a woman will be more isolated in the new unfamiliar unwarm house in the new environment. Another problem to consider when developing a new community. (RJD)

TOMEH, AIDA K.
"Informal Group Participation and Residential Patterns"
American Journal of Sociology, July 1964, **70,** 28–35.

A study dealing with the nature and extent of informal social interaction as it is related to residential patterns in metropolitan Detroit. From her analysis of a precision matched sample the author concludes that informal social relationships are influenced by place of residence and that both social characteristics and residence location are important factors in determining social contact. Previous studies have tended to emphasize the former variable alone. When some population characteristics are held constant, evidence shows that increased social participation is found in the suburbs. However, this is not the case with residents who do not fit into the general pattern of the suburban area (e.g., negroes and single people). Minority status is a barrier to participation. (NM)

1967

PERRATON, JEAN K.
"Community Planning: An Analysis of Certain Social Aims"
Journal of Town Planning Institute, March 1967, **53,** 95–98.

Three aspects of environment—sense of belonging, neighborliness and community spirit—are defined and analyzed in relation to planning. Planning policies that arrange residential areas to form clearly defined entities, design layouts to encourage neighborly conduct and social "balance," and provide community buildings and other local facilities, appear to be ineffective according to research done except in terms of promoting neighborly conduct. (SS)

1968

KRIESBURGH, LOUIS
"Neighborhood Setting and the Isolation of Public Housing Tenants"
Journal of the American Institute of Planners, January 1968, **34,** 43–50.

The author is primarily interested in the consequences of integrating low-income public housing into middle income neighborhoods. This study, a survey done on four housing projects and their surrounding neighborhoods in Syracuse, New York, is an attempt to analyze the extent to which social isolation between project tenants and residents in surrounding areas exists and is affected by socioeconomic differences between them. Concludes that residence in public housing constitutes a barrier to social interaction but that socioeconomic differences are not necessarily an impediment to social interaction. (PM)

1970
SOEN, DAN
"Neighborly Relations and Ethnic Problems in Israel"
Ekistics, August 1970, **30,** 133–139.
Reprinted in Bell, 1972.

To what extent do heterogeneous neighbors or heterogeneous neighborhoods affect satisfaction with the residential environment? He presents findings from surveys of Jerusalem. He concludes that sensible planning in full awareness of the difficulties of heterogeneous neighborhoods may not only achieve a higher degree of satisfaction of the inhabitants, but also encourages ethnic openness. This is complementary to Gans' study, 1961. (GB)

KELLER, SUZANNE
"Human Communication and Social Networks at the Micro Scale"
Ekistics, October 1970, **179,** 306–308.

She defines networks of social interaction and the three ways they work in the daily lives of people: through the diffusion of innovation; the spread of rumors; and the web of friendship. She notes that the most significant role is that of the gatekeeper who filters information. She supports the notion of holistically planning for communication in the city—at all levels.(GB)

1971
BOESCHENSTEIN, WARREN
"Design of Socially Mixed Housing"
Journal of the American Institute of Planners, September 1971, **37,** 311–319.
A survey of six families at Brookfield Farm Renewal, Boston used as a basis for drawing maps of social interaction between families of different classes. He gets a lot of mileage from a little research. (GB)

Time and Activity Budgets

From a behavioral point of view, the time budget is complementary to the notion of behavioral setting. The first provides the frequency and duration and the second the place for specific behaviors. Both provide nonmonetary quantitative data on man's patterns of living and thus bring other measurements than economic for making qualitative design judgments.

The first major time budget study in the United States came into being because of dissatisfaction with the quality of life during the Great Depression of the 1930's. P. Sorokin headed a group formed to analyze the time budgets of white collar workers, with the express purpose to evaluate hours devoted to social ends, which the authors were disappointed to find lacking. While no policies were developed from their findings and further developments of the research techniques were stopped because of the Second World War emergency, both the basic methodologies and a means of classification had been developed.

It has not been until the last decade that interest has again focused on time-budget measures as appropriate for indicators of the quality of life. This has resulted from a new discontent—not the depression of the thirties—but a new consciousness that monetary measures alone cannot guide policies within an urbanized and generally affluent society. In 1959, Richard Meier argued that time budgets should be used to parallel national income accounting. While this has not occurred as yet, concern with quality of life is leading various countries in this direction. The development of time-budget studies have been placed in three categories —methodologies, land use implications, and the uses of leisure hours.

Methodologies of Time-Budget Studies

Since Sorokin the basic technology has remained the same: People are asked to record how they use their time and this is coded into a predetermined classification of activities. More recently the computer has facilitated what had been the laborious analysis of the data making time-budget analysis more feasible (Kranz, 1970).

With greater emphasis and more research, various researchers have seen time-budget data as ways to further their own special interest areas, e.g., Szalai on international comparison, Godschalk and Mills on citizen participation, and Hitchcock on life style variations. Although the recent richness of approaches indicates a developing of interest and potential fruitfulness for these studies bringing about a greater understanding of man–environment relationships.

1939

SOROKIN, PITIRIM, AND CLARENCE BERGER
Time-Budgets of Human Behavior
Cambridge: Harvard University Press, 1939.

The time budgets of 100 white collar workers were measured for four weeks. Motives as well as activities were examined. Detailed findings in a chart form and concise text make this easy to compare with current patterns. He found single overt activity motivated by only one reason. He concluded that 20 to 22 hours a day were budgeted for hedonistic, utilitarian, and sensate purposes; that a social conscience did not really cause significant activity patterns. (ER)

1954
FOLEY, DONALD L.
"Urban Daytime Population: A Field for Demographic-Econological Analysis"
Social Forces, May 1954. Reprinted in Theodorsen, 1961.

Proposes empirical time-budget activity studies and discusses their utility. (GB)

1959
MEIER, R. L.
"Human Time Allocation: A Basis for Social Accounts"
Journal of the American Institute of Planners, February 1959, **25**, 27–33.

Studies of time budgets are suggested to be run in parallel to national income accounting. Meier suggests that improvements in income and social development are accompanied by increases in the amount of time spent in public activity and increases in the variety of life. Thus he argues that the cumulative data on time allocations can be used to indicate whether the life of various sections of the population is getting richer, and the effectiveness of programs directed to modifying the social and physical environment can be tested. (GB)

1966
GODSCHALK, DAVID R., AND WILLIAM E. MILLS
"A Collaborative Approach to Planning through Urban Activities"
Journal of the American Institute of Planners, March 1966, **32**, 86–94.

The authors suggest that urban activities surveys may be workable bases for confirming planner-citizen dialogues. The pilot study of this method demonstrated its usefulness and feasibility. The process stresses two-way communications. The activities survey provides information on attitudes, values, neighborhoods, and life styles of subcommunities. It is also suggested that citizens in being interviewed help increase the level of awareness, choice, and action. The authors are unclear as to how this method can provide an ongoing dialogue. (WP)

SZALAI, A.
"Trends in Comparative Time Budget Research"
The American Behavioral Scientist, May 1966; *Ekistics,* November 1967.

A survey of time-budget studies which is quite thorough. It sets the stage for time-budget surveys on cross-cultural bases. (GB)

1969

CHAPIN, F. STUART, AND RICHARD K. BRAIL

"Human Activity Systems in the Metropolitan United States"
Environment and Behavior, December, 1969, **1**, 107–130.

This paper relates environment and behavior in a systems framework (from 43 metropolitan areas). By use of probability sample, the life cycle, and different economic circumstances, human activity systems are measured in time and space. Concludes that in a typical weekday (if all time expended in forms of obligatory activity are excluded from typical adult's 24-hour day) about 5 hours remain for discretionary activity (of which 4 hours are spent at home). This conclusion stresses importance of home and neighborhood in allocation of public resources for leisure time facilities. (LC)

1970

KRANZ, PETER

"What Do People Do All Day?"
Behavioral Science, May 1970, **15** (3), 286–291; *Ekistics,* **178**, 203–206.

This is a report of a computerized methodology for analysis of time-activity budgets with a measureable level of satisfaction. While his study focused on behavior, it is easily adaptable to behavior–environment analysis. (GB)

1971

HITCHCOCK, JOHN R.

"Daily Activity Patterns: An Exploratory Pattern"
Unpublished manuscript, 1971.

Hitchcock hypothesises that the characteristics of outside activities, especially physical medical checkups, are correlated with a parochial-cosmopolitan life-style dimension distinct from social status. Particular attention was paid to in-the-home versus outside activities by sex. Both men were classified in terms of those having high or low levels of outside activities and women according to high or low levels of inside activities. It alludes to interesting possibilities for utilization of time-budget analysis. (GB)

1972

MARTINEAU, THOMAS R.

"The Urban Activity Model"

Environmental Design: Research and Practice, EDRA 3/AR 8, Los Angeles, 1972.

A classification system of activities was devised in order to test how well communities fulfilled the needs, desires, and life styles of their residents. Unfortunately in an area where there is a lot of research, Matineau seems to want to reinvent the 'wheel' for himself. His categories do not match other peoples, and in fact they are loaded toward peculiar lifestyles. There are some interesting thoughts but it would benefit from being related to like projects. (GB)

BULL, C. NEIL

"Prediction of Future Daily Behaviors: An Empirical Measure of Leisure"

Journal of Leisure Research, Vol. 4, No. 2, Spring 1972, pp. 119–128.

The study measures the degree to which people are able to preduct their future daily behaviors. Using a time-budget methodology, 49 married and employed males were asked to predict in a dairy what they would do in the next 24 hours. Neither age, socio-economic status, nor education were related to prediction errors. Weather did affect predictions. In addition, leisure activities were overestimated while work related activities were underestimated. This can affect research relating to planning for future recreation-demand. (GB)

Land Use and Activity Studies

F. Stuart Chapin in his well-used land use planning text of 1965 devotes a chapter to the study of urban activity patterns. In this he illustrates the relationship between human time-budget studies and land uses. Since this time, a number of his students as well as Chapin, himself, have continued to refine these concepts.

More recently others have taken on this line of research. It is doubtful, however, when it will be fully operational at an urban scale. The cost remains high to get a reasonable sample and the inferences from time to space decay as both dimensions constantly change making the technique most applicable to special projects to be installed at specific places for specific populations. See for example the study by Ray Maw cited in the next subsection on leisure.

1965
CHAPIN, F. STUART
"The Study of Urban Activity Patterns"
Urban Land Use Planning, Chapter 6, Urbana: University of Illinois Press, 1965.

Chapin is primarily concerned with various kinds of urban activity systems which take spatial form in the metropolitan area, especially systems which assume importance in the structure and organization of the area. Activity systems are defined as "behavior patterns of individuals, families, institutions and firms which occur in spatial patterns that have meaning in planning for land use." Techniques for studying activity systems and the definition of spatial patterns these systems take are the prime concerns. Chapin also discusses content of activity surveys and some forms of data summarization. Good description of game technique for surveying. (PM)

CHAPIN, F. STUART, AND HENRY HIGHTOWER
"Household Activity Patterns and Land Use"
Journal of the American Institute of Planners, August 1965.

A study of the activity patterns of groups, e.g. households, institutions, and firms, and how evaluation and analysis of these patterns can be used to isolate inputs useful in the physical planning process. The study was conducted by the use of an interview game technique that covered several areas of household activity (religious, social, political) and hoped for value in the household in terms of allocation of spare time. This article was well written and should be useful in the formulation of methodology. (LM)

1968
CHAPIN, F. STUART
"Activity Systems and Urban Structure: A Working Scheme"
Journal of the American Institute of Planners, January 1968, **34**, 11–18.

Describes a conceptual system which utilizes choice theory to describe and convert human motivations into human activity in the city. No matter what level model, he relates this to why people move residence location and the procedure of decision-making they actually follow. A systems approach to urban structure. (RL)

1969
BATCHELOR, PETER
"Residential Space Systems: Generic and Specific Concepts of Urban Structural Analysis"
EDRA One, Evironmental Design Research Association, First Annual Conference, Chapel Hill, North Carolina, 1969.

This is a fairly technical paper which attempts to develop standards for creating models of residential space. Batchelor defines two "surfaces" or topological conditions which describe the urban environment. "Behavioral surfaces circumscribe the sum of all activities within a given area." Cultural surfaces include codes, land use, and functional division standards which control the structural disposition of that area. Cultural surfaces are static while behavioral surfaces fluctuate daily. Accurate models must include definition of interrelationship between these two surfaces. (MT)

1970
HEMMENS, GEORGE C.
"Analysis and Simulation of Urban Activity Patterns"
Socio-Economic Planning Sciences, 1970, **4**, 53–66.

This is a report of an on-going effort to use computers for simulating the out-of-the-home activity patterns of the resident households of a metropolitan area over a 24-hour day. The first section discusses the conceptual framework proposed for structuring the analysis and simulation of activity patterns and relates both person and household activity patterns to land use and transportation planning. The second part discusses some empirical results from preliminary analysis of these activity patterns. Particularly the data on activity linkages point out potentials for design links. (GB)

1971
MACMURRAY, TREVOR
"Aspects of Time and the Study of Activity Patterns"
Town Planning Review, April 1971, **42** (2).

MacMurray sets up a framework for relating time studies to environmental requirements. He particularly suggests their utilization for the investigation of various life style patterns in the determination of land use needs. His review of the literature of existing time studies is incomplete but his framework would be interesting to test. (GB)

1972
POLLOWY, ANNE-MARIE, AND MICHEL BEZMAN
"Design-Oriented Approach to Development Needs: An Operational Framework Relating Activity Patterns to Environmental Requirements through the Performance Approach"
Environmental Design: Research and Practice, EDRA 3/AR 8, Los Angeles, 1972.

A methodology for setting performance specifications for designers The programming process described includes goal statement, attainable objectives, performance requirements according to activity patterns and needs, and performance criteria, and finally feedback. (JR)

Leisure Time Analysis
Time is the equivalent of money, especially during those periods when people have choice: when they are not devoting themselves to hygiene, eating, sleeping,

housekeeping, working, or forced learning. This is the discretionary period when choices are available. And furthermore it is the emphasis on one choice over another that can provide the peculiar amenities or characteristics of a city: tennis courts, football stadiums, and beer taverns in Australian towns; bocci courts and streetside cafes in Italy; and shopping centers in the U.S.A. Existing patterns change when new forms of leisure activity develop, such as watching the TV, when access brings a new beach or ski slope into the potential for use, and when there is more time available.

The research done in this area to date reflects many of these different concerns, as well as the more basic ones: Can the use of leisure time indicate the quality of life? And, can a rearrangement of environments for leisure activities feed back on people's everyday satisfaction?

1961

PITT, GILLIAN M.

"Leisure in a New Town: A Survey of the Leisure Habits of Tenants in Crawley" *Town and Country Planning,* March 1961.

Survey made in 1960 in Crawley, Sussex, England to discover how the people who have come to live in the town use their leisure time. The sample was small and restricted to occupants of the houses built and rented by the development corporation. For the purpose of the research leisure was defined as "that time when the individual has some effective choice of activity." The study concludes that the young family is largely home-bound and the number of people involved in community life of the town has gained over the years as a result of the fact that as people pass the mid-thirties home ties slacken and leisure activities move to a wider sphere. (LC)

1969

MAW, RAY

"Construction of a Leisure Model"

Official Architecture and Planning, August 1969; *Ekistics,* March 1971.

In constructing a model for the use of leisure time within the working week and over the normal weekend, Ray Maw starts by considering the time budgets of various subgroups of an urban population. He interviewed in Northeast London in an attempt to couple time budgets with the accessibility of a large indoor swimming pool to its potential users. He suggests that the resulting model can be usefully employed to test the most effective location of new recreational facilities, as well as to test the effect of changes in the transportation network or other aspects of accessibility upon existing facilities. (GB)

NAKANISHI, NAOMICHI

"Changes in Living Patterns Brought about by Television"

The Developing Economics, December 1969, **7** (4); *Ekistics*, September 1970.

The author looks at time budgets of Japanese families before and after the introduction of television. Changes have occurred in the timing of activities and in the number of concurrent activities pursued in the dwelling. (GB)

1971

BURTON, THOMAS L.

"Identification of Recreation Types through Cluster Analysis"

Society and Leisure, 1971, **1**, 47–64.

Respondents to a recreation activities survey were asked to indicate how many of 60 activities they had ever participated in during 1968. The responses were grouped. Fourteen activity groupings were identified. The implication is made of how these could be used for planning appropriate facility clusters. (GB)

JANISOVA, HELENA

"Leisure Time of City Residents in the Light of Urban Living Conditions and Environment"

Society and Leisure, 1971, **1**, 121–144.

Over 2,000 residents of Prague were asked questions concerning choice of leisure time activities both after working time on a regular working day and on free days. Fourteen tables are included in the article: (1) way leisure time is spent; (2) differences in leisure activities by sex, (3) by employment, (4) by age, (5) by education, (6) by family types; (7) weekend leisure by housing estate versus city residents, then (8) by employment, (9) by education, (10) by age; (11) reasons for not going away on weekends by sex and then (12) by employment; (13) reasons sport is not participated in, by sex, and then (14) by age. It is noted that this is going to be incorporated in the planning of the city. (GB)

CHAPIN, F. STUART, JR.
"Free Time Activities and Quality of Urban Life"
Journal of the American Institute of Planners, November 1971, **37** (6), 411–417.

Using two measures—the amount of time and the variety reflected in discretionary activities—living patterns of Washingtonians from differing life situations are compared with those of urbanites in the same situations for the nation as a whole. Very distinct differences appear along racial-income lines. While this a larger scale than Chapin's other activities studies, it breaks into the area of developing national approaches to urban plans. (GB)

SOCIAL SCIENCE METHODOLOGIES

These citations pertain to the traditional social science research techniques which have been applied to behavioral studies, that are useful to designers, leaving out the general research books relating to logical or statistical methods.

Two concepts demand special distinction. First, the work of Charles Osgood *et al.* on the semantic differential is important because it has been utilized to translate verbal images into environmental responses, relating behavioral or perceptual connotations to words which signify design parameters. Because the language of design is graphic, its translation to those who are not visually literate provides one of the greatest hurdles in environmental research. To date the semantic differential is one of the best means of bridging this gap.

Second, incorporating the client group into the design process has gained scientific respectability, as well as become a necessary practice. Participation in design per se is discussed in detail as a design methodology. In the context of social scientists who prepare the predesign program and carry out evaluative studies, incorporation of the "client" means blurring the distinction between the observer and the observed. Both Margaret Mead with her long and rich experience as a field anthropologist and P. K. New, reflecting the younger generation, emphasize the advantages of involving the community affected by research. They also point out that there is nothing sacred nor proven particularly beneficial as a result of antiseptic, statistical, and "unbiased" observations of communities by researchers. Social science is working with human beings, who unlike atomic particles, protozoa, and even chimpanzees, are capable of conceptualizing and articulating their understanding of situations.

The 1968 article of William Michelson summarizes a much broader range of approaches that have been carried out by the social scientists. This brief review by Michelson is appropriately supplemented by his book (1970) which deals primarily with residential environments and is discussed in that section.

1955
LAZARFELD, P. F. (ED.)
Language of Social Research
Glencoe, Illinois: Free Press, 1955.

This book deals with social research methodology, concentrating on a limited number of problems, each of which is illustrated by a set of related articles. Sections on formal aspects of research on human groups and empirical analysis of action are relevant though dated. (PM)

1957
OSGOOD, CHARLES S., GEORGE J. SUCI, AND PERCY H. TANNENBAUM
The Measurement of Meaning
Urbana, Illinois: University of Illinois, 1957.

"Meaning," the authors state, "is one of the most significant pivotal variables in human behavior." This book is a progress report of what has been done so far in the measurement of meaning by means of the semantic differential. Research on measurement is based on the simplest of conceptual models which asserts that "most of variance in human semantic judgments can be explained in a relatively small number of orthogonal factors, these being completely general over both subjects and concepts and always represented by the same set of scales." An interesting section of the book deals with the congruity principle which relates to the "interaction of cognitive events that occur more or less simultaneously." The book also includes a good representative sample of applications of semantic measurement including "attitude assessment, study of personality traits, and dynamisms, measurement of the course of psychology, studies in psycholinguistics, in aesthetics, in advertising, and in other mass communication." (PM)

1968

Michelson, William

"Urban Sociology as an Aid to Urban Physical Development: Some Research Strategies"

Journal of the American Institute of Planners, March 1968, **34**, 105–108.

Describes his idea of the sociologist's contribution to the building of the future city and the strategic approaches. Recognizes lack of precedent for research linking social to physical variables and suggests two approaches: (1) mental congruence, i.e., the attitude of individual toward particular spatial pattern and (2) experiential congruence, i.e., how well the environment actually accommodates the character and behavior of people. Research strategies related to empirical study of social and physical phenomena include (1) survey research, (2) semi-projective game situation, (3) longitudinal studies of movers, (4) time and activity budget. Very relevant and strongly recommended. (PM)

1969

MEAD, MARGARET

"Research with Human Beings: A Model Derived from Anthropological Field Practice"

Daedalus, Spring 1966, 361-368; *Ekistics,* July 1969, **164**, 9–13.

In the words of the author, "I submit that the intense willingness of an individual of any level of education to participate in an enterprise . . . is related to the degree of the involvement of the subject. Because he is personally involved . . . he is removed from the demeaning status of guinea pig. We can further adopt the position that the failure to do research, to experiment, and to learn is reprehensible. We can cease to try to limit and curtail experiments on human beings, while we devise more and better experiments with human beings who, as participants, are collaborators." Margaret Mead.

1970
HUTT, S. M., AND CORINE HUTT
Direct Observation and Measurement of Behavior
Springfield, Illinois: Charles C. Thomas, 1970.

The Hutts of Oxford present an ethiologic or psychological approach to the exploration of attention, learning, and behavior in young children. They present their own experience in attempting to record and measure behavior focusing on the techniques of tape recordings, check lists, and event recorders, and motion pictures and videotapes. As one progresses from animals to children and to adults these processes of recording and analyzing behavior become more complex and difficult. Here is some worthwhile experimentation to learn from. (GB)

1972
LOWENTHAL, DAVID
"Methodological Problems in Environmental Perception and Behavior Research"
Environmental Design: Research and Practice, EDRA 3/AR 8, Los Angeles, 1972.

A discussion of the fragmentation of research by social scientists. This is seen as a result of the lack of commonly agreed definitions, objectives, and mechanisms and a systematically organized theoretical basis. Basic problems are the method that determines research and objectives, utilization of the research, presentation of the research findings, and the single disciplinary nature of most research projects. A recommendation is made that interdisciplinary educational programs are developed to train researchers to conduct environmental perception and behavior studies. (JR)

1972
NEW, PETER KONG-MING, RICHARD M. HESSLER, AND LUIS S. KEMNITZER
"Community Research, Research Commune?"
Environmental Design: Research and Practice, EDRA 3/AR 8, Los Angeles, 1972.

A proposal to involve the subjects of behavioral research in the design of the research project. The subjects become members of the research team. The purpose is to eliminate the researchers' bias, particularly in doing community studies, i.e., the neighborhood. (JR & GB)

PART 3. THE FRAMEWORK OF THE URBAN ENVIRONMENT

The purpose of both the designers and the social scientists is to create a better urban framework. The two approaches—treated separately—come together in this third section, in which the city itself is broken down into its component parts.

The largest unit treated is the urban subcenter, above that scale behavioral patterns are either programmed (in parades and mass meetings) or extended by mechanized means. The smallest unit is the room, the basic bit from which cities may be built. In between the divisions are those that developed empirically, i.e., the units on which there is some consensus in the literature.

The subsections of the urban framework do bear some similarity to the hierarchical patterns of settlements which provide the basis of C. A. Doxiadis' concept of Ekistics. The two breakdowns compare as shown in Table 1.

TABLE 1

Ekistics	Population	Environmental Design Fit
man	1	
room	2	room
dwelling	4	dwelling
dwelling group	40 ⎫	dwelling group
small neighborhood	250 ⎬	small neighborhood
neighborhood	1,500 ⎭	
small town	9,000	neighborhood
town	50,000 ⎫	urban centers
large city	300,000 ⎭	

In the breakdown, the populations are considered approximate. As human behavior is our independent variable, the unit man was left out. In terms of room and dwelling the distinction is clear, but above that it begins to blur.

The dwelling group has grown in size as a significant amount of literature deals with the management and problems of living in inhumane high rise buildings. Thus, the artifact of the single high rise pushes the number of people compacted in one dwelling group up to 250 and even more.

Depending on density, the small neighborhood may range from 200 to 5,000 people, but reflects the territory which can easily be traversed by the pre-school child and the aged.

Although the neighborhood itself has more annotation than any other subunit, it is the most elusive. On the one hand, it is reflected in community studies on "natural" areas of cities. Because researchers often start with agglomerations of 100,000 people or more they seldom find anything more fine-grained than an area of 5,000–15,000 population which is also the size of census tracts. The planner presented with the same complexity finds this size suitable for analyzing and programming community needs. But neither of these two methods comes to grips with "the neighborhood" that might be defined by the resident.

The urban subcenter has taken on greater significance with the demand for variety and choice conveniently available to the home. It is in the range of size of successful new town ventures and segments of megalopolises which can retain some uniqueness for their inhabitants.

The discussion of the urban framework begins with the subcenter and ends with the room which relates directly to the "fore thought" on human needs.

The Urban Subcenter

The largest scale chosen for cataloguing purposes is the urban subcenter and from there the entries are grouped in decreasing scales, ending with the room. The general concern of the entries is for establishment of equilibrium both internally and externally for the subcenter and the problems of artificially interceding at such a scale. This scale unit offers a conceptual framework, both physical and social, to maintain focal strength to avoid the alienation of large scale urbanization.

The ancient Greeks also wrestled with an urban conceptual framework for deliberately establishing cities with a healthy equilibrium. The population ideal was based on human scale and human needs. The population maximum of twenty thousand allows all citizens to gather at one public forum and corresponds to the draw of a population for our modern day facility, the high school (where such events as graduations demand massive gatherings).

Industrialization has led to a new world phenomenon which Lewis Mumford so aptly termed "mis-urbanization." The force of the new work system disturbed the naturally based equilibrium of a thinly spread population in village and towns, with their hierarchies of roots and order. New populations with new urban problems in larger scale settlements grew with no historical precedents. Peter Laslett, in his reconstruction of pre-industrial England in *The World We Have Lost,* describes a stable, well-organized network of small settlements prior to the Industrial Age. While this no longer exists, it gave birth to new production methods and the growth of industrial cities. England was one of the first countries to experience the large scale "mis-urbanization" that continues today. It was here that some of the first rumblings of discontent were voiced in Utopian thinking and industrialists experimented in hygienic company housing, which culminated with such turn of the century utopists as Robert Owen and Ebenezer Howard.

Howard's Garden City was dependent on metropolitan industrialization, but it echoed the goal of decentralization of the ancient Greeks. It was the Industrial Age's version of a balanced community. Since the turn of the century, growing interdependency has pushed larger and larger governments into urban policy making decisions and has developed a growing body of planning specialists to help direct development.

Problems of the urban subcenter relate to the experience of deliberate governmental intervention. The entries are arranged under four major topics—the Central Node, the Shopping Center, the New Town, and Spatial Perceptions of the Pedestrian—preceded by an annotation of the comprehensive spatial analysis of towns made by Camillo Sitte at the end of the 19th century.

1889

SITTE, CAMILLO
The Art of Building Cities
New York: Reinhold, 1965. Originally published in 1889.

Sitte, writing in 1889, strongly believed that city planning should not be a technical matter but an artistic enterprise. Ancient and modern cities were analyzed "in a purely artistic and technical manner, so as to discover their compositional elements—which can lead on the one hand to harmony and enchanting effects, or to disunity and dullness on the other." Relationships between buildings and plazas; the size and shape of plazas; location of monuments; and streets are discussed only according to their function and aesthetic appeal. (HS)

The Central Node

Although there is a solid literature on central place theory and quite a little interest and dismay as to the disappearance of community as a place phenomenon (as the next section on the neighborhood indicates), there are only three entries listed which relate to the nodal subcenter. (Subcenters of cities in contrast to their central business district centers have less ability to provide larger-than-life identification of place for either orientation or identity.)

One entry (Harvey) does deal with the focal point of the County Courthouse. As our older subcenters, as well as our urban centers, lose their centrality, there is decreasing opportunity for civic leadership to encourage the "grand" accent for the locality. With the introduction of the automobile, more naturally formed subcenters are loosing both the pull of their central location internally and their strength to maintain themselves from external forces. Some investigation is needed to uncover the "formula" or climate which encourages great, rather than gross public solutions. Some factual evidence (the decision makers' food) in the way of measurement is needed to prove how the image of physical excellence encourages focality. As amenity has increasing economic draw, the means with which this is achieved becomes a salient point for investigation.

One entry (Jones) has uncovered some historical precedents for "gypsy social structures" which are not focal in the sense of place. This author sees in temporary gatherings the focus of interest and points out that some civilizations in the past have viewed the city as ceremonial in nature. The integrative possibilities of temporary gathering (especially with specialization and instant communication) have not as yet been explored for their relevance in our transient society. In the temporary "on location" gathering there is, with the help of the media, not only a forging of the image of the interest but also the place.

A. E. Parr sees the necessity for the child to identify with the scale of the subcenter for his own development needs. From the increase in juvenile delinquency and drug use and more painful identity crisis at concurrent maturity with the decline of the subcenter, the points this author makes may be seen to be more important than just a satisfaction of nostalgia. The school bus would never have been an issue if the automobile had not robbed the child of the freedom of his two legs. Even the towns and villages are robbing the child of this former freedom. It has been the scale of the subcenter which has traditionally fed the cities with their creative energies. If these are not kept vital, then both the large city and smaller neighborhood will suffer.

1967
PARR, A. E.
"The Child in the City: Urbanity and the Urban Scene"
Landscape, 1967, **16**, 3–5.

The author briefly describes his childhood in a town in Norway and the interesting activities that can be found in a city. He speculates that, since the most formative years of a person's life are before he reaches the age of 12, children should be considered the most important segment of urban populations. As cities become larger and more hazardous, children's mobility has become increasingly restricted, with a corresponding narrowing of experiences. As cities grow, cultural facilities and heterogeneity are declining. (LG)

1971
JONES, EMRYS
"A Note on Some Aspects of Location and Network Activities"
Ekistics, January 1971, **31**, (182), 42.

Historic examples of activity networks illustrate a lack of centralized form with central-like activities. "This is a plea for a freeing of society from the economic straight jacket and for thinking twice before allowing the physical form of our settlement to be dictated by a too-mechanical hierarchial system." He illustrates his point by activities in Wales which create their own behavioral settings in different locations in different years. This society does not depend on behavior contingent forms but peripatetic activities. (GB)

1972
HARVEY, W. LAWRENCE *et al.*
"The Square, Descriptive Modeling of Central Courthouse Square Towns of the
South Central U.S."
Environmental Design: Research and Practice, EDRA 3/AR 8, Los Angeles, 1972.

An analysis of the use of public squares in small agricultural county-seat towns
to determine causal relationships in the location of activity zones. A notation system
was developed which allowed multidisciplinary participation and lessened the difficulty of holistic conclusions. However, the present development of the technique
needs refinement as well as more data in order to arrive at substantive conclusions.
(JR & GB)

The Shopping Center

Although there are sophisticated mathematical and geographic theories for
efficient placement of facilities from the consumption point of view and mountains
of market research to ferret out human response, there has been little uncovered
in the human use of available shopping space or its social implications. To our
knowledge as yet no one has measured the extent of the noncommercial activities
in the new suburban shopping centers or the social costs of self-service. Comparative studies would be useful to measure the extent to which nearby public
or private recreational facilities or programs reduce petty crime and create social
groups.

The internal "street" in the new fortress styled shopping center does seem
to be introducing the pedestrian pleasures formerly available along main street.
These facilities do work to emphasize the newer subcenters but as yet to the
detriment of the Central Business District, as well as older subcenters.

As shopping has traditionally been a major activity of the industrial urban dweller
and Americans have been exceptional in their consumption, the public benefits

and losses of the shopping activity could well use a Nader type of investigation and some facts to impress the decision makers and the general public as well with the social significance of intermediate areas to serve the needs particularly of teenagers and the elderly.

1954

STONE, G.

"City Shoppers and Urban Identification; Observations on the Psychology of City Life"

American Journal of Sociology, 1954, **60**, 36–45.

Through the use of a questionnaire, the author found that housewives from Chicago's N. E. section comprised four types of shopper: economic, personalizing, ethical, and apathetic. Each type of shopper is distinguished by specific social characteristics, reflecting her position in the social structure of her residential community. Personalizing shoppers were found to draw on their relationships with clerks to form subjective identifications with a community in which they had restricted opportunities for participation; such relationships were found to help integrate a person into a larger urban setting.

1970

DOWNS, ROGER M.

"The Cognitive Structure of an Urban Shopping Center"

Environment and Behavior, June 1970, **2** (1).

Using the cognitive behavioral approach to location theory and consumer behavior, the author studied a downtown shopping center in Bristol, England to determine how consumers evaluate and assess a segment of the spatial environment in which they live and with which they frequently interact. It was hypothesized that the cognitive structure of a shopping center is nine dimensional; the hypothesis was operationally defined by a set of 36 semantic differential scales. The study concludes that the findings in general support the hypothesis and that the image is a complex construct. There are significant interrelations between spatial cognition, urban form, and human behavior of which we are almost completely ignorant. (LC)

1972
BELL, G., AND MARGRIT KENNEDY
"Age Group Needs and their Satisfaction: A Case Study of the East Liberty Renewal Area, Pittsburgh"
Environmental Design: Research and Practice, EDRA 3/AR 8, Los Angeles, 1972.

Considering a renewal of a neighborhood area, the authors defined a lack of sensitivity to the needs of the residents and the users on the part of the designers. The importance of post-renewal feedback action monies are enunciated to promote the effectuation of plans that in fact suit the uses of the people. The needs of both people in the residential areas and in the shopping areas were looked at in making this subsection of the city come together as a whole. (GB)

New Towns

With the earlier impetus for New Towns in England and Howard's concepts translated into actual settlements, their development over time have been evaluated by Kuper, Pritchard, McKie, Taylor, Willis, and Broady. Similarly, because of the large scale building of subdivisions in the United States, the new satellite cities have been compared with large scaled subdivisions by Lansing and Zehner.

As in other scales, there is consensus for relating the physical to the particular people for which it is planned, and most of the studies evaluate the public spaces and their use.

There is a large literature relating to land use planning, legislation, financing, and the economic viability of new towns that has been excluded. Additional references dealing with neighborhoods within new towns are in the next chapter.

1953

KUPER, LEO

Living in Towns: Selected Research Papers

Urban Sociology of the Faculty of Commerce and Social Science, University of Birmingham, 1953.

Conclusions reached include: (1) Each new town plan should be related to the people for whom it is made (activities, values, and attitudes); (2) new town planners are prone to work with too rigid specifications and general values (i.e., idealization of the village community), based on the following questions: (a) what happens to people when they are thrown together in a planned neighborhood? (b) what is the influence of physical structures on behavior of people living in them? (c) is there any mechanical determination of social life by its physical environment? (d) can a blueprint of a town planner determine a blueprint for the social life of the people? Interesting in terms of methodology—direct conversations, not questionnaires, between investigators and residents. (AT)

1964

LAMANNA, RICHARD

"Value Consensus among Urban Residents"

Journal of the American Institute of Planners, November 1964, **30**, 317–323.

In an effort to bridge the sociocultural values gap and facilitate meaningful communication between planners and their clients, the author attempts to analyze the value orientations of residents of Greensboro, North Carolina. Residents were asked the physical and social qualities they desire in an "ideal" town, then were asked to assign priorities to these "livability values." Their preferences were evaluated in terms of respondents' race, sex, age, class, level of education. (AW)

1967

PRITCHARD, NORMAN

"Planned Social Provision in New Towns"

Town Planning Review, 1967–1968, **38**.

Providing the necessary social amenities for the residents of new towns will be resolved by the nature of the plan. He wants to provide communications and the provision of space to serve the needs of the community in all aspects of living together. You cannot plan people, but you can plan an environment in which they can work out their own problems. (RB)

1969

MCKIE, ROBERT
"Peterborough Amenities and Social Change"
Town and Country Planning, Jan.-Feb. 1969, **37** (1–2).

A survey of Peterborough, an expanding English community, to determine residents' attitudes towards existing amenities and the quality of the environment. Revealed three areas of the city with distinct ethnic and social identities. Conclusion reached was that centralized amenities are the key to unification of a fragmented community. (AW)

TAYLOR, G. BROOKE
"Telford's Social Relations Department"
Town and Country Planning, Jan.-Feb. 1969, **37**.

The design unit of Telford New Town (England) is discussed in relation to social conflicts of open space versus convenience to work and services, adult quiet environment versus child's need for noise and action, newcomers versus established residents, shopping needs, pedestrian versus automated transport. Design included. (BB)

WILLIS, MARGARET
"Sociological Aspects of Urban Structure"
Town Planning Review, Jan. 1969, **39** (4); *Ekistics*, September 1969.

A comparision of residential groupings proposed in planning new towns. Notes that provision of amenities and services are affected by size and density of residential units. Desires of residents vary according to age, class, life style. Physical plan must be flexible to allow for adaptation to change as time and demand vary. Social assumptions of planners concerning neighborliness, convenience, and accessibility of amenities may have to be re-examined. Planners have to take quality as well as quantity of facilities into consideration. (AW)

1970

LANSING, JOHN B., AND ROBERT W. MARANS
Planned Residential Environments
Ann Arbor: Institute for Social Research, University of Michigan, 1970.

This book describes the outcome of a survey designed to appraise resident satisfaction with the planned environment and some particular aspects of planned communities: accessibility to outdoor recreation, dwelling unit density, neighborhood noise level, privacy in the yard, and adequacy of outdoor space for family activities. The additional factor of transportation needs of these residents was measured and compared to needs of people living in older, unplanned communities. Ten communities were selected for this survey, including Reston, Colombia, Radburn, Glen Rock and others, as they reflected varying degrees of planning. Data were collected by interview of family household head or wife of head in single family or town houses. (MT)

BROADY, MAURICE
"The Sociology of the Urban Environment"
Ekistics, March 1970, **172**, 187–190.

For the sociologist author, it is on the understanding of the social structure and the architectural design that the planning of the urban environment must rest. In his investigation of the new town of Harlow in England (a particularly "lively" town), he was able to construct a system of organization for the purposes of prediction. The major reasons for "Harlow's Health" he uncovered were: "People with something to contribute to the town's development and the characteristics of the administrative, political and social organization of the town which made this potential effective." Major factors which contributed to Harlow's vitality were: public policies for industrial selection, housing application, and the selection of teachers. (ER)

1971
ZEHNER, ROBERT B.
"Neighborhood and Community Satisfaction in New Towns and Less Planned Suburbs"
Journal of the American Institute of Planners, 1971, **37** (6), 279-285.

Using results from interviews with residents in two highly planned new towns —Reston and Colombia—and two minimally planned but otherwise comparable suburban communities, this report compares several measures of neighborhood and community satisfaction and attraction. At the neighborhood scale, the best predictor of satisfaction was the respondents rating of maintenance level. At the community scale, extent of community planning in the new towns and accessibility to work and local facilities in all four communities were important components of appeal and satisfaction.

Spatial Perceptions of the Pedestrian

The perception of space when the body is in motion is an often overlooked but very significant phenomenon. Some research has been done in the area of acuity of the driver (see the section on perception studies), but the perception of the pedestrian has largely been neglected. Most designers are intuitively aware of and consciously consider the reactions to space that pedestrians will develop; certainly the history of architecture and urban design demonstrates that it is in the perception of space by the pedestrian that great design is perceived. The great piazzas of Italy are to a large degree appreciated because of the delight of the approaches and the surprise engendered by the change in scale and materials as one reaches the piazza. The mechanization of movement has apparently altered the appreciation of the regard for the pedestrian as an observer, but it is at the pedestrian scale that space is most acutely perceived. Many of the studies of perception deal with the pedestrian; the following selections attempt to set standards for the designer to apply in creating spaces for pedestrians.

1962
MORRIS, ROBERT, AND S. B. ZISMAN
"The Pedestrian, Downtown, and the Planner"
Journal of the American Institute of Planners, **28** (3), 152–158.

An analysis of the pedestrian requirements of center city design, including a trip survey similar to the trip requirements usually taken for auto and transit studies. The authors' point is that most downtown trips commence when the car is garaged or the transit trip is ended, whereupon the pedestrian role becomes active, and that planners and urban designers should be more aware of the importance of the pedestrian in designing for downtown.

1968
STUART, DARWIN G.
"Planning for Pedestrians"
Journal of the American Institute of Planners, January 1968, **34** (1), 37–41.

"Regardless of the intensity of pedestrian use, the paths and spaces provided for urban walking present an extensive ad hoc and largely disorganized circulation system . . . though pedestrians and the paths provided for their movement represent a clearly important topic for urban study, these considerations have been long neglected." Stuart represents a planning framework for the design of pedestrian routes based on either pedestrian-vehicle separation or pedestrian-vehicle coordination. (JR)

1969
MARTIN, ANN
"The Pedestrian in the City: A Bibliography"
Ekistics, September 1969, **28** (166), 212.

A title listing of 26 works that are specifically devoted to the behavior and considerations needed in understanding the pedestrian. (GB)

RUDOFSKY, BERNARD
Streets for People
Garden City, New York: Doubleday and Co., 1969.

As the author says, "This book is about the great outdoors, the pedestrian streets, and the people one meets there." It is beautifully illustrated and takes an historic approach that relates street design to differing pedestrian activities. (GB)

1971
FRUIN, JOHN J.
Pedestrian Planning and Design
New York: Metropolitan Association of Urban Designers and Environmental Planners, Inc., 1971.

An interdisciplinary approach to pedestrian traffic planning. Human physiological and psychological factors often overlooked in the planning and design of pedestrian spaces are included. Other areas in this comprehensive pedestrian study are: traffic and space characteristics of pedestrians, level of service design standards, guidelines for planning and design, and some aspects of pedestrian movers. Several examples of people-oriented planning cited in the book include pedestrian walkways in the Barbican section of London and the Cincinnati skyways. (CH)

GARBRECHT, DIETRICH
"Pedestrian Paths through a Uniform Environment"
Town Planning Review, January 1971.

Research findings on the pedestrian's path-choosing behavior in a built environment. Various paths taken through an at-grade parking lot in Boston are studied in terms of such decision variables as intersection, direction, barriers, and pedestrian group size. The statistical analyses showed that the probabilities of a pedestrian's remaining on a boundary are considerably higher than that of his straying into the bounded area, and that a man walking along the line connecting origin and destination is likely to stay on the same side of the line on which he started the trip. Such findings may partially explain the high pedestrian frequencies on the boundaries (or edges in Lynch's term) of shopping areas. (CH)

The Neighborhood

The neighborhood furor may have been started by Ebenezer Howard but it was certainly fed by Robert Park and the social ecologists. These two people reflect the two major dimensions of neighborhood: a physical planning construct and a social-ecological approach to sub-urban groupings.

During this century, the social ecologists have reacted to the concept of planned neighborhood units and the planners have been influenced by the findings of the community studies. Only recently have bridges been built between the two approaches by such people as Herbert Gans and Suzanne Keller. Both of these sociologists have taken as their mission to influence and "teach" the planners.

These two streams are approached separately. The first part of this section is devoted to community studies and the second half to planning the neighborhood.

Community Studies

The study of population in the local habitat is traced to its biological analogy and was made popular by the social ecologists, particularly McKenzie, Park, and Hawley. Other sociologists, of the so-called ecological school, really went beyond the scope of "community" (e.g., Wirth) and are discussed in the section on "Social Science Approaches."

While the early writings are general statements of the purpose of developing community studies, the later ones are case studies themselves. In fact, the most recent ones are both the most literate and the most successful in synthesizing in writing the complicated feedbacks between environment, population, culture, and social structure. Only some of the many case studies are annotated, but the books by Stein and Frankenberg summarize major studies in the United States and Great Britain, respectively.

Jane Jacobs sticks out like a sore thumb—the stinging asp in the bouquet of sociologists—analysis of and description of community is her strong point. Furthermore her message of the exuberant diversity possible in high-density communities near downtown rather than in rural and suburban settings predominating most of the other studies, makes a very important, if not unique, contribution, in our search to understand the importance of community within megalopolitan life.

1926
MCKENZIE, R. D.
"The Scope of Human Ecology"
Journal of Applied Sociology, March 1926, **10**, 316-323
Reprinted in Theodorsen, 1961.

This essay which precedes Park's by ten years, discusses urban ecological processes without drawing the direct analogies. He hypothesizes that behavioral choice increases with progress of civilization. Less interesting to read than Park. (GB)

PARK, ROBERT EZRA
Human Communities: The City and Human Ecology
The Free Press, Glencoe, Illinois 1952

This book reprints a series of Park's essays, including:

"A City as a Natural Phenomenon" in which he refutes a general index for rating the environment. His major point is that "high grade" communities fail to be either self-reproducing or self-sufficient and must depend on·"low grade" communities for survival.

"Community Organization and Juvenile Delinquency", written in 1925, in which he points to the child as the real neighbor in the local community and emphasizes play as the format for finding and establishing social associations.

"The City: Suggestions for the Investigation of Human Behavior in the Urban Environment", a 1916 essay with prophetic insights into social/urban order.

"Symbiosis and Socialization: a frame of reference for the study of society", in which he analyzes institutions and collective behavior in the city. (ER)

1936
PARK, ROBERT EZRA
"Human Ecology"
American Journal of Sociology, July 1936, **32**, 1–15.
Reprinted in Theodorsen 1961, Warren 1966

Park takes an ecological approach to the human community in which, "human beings occupying the same habitat come into competing but reciprocally meaningful relationships to each other and the natural environment" and those relationships constitute a "community in that their activities become intertwined in a natural economy." Park sees the forces of competition, dominance, and succession as operating to determine the shape and form a human community takes. "Human ecology" is defined as "an attempt to investigate the processes by which the biotic balance and the social equilibrium (1) are maintained once achieved and (2) the equilibrium are disturbed, the transition is made from one relatively stable order to another." (PM)

1950

HAWLEY, AMOS H.

Human Ecology: A Theory of Community Structure

New York: Ronald Press, 1950

   Hawley's human ecology social theory of community development is circuitous but condenses sociological, economic, and anthropological contributions of mobility, settlement patterns, caste systems and urbanization. (AT)

1957

WYLIE, LAURENCE

Village in the Vaucluse

Cambridge: Harvard University Press, 1957.

   Study of all facets of life in a modern French village by an American professor who lived and observed the village for one year. Major conclusion is that life in the village is not economically easy but people who live there manage to live within the constraints rather successfully. The physical plant of this remote historical monument contributes to the sense of identity and roots as it furnishes a measure of control. The policy of family allowance is examined and found not to encourage large families (the devout Catholics having fewer children than the village Communists). The few who succeed in school (which has central control) drain the village of leadership for change. Professor Wylie provides a vivid description of the cafe as a social communication center of the village. (ER)

1960

STEIN, MAURICE R.

The Eclipse of Community

Princeton: Princeton University Press, 1960; New York: Harper and Row, 1964.

   This book summarizes the research of Park, the Lynds, Lloyd Warner, Whyte, and others who studied the community. It is a search to find the perspective through time on the evolving American community, from anthropological, psychoanalytical, and sociological viewpoints. These approach many of the assumptions made by planners dealing with and planning for "neighborhood/community." It is an easy way to get a lot of the sociological background. (GB)

1961

JACOBS, JANE

The Death and Life of Great American Cities

New York: Vintage, 1961.

Ms. Jacobs' book testifies vividly against traditional philosophies of city planning and rebuilding. Her attack is supported by her personal accounts of neighborhoods whose social ecology and cohesiveness fell to disorder after the policies of middle class planners imposed physical change under the guise of "renewal." Her examples are drawn from communities in Boston, Chicago, Baltimore, New York, and other major American cities. This carefully written book is recommended for its strong, albeit controversial point of view, in its conception of the stability of "neighborhood place" in contemporary American culture. (MT)

1965

FRANKENBERG, RONALD

Communities in Britain: Social Life in Town and Country

Pelican Original, 1965.

Frankenberg does for British community studies what Stein did for U.S. ones. Frankenberg seems to understand the internal and external social networks which support the spectrum of communities (holding time constant) from the rural to the urban. This holds an important message to all those planners that see the neighborhood as the village in the city. He shows that this is impossible and analyzes the continuum of differences, pointing out the shortcomings of both rural and urban community life. (GB).

1970

BLYTHE, RONALD

Akenfield: Portrait of an English Village

New York, Delta Books: 1970.

A profile of a contemporary English village constructed in the words of the inhabitants. This methodology adds a measure of credibility (which scientism seems to require) as it develops a comprehensive statement of some literary distinction. It is a rare view into an industrial farming village and the changes that have taken place in its physical and social structure with the input of technology. Starting with the oldest villagers—who are almost from another world—to the young moderns, it uncovers the attitudes regarding place and activities, the village and the outside world. (ER & GB)

Planning for the Neighborhood

Many people have tried to bury the neighborhood unit, but it remains with us. The sociologists have proved the viability and strength of the concept of community which by necessity almost always gets translated physically into a spatial organization not unlike a "neighborhood."

The delimitations of neighborhood size have ranged from the level of 100 to 2,000 families or 300 to 10,000 people. The differences are so great that our discussion has been divided into two sections: one considering the planners neighborhood unit with an average population of 5,000 whose size allows the provision of services as one of the major concerns; and the other, the small neighborhood where identification and sociability are primary factors. Confusion between the two concepts (with the same name) has in fact led to some of the debate. Agreeing with Cristopher Alexander that the city is not a tree but a complex interlocking mesh of associations and facilities, then the large scale unit which bases the planning of such services in a simplistic fashion certainly can be criticized. But the same criticism does not hold for the symbolic meaning that people still attribute to their home territory—the small neighborhood, or the need for children to explore an intimate territory before they are unleashed to investigate the city. For human beings none of these areas are necessarily precisely defined through all of the time and their discrete representation on "planners maps" also brings some difficulty. Studies on perception show that neighborhoods are different to different people. Thus, the neighborhood does not provide an easy rubber stamp for planning cities.

The major themes of neighborhood unit planning are each grouped separately. These are:

1. definitions and criticisms of neighborhood
2. the size of the neighborhood
3. neighborhood boundaries
4. planning for facilities and amenities
5. population balance within the neighborhood

Then the following chapter on "The Small Neighborhood" continues material on the social questions that are raised in the last part of this section.

Definitions and Criticism of Neighborhood

Every twenty years there is a new definitive work on the neighborhood. At the turn of the century it was Ebenezer Howard; in the twenties, Clarence Perry; in the forties, James Dahir; and in the sixties, Suzanne Keller. And for each of these, there are critics. With each revolution, the theme develops a few more variations.

1898
HOWARD, EBENEZER
Garden Cities of Tomorrow
London: Faber and Faber, 1946
(first published 1898, *To-morrow: A Peaceful Path to Real Reform*)
Howard implicitly believed that environment determined behavior and thus proposed the garden cities. His statement remains clear. (GB)

1929

PERRY, CLARENCE

"The Neighborhood Unit"

Neighborhood and Community Planning, Regional Survey No. 7, New York, Regional Plan Association, 1929.

This important monograph outlines Perry's influential theory of neighborhood planning. Aspects of its spatial and social justification are detailed. Perry gives special attention to the following features of the neighborhood unit: size, boundaries, open spaces, institutional sites, local shops, and the internal street system. Recommended reading for all planners and sociologists. (MT)

1939

PERRY, CLARENCE

Housing for the Machine Age

New York, Russell Sage Foundation: 1939.

The active promotion of community life was suggested as an alternative to building and rebuilding total large cities. Emphasis was placed on articulating the neighborhood unit to encourage well rounded family life. Specific examples and details are included for neighborhood services and their placement. Actual scale, density, and percentages of open space are indicated. Unfortunately this recipe has often been tried to be applied even when the chef does not understand his utensils, the ingredients, and most of all the characteristics of the invited guests.

1944

CHURCHILL, HENRY S., AND ROSLYN ITTLESON

Neighborhood Design and Control

New York: National Committee on Housing, Inc., 1944.

A planners' study which anticipated the problem of urban sprawl and laid out a strategy for orderly community growth through the neighborhood. They present specifics in differing neighborhood needs for high, medium, and low income families: the lower the income group, the more community facilities needed, i.e., everything from more playgrounds to more adult centers. Similar to more recent suggestions that as private, indoor household or house-yard facilities are low, then demand on community services will be high and vice versa. (ER & GB)

159

1947

DAHIR, JAMES

The Neighborhood Unit Plan: Its Spread and Acceptance

New York: Russell Sage Foundation, 1947.

This is basically a selected bibliography on the neighborhood·unit. The author comments in the form of a review of the literature and the state of neighborhood planning and plans up to 1947. His concept of the neighborhood is expressed in the foreword: "The builders of American cities have customarily erected housing with little regard to the groupings of people into neighborhoods for constructive social living. The neighborhood unit plan proposes a means of correcting this laissez-faire trend in city growth." Although Dahir brings in material from the Michael Reese Hospital plans which considered the adjacent "ghetto" area as part of the "neighborhood," his approach is primarily suburban and reflects the concern for "postwar housing growth" in the U.S. It is very clearly written and organized. (GB & ER)

GLASS, RUTH

The Social Background of a Plan: A Study of Middlebrough

London: Routledge and Kegan Paul, 1947.

This book describes a social survey undertaken in the early 1940's for the purpose of replanning the physical and social aspects of Middlebrough, England, a then declining industrial town. It contains several chapters dealing with the definition of neighborhoods, their social and geographic components, as well as an evaluation of health and education services needs. Represents earlier efforts at town planning which attempted to integrate social data into the physical planning process. (MT)

1948

ISAACS, REGINALD

"The Neighborhood Theory"

Journal of the American Institute of Planners, 1948, **14.**

An examination of the historical neighborhood concept and a demonstration of the inadequacies and impediments it causes. (See the next annotation.) (RJD)

ISAACS, REGINALD
"Are Urban Neighborhoods Possible?"
Journal of Housing, July 1948, **5**, 177–180.

The adequacy of the neighborhood concept is questioned based on the fact that units of this size cannot support, individually, the necessary facilities such as churches, schools, and shops. He observes that the neighborhood unit cannot contain all the activities of a family group. He doubts the value of homogeneous neighborhoods as a cure for social disorganization, and further he states that the visonary neighborhood is impossible by virtue of the nature of the city—a place of mobility and constant change. (BJ)

DAHIR, JAMES
"Neighborhood Planning is a 'Three-in-One' Job"
Journal of Housing, October 1948, 270–272.

His three neighborhood categories are similar to those defined by Suzanne Keller some 20 years later. He is definitely a devotee and ends up with an argument for planning on neighborhood grounds as it best supplies "what people want." (GB)

TANNEBAUM, JUDITH
"The Neighborhood: A Socio-Psychological Analysis"
Land Economics, November 1948, **24** (4).

The article poses the question: In what ways, and to what extent does the neighborhood concept propose to deal with the nonphysical problems of city life? Judith Tannebaum uses the concept of anomie to describe acute social disorganization. She defines the relation of the physical and nonphysical input into neighborhood planning. The concept of increasing urbanization has been foreseen in such concluding statements as: "Individuals cannot be citizens of the world in any real sense for such status provides for non-concrete identification." And "a physical environment that is too overpowering can serve to dwarf the individual personality into inconsequence. To a large extent this has been the actual effect of megalopolitan living on individuals." The article is well written and conceptually still valid. (GB)

1949

ADAMS, F. J., S. RIEMER, R. ISAACS, AND R. B. MITCHELL
"The Neighborhood Concept in Theory and Application"
Land Economics, Feb. 1949, **25** (1).

This is an invited panel on the neighborhood concept. Their papers are not as articulate as each of them has published elsewhere. In some ways they play fashionable academic games and do not come to the crux of any issues. (GB)

1950

RIEMER, SVEND
"Hidden Dimensions of Neighborhood Planning"
Land Economics, May 1950, **26**, 197–201.

The utility of the traditional concept of neighborhood is questioned with respect to its use in an urban setting. Reimer observes that transportation advances make possible other settings for primary face-to-face contacts than the neighborhood. He notes that neighborhood awareness ranges from a spatial unit, to be based on routes, shared activities, or voluntary associations. Reimer suggests that the emphasis should be placed on adequate urban facilities for given areas and suggests a high school sized unit as the smallest. (BJ)

DEWEY, RICHARD
"The Neighborhood, Urban Ecology and City Planners"
American Sociological Review, August 1950, 502–507.

A criticism of the over-use of Perry's neighborhood concept without understanding its sociological principles. Many of Dewey's predictions came out wrong, so this is rather fun to read. (GB)

1951

STEIN, CLARENCE
Towards New Towns for America
New York: Reinhold, 1951.

This book clearly explains with text, photos, and plans, the objectives of 12 experimental housing neighborhoods built between the two World Wars. The book was written in the spirit of continued research: "When an idea becomes conventional it is time to think it through again." Thus, this volume both outlines a heritage for U.S. residential unit planners and has a message for the future. (GB)

KUPER, LEO
"Social Science Research and the Planning of Urban Neighborhoods"
Social Forces, March 1951.

Kuper suggests that the social scientist may contribute to the planning of neighborhoods in two ways: (1) unmasking the values and assumptions indigenous to particular communities to reveal their derivation and ambiguities and (2) assessing direction of social change in communities and offering guidance for planned change. Article also contains a sociologist's definition of "neighborhood." (MT)

1954

MUMFORD, LEWIS
"The Neighborhood and the Neighborhood Unit"
Town Planning Review, 1954, **24**.
Reprinted in Elias, 1964.

Mumford advocates neighborhood units of 5,000 people of mixed ages and economic strata. Since he thinks that "Neighborhoods exist, as a fact of nature," he urges planning to fulfill their particular functions, for example, planning the local school to serve as community center. He praises the contributions of planners, especially Clarence Perry, who developed the theory and practice of the planned neighborhood unit. In planning amidst the counterforces of decentralization desires and increased mobility in autos, one should consider Mumford's argument that "if the problem of urban transportation is ever to be solved, it will be on the basis of bringing a large number of institutions and facilities within walking distance of the home, which will also be a 'guarantee of their being steadily used by all members of the family.'" (EW)

1965

MANN, PETER H.
"The Neighborhood"
An Approach to Urban Sociology, Chapter 6, London: Routledge and Kegan Paul, 1965.
Reprinted in Gutman, 1970.

Mann examines the role of neighborhoods in different ages of the life cycle. He bridges sociological and planning ideas. His concepts are similar to Michelson's. (GB)

1966

KELLER, SUZANNE
"Neighborhood Concepts in Sociological Perspective"
Ekistics, July 1966, **22**, 67–76.

   A prelude to the book of 1968. Shorter and covers much of the same ground. (GB)

1968

KELLER, SUZANNE
The Urban Neighborhood
New York: Random House, 1968.

   Ms. Keller's book is a penetrating exploration into the sociological dimensions of the urban neighborhood. She deals with the ambiguities inherent in the concept of neighborhood and describes the activity of neighboring and the changing role of "neighbor" in contemporary urban culture. Book cites the necessity for a redefinition of the neighborhood as a spatial and social entity with valuable implications for planning our urban environment. (MT)

1969

SOLOW, ANATOLE, CLIFFORD HAM, AND E. OWEN DONNELLY
The Concept of the Neighborhood Unit
Environmental Health Planning Report 1, Graduate School of Public and International Affairs, University of Pittsburgh, 1969.

   This paper was prepared as part of a study undertaken by the American Public Health Association to evaluate the "validity and relevance of existing standards for residential neighborhoods and to formulate up to date criteria for the planning, design and management of the urban and residential environment." Provides comprehensive analysis of neighborhood in historical and cultural context with the major concepts of Howard, Perry, and Le Corbusier offered in some detail. A useful publication. (MT)

PIORO, ZYGMUNT
"An Ecological Interpretation of Settlement Systems"
Architectural Association Quarterly, July 1969.

   Research on spatial organization of man's habitat (technical equipment systems of production and services) is a step in the investigation of more difficult processes within community or settlement systems. Good for its precision in defining relationships between man's physical environment and social structures or an ecological theory of development and suggests research methods. Author distinguishes seven major groups of factors for change: (1) natural geographic environment; (2) man-made geographic environment; (3) population; (4) economic structure; (5) noneconomic structure; (6) social organization; (7) culture. (SES & MT)

The Size of the Neighborhood

In defining neighborhood in the last section, many of the authors also put size parameters around it, especially Perry, Mumford, and Stein. This literature is complementary to the economic-geopraphic theories relating to hierarchies of service areas of cities, all of which is left out of this bibliography.

The last article was written in 1963, and more recent treatment of this subject is included in the monograph by Solow, Ham, and Donnelly, listed with the previous section and in Bell and Tyrwhitt listed in the bibliography section.

1948

BLUMENFELD, HAN
"'Neighborhood' Concept is Submitted to Questioning"
Journal of Housing, December 1948.

Blumenfeld defines the various numbers of families appropriate for forming into neighborhoods. He justifies a grouping of 6 to 12 families who "keep each other company while resting in the evening"; 50 to 100 families who can all know each other by first names; then upward from 100 to 500 families is the maximum size of a group which has a "human scale"—with the children knowing each other; then he says there is no qualitative difference between 500 families and 10,000,000. He counters the standard neighborhood size of 5,000 to 10,000 people as only having the "parent-teacher council" in common; and anyone knows how effective this group is! (GB)

1949
TYRWHITT, JACQUELINE
"The Size and Spacing of Urban Communities"
Journal of the American Planners, Summer 1949, **15**, 10–15.

The author defines the concepts of "garden cities" and "neighborhood units." She suggests that the latter is too small in size to meet the needs of a modern family. As an alternative, it is suggested that the unit of 5,000 to 10,000 be replaced by an urban unit, of 30,000 to 70,000 people who are reasonably mixed racially and economically. This is a reinterpretation of the "garden city" and "neighborhood unit" concepts in terms of human needs and the technical trends of the twentieth century. (BJ)

1951
BARDET, GASTON
"Social Topography, An Analytical-Synthetic Understanding of the Urban Texture"
Town Planning Review, Oct. 1951, 237-260.
Reprinted in Theodorsen, 1961.

Bardet classified all buildings in terms of human behavior to achieve the "social topography" of a town. From observations he suggests three levels of a neighborhood: patriarchal (5–10 families), domestic (50–100 families), neighborhood (500–1,500 families). "It will be easier and safer, and the results will be of longer duration, if we seek to cure our towns of the serious disease from which they suffer by the use of microgroups and micro-organisms instead

of by vast, blind plans that must be constantly revised." (concluding sentence)
(GB)

1960

HIGASA, TADASHI
"A Study of the Planning Unit and the Organization of Facilities of the Residential
Unit"
Report, Building Research Institute, Ministry of Construction, Japan, No. 32, 1960,
65 pages; *Ekistics,* October 1960, **60**, 232–234.

This is a report for placing facilities in residential units from small neighborhoods
to subcenters of cities and altering the positioning of facilities according to densities.
(GB)

1963

MANN, LAWRENCE D.
"The Internal Hierarchy of Sub-Areas in Urban Settlements"
Ekistics, January 1963, **86**, 34–38.

A comparative review of different ways to break down appropriate sizes of
"neighborhoods" and the like for planning purposes. Each of the systems reviewed
assumes an hierarchical ordering: Doxiadis, Christaller, Bardet, and Chombart
de Lauwe. (GB)

PEARSON, NORMAN
"Planning a Social Unit"
Ekistics, January 1963, **86**, 39–42.
Reprinted in Bell, 1972.

A summary of a variety of planners' and utopian concepts for the smallest
scale urban units—neighborhoods or communities. He includes a review of a
variety of little known examples—Kampffmeyer on Soviet Russia—which are interesting to compare with Stein, Perry, etc. (GB)

Neighborhood Boundaries

The studies that seek to define neighborhood boundaries overlap with those classified under "Perception." These often relate back to the basic work of Lynch asking residents to define their own "district" and denote its "edges." Two items are listed here as they are more concerned with the notion of neighborhood than the problems related to the process of perception. Other items can be found in the perception section.

1968
LEE, TERRENCE
"Urban Neighborhood as a Socio-Spatial Schema"
Human Relations, August 1968, **21** (3), 241–267.

Lee attempts to join the physical and social aspects of neighborhoods through a phenomenological approach. The study is based on interviews with housewives in Cambridge, England, which examined their social behavior background and attitudes. In addition, each was asked to delineate their neighborhood on a map. From this data "neighborhood quotients" (NHQ) or schemata (mental representations of physical-social space) expressed as ratios of physical properties of the prescribed environment were derived. The study indicated that an individual's NHQ is determined by factors such as length of residence, age, location of husband's work, house type, and number of children. From this evidence the author concludes that planning should be directed toward heterogeneous physical and social layouts, deliberately emphasizing the local satisfaction of needs. (NM)

1970
SANOFF, HENRY
"Social Perception of the Ecological Neighborhood"
Ekistics, August 1970, **177**, 130–132.

In 100 interviews in southeast Raleigh, respondents were asked to locate their neighborhood boundary, neighborhood center, three best friends, closest relatives, previous residence, place of work, major social organizations, and primary shopping areas. Since there was considerable identification with friends in the neighborhood, the author pleads for relocation to take such items into consideration and cites similar findings by Fried and Gleicher. (GB)

Planning for Facilities and Amenities

There are many articles on economic approaches to determining the placement of community facilities and other amenities, such as schools, local shops, parks, health clinics, fire stations, etc., but there are few behavioral models. Admittedly, there is an overlap between the two and no matter how socially desirable it may be, a corner shop will not stay in existence if it is not economically viable.

The articles selected here have only a behavioral approach. Clearly if one were planning for these facilities, marketing literature is also needed, but that is readily available. The listings here are obscure, have never been organized together, and clearly do not present a unified approach.

Ray Maw's model of activity patterns and facility use provides a methodology that can begin to tie behavioral data together. To complement this, the anthropological detail of such researchers as Cara Richards on "City Taverns" continues to be important. In the future research on behavioral patterns will play increasing roles in developing plans to meet community needs as the economic necessities become less important in post-industrial societies.

1957

RAVITZ, MEL J.
"Use of the Attitude Survey in Neighborhood Planning"
Journal of the American Institute of Planners, 1957.

Using a survey of a neighborhood in Detroit, Ravitz determined the satisfactoriness of amenities. (GB)

GOTTLIEB, DAVID
"The Neighborhood Tavern and the Cocktail Lounge"
American Journal of Sociology, May 1957, **62**, 559–562.

The neighborhood tavern and the cocktail lounge exhibit a relationship between use of leisure and its meaning to the individual. The lounge caters to a transient clientele that does not form a cohesive group. The tavern, however, is a product of the neighborhood. It caters to individuals with similar backgrounds. It becomes the center of a voluntary association enforcing group norms and organizing group action. The taverns have been found to be sources that prevent social change. Instances are recorded where block clubs to resist neighborhood invasion have arisen from among the patrons of the neighborhood tavern. (BJ)

1961

GOSS, ANTHONY
"Neighborhood Units in British New Towns"
Town Planning Review, April 1961, **32** (1), 66–82; *Ekistics,* September 1961, **71**, 211–217.

Goss compares the plans and facilities for the neighborhood units in 10 English New Towns. He also evaluates these as residential units versus the housing estates built before the war. In his discussion, he interrelates the question of density with that of the provision of neighborhood facilities. (GB)

1964

RICHARDS, CARA E.
"City Taverns"
Human Organization, 1964, **22**.

A study of city taverns and the type of face to face group formed regularly in this environment. Importance of taverns in the lives of urban dwellers and in theoretical formulations about the urban environment in general. Study done in Queens and Nassau counties in New York. The tavern provides one way for the urbanite to overcome the social isolation which might be imposed by the environment and to make meaningful social contacts. (RB)

1966
ATHENS CENTER OF EKISTICS
"Participation of Residents in Local Community; Use of Common Facilities"
Ekistics, July 1966, **128**, 60–63.

A study of how 18 communities in Greece use the common community facilities (churches, theaters, parks, gyms, sports arena, coffee shops and confectioners, taverns, restaurants, night clubs). The premise was that size and spacing of community facilities is a problem, and it is important to find out who uses them and how often. Mildly interesting. (MS)

1969
MAW, RAY
"Construction of a Leisure Model"
Official Architecture and Planning, August 1969; *Ekistics,* March 1971, **184**, 230–238.

In constructing a model for the use of leisure time within the working week and over the normal weekend, Ray Maw starts by considering the time budgets of various subgroups of an urban population. He interviewed in Northeast London in an attempt to couple time budgets with the accessibility of a large indoor swimming pool to its potential users. He suggests that the resulting model can be usefully employed to test the most effective location of new recreational facilities, as well as to test the effect of changes in the transportation network or other aspects of accessibility upon existing facilities. (GB)

1970
ANDREWS, FRANK M., AND GEORGE W. PHILLIPS
"The Squatters of Lima: Who They Are and What They Want"
Journal of Developing Areas, January 1970, **4**; *Ekistics*, February 1971, **183**.

In a survey, 361 selected barriada households were interviewed with regard to their characteristics and how they perceived the needs for various facilities in their community. Both the intensity and extent of their dissatisfaction were measured. (GB)

PAPPAS, P.
"Trip Lengths in Relation to Facilities"
Ekistics, August 1970, **177**, 87–103.

Based on a 1963 survey of Athenian households, this report analyzes the distances residents would travel for 12 services and facilities, some of which are peculiar to the Greek environment, e.g., sit-down outdoor theaters. The tables have extensive data, but the survey is too detailed to be replicated. (GB)

CLARK, W. A. V., AND G. RUSHTON
"A Method of Analyzing the Relationship of a Population to Distributed Facilities"
Environment and Behavior, Sept. 1970, 192–207.

They develop a method to measure the distribution of facilities to a population and the relationship between a theoretical and actual distribution of facilities to a population. The paper describes a computerized method of establishing graphically, displaying, comparing, and testing these relationships. The method provides the tools for analyzing spatial patterns that have behavioral interpretations. (LC)

Population Balance within the Neighborhood

From the physical questions of size, boundaries, and facilities, one comes to the more social questions of just who will live within the neighborhood. Certainly, Howard's first conception was of a suburban unit to allow good middle class families to leave the dirty city.

Ever since, one group has looked at the neighborhood as being a tool of class, ethnic, age, and racial segregation. But, say the neighborhood proponents, if it is planned right, the neighborhood can provide for a diversity of people, with an environment to enculturate the children with a broad range of social models. The critics include Peter Mann, Reginald Isaacs, and Herbert Gans, while those that think the concept possible include Catherine Bauer, Peter Marcuse, and Francis Hendricks.

The arguments on both sides relate primarily to two factors: appropriate sizes for heterogeneity and patterns of social interaction between people. The proposal by Hendricks and MacNair to develop small groupings based on homogeneous interest, overcomes the usual criticisms, in recognizing the increasing "role" and leisure time interest identifications which could be meaningful bases on which to plan neighborhoods. Their approach is complemented in some of the reports selected in the chapter on "The Small Neighborhood."

The second factor—social interaction—is treated in a section all on its own. Gans has made the point that people will only talk to each other if they have something to say, and by definition then nonhomogeneous people will not interact. But Soen (1970) in a survey of heterogeneous versus homogeneous communities in Israel, showed that the interplay occurring in the mixed grouping worked toward decreasing racial prejudice. He finally proved the point that Catherine Bauer made in 1945.

1945

BAUER, CATHERINE

"Good Neighborhoods"

The Annals of the American Academy of Political and Social Science, November 1945, 104–115.

An analytical discussion of neighborhood from a sociological point of view. The article favors diversification in neighborhoods versus segregation and race discrimination from the social point of view. (GB)

1958

MANN, PETER H.

"The Socially Balanced Neighbourhood Unit"

Town Planning Review, July 1958, 91–98.

He concludes: "The concept of the socially balanced neighbourhood unit, therefore, is based upon an erroneous analysis of the social structure of urban society, and, apart from its amenity aspects, is an ideal that is unlikely to be attained without a complete change in the structure of our society. Let us bury it quietly, and begin to think again from a sociological rather than an ideological basis." (GB)

1961
GANS, HERBERT J.
"The Balanced Community, Homogeneity or Heterogeneity in Residential Areas" *American Institute of Planning Journal*, August 1961, **27**, 176–184.

Heterogeneous population offers no real advantages over homogeneous population. The planner and developer, etc., should attempt to achieve a mix which will best serve the community in the solving of problems or the implementing of programs. Enough homogeneity should be provided to allow institutions to function and interest groups to reach workable compromises. Enough heterogeneity should be present to prevent undesirable inequalities in the level of services which may exist in a completely homogenous community. The planning professions should pay more attention to the environment of the deprived population. (RM)

1969
MARCUSE, PETER
"Black Housing: A New Approach for Planners"
"Urban Housing: Issues and Problems," *Connection*, Spring 1969, Harvard Graduate School of Design, Cambridge.

A strong case is made for the improvement of diversity in the United States. Planning should be for positive interaction and in an effort to minimize friction. Although it is known that people prefer homogeneity, the question unanswered is at what scale? Is homogeneity healthy? Is homogeneity wrong for a whole racial group? The author believes that twentieth century insecurity fosters homogeneity. (ER)

1970
HENDRICKS, FRANCIS, AND MALCOLM MACNAIR
"Concepts of Environmental Quality Standards Based on Life Styles"
Ekistics, August 1970, **177**, 139–144.

The authors develop a neighborhood model where there is both high mobility and a wide range of life styles. They contend that only a wide diversity of neighborhood sizes and patterns, each homogeneous within itself, can meet the needs of the increasing variety of life styles that will continue to arise within metropolitan and megalopolitan frameworks. (GB)

The Small Neighborhood

Children are indeed the true neighbors. Their socialization through play accounts for approximately half of the entries and the rest of the studies deal with the emotional value of the local environment. As we all, more or less, view the world from our childhood, this scale takes on a double significance.

Four authors have effectively integrated an appreciation of the needs of children with an appraisal of the emotional value of the small neighborhood. Madeleine Kerr in England and Herbert Gans in the U.S. established the significance of appreciating the local environment for the well-being of a community. Each of them studied slum neighborhoods and determined that the nonphysical, emotional ambience provided for the district viability—not the plumbing standards. In the contemporary city where the poor do not often have the opportunity to establish roots through ownership, the street or group of streets provide them identity with place. In the West End of Boston reported on by Gans and on Winston Street described by Hannerz, the areas were considered as home with movement from one apartment to another within these boundaries. The apartment itself was considered as interchangeable with another; but the area was not replaceable. Roots and place identification are evidenced in this small area.

The importance of roots was made explicit in the specific discussion of human needs. Robert Coles, in his compelling account of life in the Appalachian hills, emphasizes the strong ties of the children and adults to the ground itself. This is in all of our heritage. And for many people of the city, this heritage is not far removed. While it is impossible to go back—to recreate the country village—and it is also clear that no one really wants to do that, it is of utmost importance that the planner recognize manifestations of the development of roots in communities and that the designer create opportunities for their development.

Four books are singled out as easy to read and these provide a significant "feeling" for the problem as a whole. (Every well-informed urbanist should have read them—or claim to have read them!) The remainder of the material is considerably more technical and divided into two sections: child/space and emotional attributes of the small neighborhood. Other entries which touch on this particular scale and its activities, often importantly, are classified at the scale of the neighborhood or the dwelling group.

1958
KERR, MADELEINE
The People of Ship Street
New York: Humanities Press, 1958.

In this five-year in-depth study of life styles and behavior patterns of Liverpool residents, an analysis is made of their personality configurations and subculture. Residents were found to adhere strongly to local customs and remain fiercely attached to the community although housing conditions were substandard and the area was earmarked for renewal. The central figure is the mother (Mum) who dominates all aspects of life. The study supports the hypothesis that deprivation has an effect on personality, especially nonintegration and immaturity. An explanation is given of how this separate subculture can survive and function within the wider urban society. (ER)

1962

GANS, HERBERT J.

The Urban Villagers

New York: The Free Press of Glencoe, 1962.

A detailed and sympathetic study of Italian-Americans in Boston's West End prior to the area's demolition. Gans brings alive the peer group culture of the working class and shows how its values affect the ambitions and self-image of the people as well as determining their attitudes toward housing, work, education, mobility, etc. The comparative analysis of the identifying characteristics of the lower, working, and middle classes makes it clear that middle class planners must devise neighborhoods congruent with the needs and desires of the area residents. Distinctions between slums and low rent housing should determine the type of renewal necessary. (AW)

1969

HANNERZ, ULF

Soulside: Inquiries into Ghetto Culture and Community

New York and London: Columbia University Press, 1969.

A Swedish social anthropologist's study of black life in a Washington, D.C., street within the ghetto. While the wider social constraints encircling the black life style are described, the richness comes from the detailed account of the complex intertwined lives of the Winston Street residents. The author identifies four different subtypes: the mainstreamers, the swingers, the street families, and the street corner men. But he also points out the mobility from one of the groups to another and the range of intermediate types. Each group is described with detail according to their habits, attitudes, and use of public and private space. The first half of the book has most of the meat. Good scholarship, good reading. (GB)

1972

COLES, ROBERT

The South Goes North

Children in Crisis, Vol. III, Boston: Atlantic Monthly Press, Little, Brown & Co., 1972.

The third volume of the author's series on American children in crisis. The major message is: We want and anticipate satisfaction in life. Coles finds little satisfaction for the urban poor. The actual words of the poor in the aggregate of the total book add to the author's outcry against our urban industrialized society. He finds our remedial efforts have failed to impress the young with their sincerity. Some fascinating information but more pessimism than Coles has exhibited in his other works. (ER)

Childspace in the Small Neighborhood

The entries in this section emphasize the socialization of children which occurs from their contact with the environment beyond the family in the small neighborhood. Behaviorally, children act out this process through play.

The entries make two major specific points: the function of play and the areas for play. In each case, there is general consensus that the children's needs in their local environment are not being adequately considered. Many of the articles make specific suggestions for making the small neighborhood an appropriate area for the integration of children into social life beyond the limits of the family.

All the entries are listed in chronological order. It is clear that many are redundant, at least in part. These listings have been included purposefully so that if one of the reference is unavailable, another can be found.

1937
PLANT, JAMES S.
"The Personality and an Urban Area"
Personality and Culture, chapter 8
London: Oxford University Press
Reprinted in Hatt, 1957.

This essay of the thirties is based on observations on the effect of a dense area of Newark on children. Of particular interest is a discussion of street play and of the effects of crowding. There are clear implications for the development of play streets and playgrounds and for the urgent need of a child to have a room or a corner of his own. (GB & ES)

1949
MCKAY, HENRY
"The Neighborhood and Child Conduct"
Annals of the American Academy of Political and Social Science, **261,** 32–41, January 1949.
Reprinted in Hatt, 1957.

McKay makes the case that the neighborhood socializes the child, and it is the appropriate arena for positively reinforcing behavior patterns. (GB)

1959
COBB, EDITH
"The Ecology of Imagination in Childhood"
Daedalus, Summer 1959, **88** (3), 537–548.

The author hypothesizes that from the ages of 5 or 6 to 11 or 12, the natural world is experienced in some special way, producing in the child a sense of some profound continuity with natural processes and presenting overt evidence of a biological basis of intuition. She has collected over 300 autobiographical works which support this. In experimenting with play patterns of children of this age, she found the greatest desire was to make a world in which to find a place to discover self. (GB)

1966
HOLE, V., AND A. MILLER
"Children's Play on Housing Estates"
National Building Studies, Research Paper 39, London Ministry of Technology
Architect's Journal, June 1966; *Ekistics*, November 1966, **22**, 365-370.

Comparative study of play areas in English housing developments of both high and low densities. All areas of the estates were classified in terms of utilization for play, the kind of activities, characteristics of supervision, and changes during the day. By the use of site utilization analyses in the field and on paper, interviews with residents and care-takers, the authors conclude that the design of the facility, with a mix of passive and active uses, will determine its ultimate usefulness. (DW)

FRICKER, L. J.
"A Pedestrian's Experience of the Landscape of Cumbernauld"
David Lewis, Ed., *The Pedestrian in the City,* D. Van Nostrand Company, 1966.

An individual's evaluation—as a pedestrian—of the built environment of Cumbernauld. While he does not do a scientific study he notes the effect of paving material on pedestrian habits, the integration of playing equipment into a progression rather than a playground, and the role of the gardens. (GB)

MEAD, MARGARET
"Neighborhoods and Human Needs"
Ekistics, February 1966, **21,** 124–126.

There are certain basic human needs, common to all. Foremost among these are privacy and continuity of human relationships; the latter being especially vital to young children. In building a neighborhood that meets human needs, we start with the needs of infants. They must learn about danger, strangeness, multisensory discrimination, and the world of the nonhuman. In this way, children can relate to their habitat so that the individuals' full humanity can be reached. (BO)

MARANS, A. E.
"Towards Preparing Man for a Changed Environment"
Ekistics, November 1966, **22,** 319–323.

Marans presents the hypothesis that many of the problems of the urban poor will ultimately be faced by the many people making the rural–urban transition, and deals specifically with the environmental problems of children in the "critical period" of the first couple of years of life. Previous and current experimentation is reviewed along with the results. Several conclusions are made on that basis in relation to daycare centers. (GB)

1968
ABERNATHY, W. D.
"The Importance of Play"
Town and Country Planning, October 1968, **36,** 471-475.

The playground, to be successful, must provide "light, movement, color, people, noise, adventure, and above all, danger"—the elements of a street—if it is to attract children. (GB)

LINN, KARL
"Neighborhood Commons"
Architectural Design, August 1968.

From observations of children, teenagers, and grownups, the author designed a "commons" for the neighborhood. He concludes that it is important that each group work to provide such facilities as it is too easy to "confuse perception with projection and to superimpose one's own frame of reference on that of others." (GB)

1969
BETTLEHEIM, BRUNO
The Children of the Dream
New York: MacMillan, 1969.

A child specialist's analysis of the life in a kibbutz, especially in regard to the new generations, not the founding ones. He gives a clear description of both the social and the physical arrangements and concludes that life patterns may be changed in one generation if children are raised outside of the family nest. He both shows the benefits of these life arrangements, such as no delinquency, and the social costs, such as an unexpected loss in the ability for adult intimacy. He implies that the kibbutz formula for raising children could be applied in a modified version in the U.S. to break the poverty syndrome. (ER)

ROSENBERG, GERHARD
"The Landscape of Youth"
Ekistics, September 1969, **166,** 210–212.

Makes a plea, which he supports with some data, that children will play everywhere and everything has to be judged as a potential play opportunity. (GB)

SPIVACK, MAYER
"The Political Collapse of a Playground"
Landscape Architecture Quarterly, July 1969.
Reprinted in McQuade, 1971, **59** (4) 288–291.

In an old dense neighborhood in Boston where the children had little private indoor space, Spivack and the children devised a playground which could be manipulated and controlled by the children. The children had to equal the work of the professional, and each day they put in a great deal of effort—building the playground and rebuilding it became the play. Although some of the children already had court records there was no vandalism. However the playground was not pretty. It did not meet the standards that some of the neighbors desired. One morning it was paved over with asphalt; and then fenced with chain link; and the equipped with devices for play; and then the vandalism and the defacement started. The author hopes that the children learned something about the political process. (GB)

WOLFF, SULA
Children and Stress
London: Penguin, 1969.

Sula Wolff, an English psychiatrist, provides a good general reading on child development. A strong case is made for small scale solutions for children and the importance of early childhood influences, especially of parents. Aggressive and anti-social disorders are found to be caused by defective socialization, and neurotic symptons are related to experiencing excessive anxiety. She finds that limited space without privacy, day or night, in lower economic family homes tends to produce dependent children who need immediate rewards. These children are neither plagued with pangs of conscience nor plan ahead. The extra stimulation of nursery school is recommended as an aid to develop needed verbal skills of children of working adults. Other than the treatment of delinquents (who require 24 hour treatment in a permanent home to construct the conscience they failed to develop and to gain trust in other humans), she finds the segregation of the young for treatment unnecessary and even unhelpful. Sound bibliography. (ER)

1970

FRIEDBERG, PAUL M., AND ELLEN PERRY BERKELEY
Play and Interplay
New York: MacMillian, 1970.

Subtitled "A Manifesto for New Design in Urban Recreational Environment," the book describes the sociological function of urban recreation sites for children, teenagers, adults, the elderly—with special chapters on vest pocket parks, recreation and economics, and "Play and Interplay" which applies to the relationship between the user group psychosocial needs and recreational opportunities in the city. An abundance of photographs helps document the message. (MT)

COOPER, CLARE
The Adventure Playground: Creative Play in an Urban Setting
Center for Planning and Development Research, University of California, Berkeley, Working Paper 118, 1970.

The author has informally surveyed a number of playgrounds and points out the special merits of the adventure playground as a versatile behavior setting for children. (GB)

DEE, NORBERT, AND JON C. LIEBMAN
"A Statistical Study of Children at Urban Playgrounds"
Journal of Leisure Research, Summer 1970, **2** (3).

The purpose of the study was to obtain information on a segment of the recreation system—urban playgrounds—in Baltimore, in order to make intelligent planning decisions concerning the distribution of facilities. By using a recreation demand model and other statistical techniques the study concludes that: (1) playgrounds which had no supervision also had little or no attendance; (2) the number of children using a playground is significantly dependent on the size and type of the facilities; (3) the separation of children into age groups for the attendance calculations is very important; (4) there is no association between any age group and a specific size or type of facility. (LC)

BANGS, HERBERT P., JR., AND STUART MAHLER
"Users of Local Parks"
Journal of the American Institute of Planners, September 1970, **36,** 330–334.

A survey of small neighborhood park use in row house subdivisions in Baltimore proved that while children used these areas extensively the recreational needs of teenagers and adults in the neighborhoods were apparently not met within these small open spaces. Recommendations for improving the assessment of residential open space needs. (GB)

1971
CUMMINS, JANE
Planning for Play
Master's Thesis, Graduate School of Public and International Affairs, University of Pittsburgh, 1971.

Utilizing the framework of Michelson's intersystem congruence model, this report evaluates the interaction of inner-city children with their outdoor neighborhood environment. Playgrounds are categorized according to scope of play and needs of supervision and then criteria are set assuming various behavioral modes. (GB)

1972
RANDALL, EDWINA
The Crisis of the Child and the Crisis of the City: The Same Crisis
Master's Thesis, Graduate School of Public and International Affairs, University of Pittsburgh, 1972.

This is a very thorough study of the preschool child. The first section describes the needs for the child within the family, the housing group, the community, the state, and then in terms of rapid technological change, morality, and total learning. In the second half the author puts forward her own ideas on the relationship between the child and the physical structure of the city. Design solutions are implicit and occasionally made explicit although it stops short of actually providing plans. (GB)

COATES, GARY, AND H. SANOFF
"Behavioral Mapping: The Ecology of Child Behavior in a Planned Residential Setting"
Environmental Design: Research and Practice, EDRA 3/AR 8, Los Angeles, 1972.

A case study of children's out-of-house behavior to identify and measure the special properties of observed activities and the behavioral attributes of space. Peer group behavior based upon the developmental stages of children is predominant in locating activity centers and in selection of play equipment and game areas. The findings are tentative and need comparison in other kinds of small neighborhoods. (JR & GB)

BISHOP, ROBERT L., G. L. PETERSON, AND R. M. MICHAELS
"Measurements of Children's Preferences for the Play Environment"
Environmental Design: Research and Practice, EDRA 3/AR 8, Los Angeles, 1972.

A methodology for gathering information directly from children concerning their preferences in playground design and equipment and to suggest some design guidelines. The basic hypothesis is that playgrounds where children are the primary users are built by designers and administrators who are insensitive to the preferences of children. (JR)

Emotional Attributes of the Small Neighborhood

It was hard to determine a title for this section. At one end of the spectrum there are measurements of the perceived value of the small neighborhood and at the other there are novel-like descriptions of the sentiments felt towards one's home territory. But all agree that it is important to respect the life style and values of neighborhood-centered families. The villain, in many cases, is bulldozer renewal.

Renewal and the development of new publicly sponsored or planned housing projects triggered most of the studies in this section. Four of the studies deal with the West End of Boston: those by Gans, Freid, and Hartman. These studies in turn are interrelated in their conceptualizations with the similar problems in England as described by Mogey, Kerr, and Broady.

While these works of the early sixties were primarily negative, stressing that planners could not do right, the last four listings all stress ways in which the planner can positively effect community renewal in its totality.

1945

FIREY, WALTER
"Sentiment and Symbolism as Ecological Variables"
American Sociological Review, April 1945, **10,** 140–148.
Reprinted in Theodorson, 1961; Gutman, 1970.

Using Boston as a case study, Firey discusses the imputed values placed on neighborhoods within a metropolitan area. He makes a strong case for neighborhood identity based on concepts corresponding to the valuative, meaningful aspect of spatial adaptation. (GB)

1956

MOGEY, J. M.
Family and Neighborhood
London, England: Oxford University Press, 1956.

Using the free interview technique, this study explores social behavior of the wage-earning population in two contrasting areas of Oxford, part of the central city and a housing estate on the outskirts. An analysis of the data shows that there are many significant differences in attitudes, social outlook, social behavior, and relationships between family and house and neighborhood in the two areas. The estate family has become "family centered" as opposed to the "neighborhood centered" city family, and the estate is seen as a more favorable social environment. It is suggested that behavioral changes on the estate may be attributed to the change in physical and social environment. (NM)

1961

BROADY, M. *et al.*

"The Design and Use of Central Area Dwellings"

Housing Review, January/February 1961, **10** (1), 8–13; *Ekistics,* April 1961, **66,** 321–324.

A survey was made of relocation of slum dwellers into new housing in the Gorbals, Glasgow. They were generally satisfied with the housing itself but complained of noise from the location of the playground and seemed to be generally insensitive to the design. (GB)

FRIED, MARC, AND PEGGY GLEICHER

"Some Sources of Residential Satisfaction in an Urban Slum"

Journal of the American Institute of Planners, November 1961, **27,** 305–315.

In a recount and analysis of surveys conducted with residents of the West End in Boston, Fried and Gleicher suggest that the persistent mythology linking social instability and pathology to "slum" areas is unwarranted and often a reflection of the planners' distorted perception of the relationship between urban residential space and social interaction. While Gans' *The Urban Villagers* proposed that peer group interaction among residents was the cementing force, these authors record the dominant role of strong kinship and neighbor contacts in maintaining social cohesion. The article also presents interesting concepts of territorial space: lower class utilization of space in which barriers between home and neighborhood are permeable, making immediate vicinity a perceived extension of home. (AW & MT)

1962

BACK, KURT W.

Slums, Projects, and People

Durham: Duke University Press, 1962

This book describes a survey carried out in Puerto Rico as a result of the unexpected refusal of a majority of slum residents to relocate into public housing projects. It appears that the objectively superior quality of the public housing was of minor importance in the decisions of slum dwellers to take up residence there. More relevant as determinants were the person's overall perspective on life based on his personality, predisposition to change, perception of his present neighborhood, ages of family, and activism or passivism in respect to shaping his life. While a few of the findings might be inapplicable to the U.S., overall it gives an excellent and necessary insight into the problems of relocation from the perspective of the relocatee. (BJ)

1963
FRIED, MARC
"Grieving for a Lost Home"
L. Duhl, Ed., *The Urban Condition* , New York: Basic Books, 1963.
Reprinted in Wilson, 1966.

Fried interviewed 250 women who had moved from the West End of Boston. After two years, 26% reported that they were still depressed. He emphasizes the significance of spatial identity to maintain a health equilibrium. It is an interestingly written report with anthropological detail. (GB)

HARTMAN, C. W.
"Social Values and Housing Orientation"
Journal of Social Issues, April 1963, **19,** 113–131.

Through a study of working class persons displaced by a Boston redevelopment, Hartman learned that the surrounding neighborhood is a far more important component of the residential "life space" of the working class (p. 118). He speculates that "the extreme apartness and inward quality of so much of today's housing, the exclusive personal involvement in one's own home may be because of the lack of settings for meaningful community life" (p. 130). His general conclusion that for "certain people the accepted standards of housing quality and quantity may be of secondary importance in determining residential satisfaction or dissatisfaction, because physical factors are important, but they have no invariant or objective status and can only be understood in the light of their meaning for people's lives, which in turn is determined by social and cultural values. (EW)

1967
WOBER, MALLORY
"Styles of Home Life and Personality Among Nigerian Workers"
Transactions of the Bartlett Society, Vol. 5, 1966-7

Social anthropologist's total approach to society in regard to housing preferences as an expression of outlook. Life in a Nigerian company estate is contrasted with that in the nearby village. The estate residents are described as "cool," not demanding involvement. The "hot" vigorous life of town is a preference of those who choose to make it that way. This study should be of interest to those planning for the less individualized segments of society. (ER)

1969

BERKELEY, ELLEN PERRY
"Urban Renewal Need Not Be a Dirty Word"
Architectural Forum, April 1969

In South Arsenal (Hartford) Conn. the urban renewal springs from within and promises to rebuild not only the community's structures but the lives of those who will use them. The residents conceived of restructuring the community along the lines of a university—a place of continuous education open to all. The concept of flexible space is essential in meeting the evolving physical, social, intellectual, and economic needs of the community. The innovative spatial organization is evidenced in the "everywhere school", a school totally inter-related with the community and the modular housing which specifically adapts to each family's needs. (AW)

TAIRA, KOJI
"Urban Poverty, Ragpickers, and the Ants' Villa in Tokyo"
Economic Development and Cultural Change, January 1969, **17**, 155–177.
Ekistics, September 1969, **166**, 163–167.
Reprinted in Bell 72, McQuade 71

To quote from Walter McQuade's introduction: "The setting may sound exotic, but the comparisons are there. Certainly the average American ghetto dweller in all his misfortune has nothing on the despised and impoverished ragpickers of Tokyo. And certainly anyone familiar with the planning profession in America can only be fascinated by the Dostoevskian cast of characters who helped the ragpickers to better their lives. A ruined businessman; a wandering monk; a tubercular young lady of good family; and a somewhat mysterious promoter-intellectual—these four nonprofessionals performed for the ragpickers a function that in this country would probably be called advocacy. The story of their success is instructive and also, in a modest way, heartening."

Certainly there are two important aspects of this essay: the integration of work into family life and child raising within a small neighborhood and also the role of the advocates in finding a living environment within Tokyo—and a modernizing urban setting. (GB)

1971
SPENCER, PAUL
"Towards a Measure of Social Investment in Communities"
Journal of Architectural Research and Teaching, April 1971, **1** (3), 32–38.

This paper discusses two pieces of research which illustrate a social science approach to the problem of measuring the strength of a community (neighborhood) and the social damage that might be caused by major planning decisions. Methods to evaluate a community's strength include studying the interrelated social ties between members of a locality in relation to the tangible, physical elements of places and trying to delimit the values related to them. (GS)

1972
APPLEYARD, DONALD, AND MARK LINTELL
"The Environmental Quality of City Streets: The Residents' Viewpoint"
Environmental Design: Research and Practice, EDRA 3/AR 8, Los Angeles, 1972;
Journal of the American Institute of Planners, March 1972, **38**, 84-101.

The relationship between traffic density and noise were associated with the environmental satisfaction on a street which was then tested against social interaction. The study demonstrated that on lightly traveled streets, residents, including children, indicated that the whole street was their "home territory," while on heavily traveled streets the street was seen as a corridor and only the dwelling groupings were seen as "home range." (JR)

The Dwelling Group

At the scale of the dwelling group, we come to grips with the human need for private quarters and the new price of it. It is at this daily level of propinquity, that in times of rapid change, privacy becomes both protection and confinement. The economically advantaged have benefited from increased mobility which permits a wide geographical range of friends and interests, while the disadvantaged and children remain confined to their locale. The rapid change to urbanized living has disturbed the opportunities for the poor to comfortably dwell in rural communities as the media is not selective in sending messages on the dazzle of urbanized life styles.

The grouping of dwellings was a first step in giving birth to permanent settlement. The concept of community grew out of everyday necessity. In the permanence of settlement there was an accumulation of physical and social arrangements which defined personal obligation and identification.

With urbanization, improved choice and increased mobility were traded off for increased personal dependency at the larger rather than the smaller scales. As the scale of cities grew, there were new problems of maintaining cultural continuity and achieving satisfactions with urban life.

192

From the base of the dwelling unit, the provider ranges out for family maintenance, leaving behind diminishing group activity, other than child rearing, to sustain the confinement. This problem of confinement permeates the entries at this scale, as the personal recognition and social assistance that have been traditionally associated with housing groups have given way to anonymity. In the press for housing, the 'apart'ment building reinforces separation and impersonalization as transiency eliminates the natural formation of groups. Public interventions in housing infringe on definitions of private rights and provide the targets of social resentments.

In the two-bath condominium and ageless colonial, there has been a trade off between comfort provided by housing technology and the loss of small scale permanence of settlement which is most apparent in the 70-year transition from log-cabin to mobile home. These phenomena have robbed the family of a place for identification with small-scaled groups which have in the past buffered inner tensions, nurtured daily human contact, and emphasized man's humanity to man.

Although high-rise apartment buildings are physical dwelling groups, they seldom encourage community. The children are either stripped or overinsulated from the local environment. In either case apartment design to date has required an unhealthy amount of parental involvement in child rearing. This design failure encourages flight to private dwellings with their individual plots. The migration to the suburbs has intensified the private problems of child rearing in the city as only the disadvantaged and super-insulated children remain. Human development suffers from confinement.

Most of the material that is collected at the scale of the dwelling is concerned with high density and high-rise housing and it is subdivided into three separate sections: Health and the High Rise; Management of the High Rise; and Attitudes to High-Rise Living.

The limited number of references on middle density reflect the infrequent though successful experiments and studies of communities. Suburban housing has not been considered at this scale, but either at the level of the small neighborhood or dwelling unit.

Finally, a postscript is added on small children in the dwelling group, irrespective of density.

High Density Housing

If large cities are to continue as exciting places, it is obvious that the continuation of the overriding desire for single dwellings must be moderated. The high-rise dwelling has served the press for private dwelling but to date it has not solved the needs of the dwelling group. Solving this need could go a long way toward maintaining centrality and halting the disorder of private decentralization. Most of the entries in this group attempt in various ways to reach this root problem.

Health and the High Rise

The entries in this group are similar to the entries under Health Performance at the scale of the dwelling. Both this section and the dwelling section are related to material in the section on Human Needs.

All entries are concerned with the establishment of health criteria which seems to be easier to determine socially and physically than psychologically. Cappon, a psychiatrist, acknowledges the fuzziness of designing apartments for mental health which must await reliable research.

1951
WALLACE, A.
Housing and Social Structure
Philadelphia Housing Authority, 1952.

A research study sponsored by the Philadelphia Housing Authority with particular reference to multi-story, low rent, public housing projects. The study tries to answer two questions: (1) What are desirable standards of individual mental health and of family and community organization in the U.S., and in Philadelphia in particular? (2) What kind of housing project is most likely to facilitate the realization of these standards? In spite of the fact that the study deals with a specific problem, it presents an extensive discussion of how the environment relates to human behavior. (LC)

1971
ROTHBLATT, DONALD N.
"Housing and Human Needs"
Town Planning Review, 1971, **42** (2), 130–144.

Donald Rothblatt studied social and psychological implications of high density housing in Marlboro houses (New York State aided low rent public housing in Brooklyn), and Bouwlust I Housing Estate (publicly assisted housing project, The Hague, Netherlands). He surveyed and compared the human need variables: family needs, belongingness needs, esteem needs, and independence needs. (EB)

1972
CAPPON, DANIEL R.
"Mental Health in the Hi-Rise"
Ekistics, March 1972, **33,** 192–195.

Cappon, a psychiatrist, states that there is no incontrovertible evidence that apartment living produces impairment to mental health because (1) there are no operational definitions of good mental health; (2) impairment of mental health is too gross a condition to be a demonstrable reaction to high rise apartment living; (3) the high rise apartment environment has not been satisfactorily defined; and (4) a proper study has not been carried out. Dr. Cappon then proposes methods for meeting all the objections. At the end he makes ten "theoretical, clinical (or anecdotal) and hunchy anticipations of results" indicating specific areas in which the high rise has adverse effects on mental and social health. (GB)

Management of the High Rise

From the housing studies collected in this section, it is clear that housing management is a key factor internationally. The entries illustrate the resentment of management by tenants and how this affects the care of housing.

There is evidence and consensus that management can make a difference. In Carlson's study of public housing in Caracas, it was found that strong leadership and an educational program aided the rural immigrants in their adjustment to high-rise living. John Turner found that security of tenure makes the greatest difference in managing a housing group. This phenomena is reflected in the spurt of recent building of cooperatives and condominiums throughout the world so that the ownership and high density may coexist.

1959
CARLSON, ERIC
"High-Rise Management: Design Problems as Found in Caracas"
Journal of Housing, October 1959, **16**, 311–314; *Ekistics,* February 1970, **171**, 187–209.

A classic high-rise feedback study in which recent rural migrants cleared from squatting just had no comprehension of how to live in the high rise. From the observations, suggestions are made for alternative housing types, altering high-rise design to meet the needs of the people, and educating the people to change their life styles to high-rise living. (GB)

1960
CARLSON, ERIC
"Evaluation of Housing Projects and Programmes: A Case Report from Venezuela"
Town Planning Review, 1960.

An important evaluation of the super blocks in Caracas, Venezuela. Architecture is found to be less important than management considerations. The problem is seen as relating to the rural poor's life style and its transference to high rise living. Strong leadership, education, community facilities, and apartment ownership seem to ease some of the problems. Good reading comparable to the material on Pruitt Igoe in St. Louis. Not as anti-high rise as most American literature (this may be cultural). (ER)

1963

HOLLINGSHEAD, A. B., AND L. H. ROGLER

"Attitudes toward Slums and Public Housing in Puerto Rico"

Duhl, Leonard (Ed.), *The Urban Condition,* New York: Basic Books, 1963.

A study in San Juan of slum dwellers and their relationship to housing types. Puerto Rico is useful for study, because of the vast cultural changes that have taken place during the rapid transition from an agrarian to an industrial society. A major study was done of schizophrenia and its relation to the life style of the city's slum dwellers. A marked contrast in the public housing compared to the slums was noticed, but the slum dwellers were happier than others. Complaints against the housing authority's rules were worse than the ones against nature. This is due primarily to middle class values being imposed on a lower class culture which produced disharmony. (RB)

SCHORR, ALVIN L.

"Housing and its Effects"

Slums and Social Insecurity, United States Government Printing Office, 1963.

This is a review of literature in which Schorr asserts that the impact of physical housing on human behavior is understated. He calls for research. A general overview. (GB)

1965

FRASER, J. M.

"Choi Hung Housing Estate, Hong Kong"

Ekistics, October 1965, **119**, 194–198.

A description and discussion of behavioral adjustments made in living in one of the highest density housing projects in the world. Management is admitted to be a key, with monthly door-to-door collection of rents a time for interaction. Both problems of teenage high spirits and increasing automobile ownership and pressure on the open space are identified. (GB)

1965
WOOD, ELIZABETH
"Social Aspects of Housing and Urban Development"
Ekistics, December 1965, **121**, 325–339.
Reprinted in Bell, 1972.

Satisfactory housing for the poor is dependent upon more than new quarters. The author elaborates on the importance of: (1) a viable economic base to provide local jobs; (2) training and motivational encouragement to the poor to be able to fill those jobs; (3) a sense of involvement gained through self-help programs and/or participation in management decisions. (AW)

1972
BECHTEL, ROBERT B.
"The Public Housing Environment: A Few Surprises"
Environmental Design: Research and Practice, EDRA 3/AR 8, Los Angeles, 1972.

Behavioral setting analysis was applied to a large public housing project in a large north central city in terms of autonomy levels, penetration levels, and a general richness index. Four conclusions were arrived at that would be of use in architecture and planning: (1) the community was divided and needed a structural way for more behavioral intermingling; (2) the richest settings were not the focal point of the community and suggest that a commercial and service center is constructed at the same location; (3) the level of participation is low and it is suggested that resident-managers might break the monolithic management structure to provide a means of citizen's inputs into design decisions; (4) the richness of the nationalist marches and the cellars stand in direct contradiction to management policies—empty space will not stand unused in an environment where space is at a premium—it is the teenagers who use the cellars as they have no where else to escape direct adult supervision. (JR & GB)

BRILL, WILLIAM H.
"Innovation in the Design and Management of Public Housing: A Case Study
of Applied Research"
Environmental Design: Research and Practice, EDRA 3/AR 8, Los Angeles, 1972.

A research project to determine methods for improving tenant satisfaction in
public housing projects. The major recommendations are in revision of management
procedures and improvement of services. An interesting discussion of the problems
encountered in carrying out an applied research project dealing with a physical
environment and people in an administrative framework. (JR)

HASSAN, RIAZ
"Social Status and Bureaucratic Relationships among Public Housing Tenants
in Singapore"
Ekistics, March 1972, **33** (196), 178–181.

A survey of public housing in Singapore which examines the relationship of
tenants of one, two, three, and four–five rooms to the housing management (size
of apartment being a function of income). The lowest social group rarely comes
in contact with management and tends to tally more satisfactions with the housing
than the upper social groups. Deterioration in ten years in the one-room flat is
such that remodeling is necessary so that it would be two rooms, and the standard
of living had risen so that this could be warranted. It was felt that more space
would provide an atmosphere in which the family would not be as likely to slip
back into slum-like ways of upkeep. (ER)

TURNER, JOHN F. C.
"Housing Issues and the Standards Problem"
Rehovot Conference Paper; *Ekistics,* March 1972, **33** (196), 152–158.

This is a scientific approach to understanding housing management. The author
finds that squatter builders maximize their particular opportunities in accepting
their own responsibility for housing. Its quality *per se* is seen to be only one
dimension of the problem, the others being location and alternative forms
of tenure. The significance of physical, emotional, and financial security are

as yet ignored as housing factors. The author takes a systems approach to housing action. The report contains charts in which nonquantifiable basic needs for various income levels are included. (ER)

Attitudes to High Rise Living

A confusion in basic attitudes, both on the part of professionals and tenants, has accounted for much of the high-rise design failure. From the recent literature and in the entries included in this grouping, attention is paid to preserving satisfactions now found in high-density living (even in slums) and in looking toward examples of multi-family housing projects that work.

In 1934, Catherine Bauer wrote her classic book, *Modern Housing,* and pointed out the many European housing examples that might be tried in the United States; and recent writers continue to make the same observations. For the most part, European housing and housing research still lead that in the U.S. The English researchers describe specific effects of high-density living: Broady and Mogey on movement into new housing estates versus slums, Willis on privacy, Reynolds and Nicholson on "living off the ground," and Ravetz on tenancy patterns. Only the most recent research in the U.S. deals with such fine detail, e.g., Hall's 1972 study on needs of younger and older tenants in middle income high-rise projects.

The traditional question in the U.S. has related to the accommodation of the poor in high-density public housing projects. In his 1966 study of Pruitt Igoe in St. Louis, Rainwater chastised the architects for not paying more attention to building for "security and order" which would maintain the "self esteem, dignity, and autonomy" for lower class people. Montgomery's reply which pointed out the framework within which the architects must work has led Rainwater more recently to the conclusion that the welfare system, more than housing, is a root cause.

1934
BAUER, CATHERINE
Modern Housing
New York: Houghton Mifflin, 1934.

This volume reviews the social solutions in housing that was being built in Europe. Mumford calls it a "brilliant work in terms of its planning and architectural comments."

1955
MOGEY, J. M.
"Changes in Family Life Experienced by English Workers Moving from Slums to Housing Estates"
Marriage and Family Living, May 1955, **27** (2), 123–132.

Reports on a study of 60 families in Oxford, England—half of which lived in overcrowded, old, deteriorated housing; the other half in the newest housing project in the city. Except for differences in accommodation, the two groups were remarkably similar in age, occupation, length of residence in Oxford, etc. The study concluded that the experience of living in improved housing has profound effects on attitudes, outlook, and life style of the urban families. Specific changes noted include: (1) less rigid division of labor between husband and wife; (2) less frequent visits with immediate family; (3) increase in friendly relations with next-door neighbors; (4) increase in aspirations for better housing. (JZ)

1962
PIORO, ZYGMUNT
"The Social Environment of Two Housing Estates in Lublin, Poland"
Human Ecology and Town Planning, **14,** 217–227; *Ekistics,* November 1962, **84.**

A very through comparative study of living patterns and the desires of the residents in two housing estates. After a description of the structural and sociological patterns of each area, specific user orientations are discussed with regard to the use of the kitchen, social services, creche, nursery school, primary school, laundries, restaurants, garden plots, at the level of the housing estate. In particular the tenants were then asked to say what else they wanted on the estate. Then the relation of the estate to the city was considered and here questions discussed were—connecting links to the city, participating in cultural life, frequenting recreation places, and elements of social bonds. In his conclusions, the author emphasizes the symptoms of social pathology and suggests both design changes and further research. In some ways, he covers the waterfront of what this whole bibliography is about. (GB)

1963
KATZ, ROBERT D.
"Intensity of Development and Livability of Multi-Family Housing Projects"
Technical Study TS 7.14, University of Illinois, 1963; *Ekistics,* January 1964, **98,** 59–66.

This is a comparative study of a number of West European and American housing projects on the following factors: privacy, useable open space, individuality of "dwellings," diversity of housing types, location, proximity to community facilities, safety and health, circulation, automobile storage, blending into its surroundings, site details, and views from and to a site. The author concluded that the most significant variables affecting livability were density, building type, and size. He stopped short of actually doing research on "behavior" although he tried to get at livability. His comparative data, however, are useful for others to refer to. (GB)

1964
WILLIS, MARGARET
"Designing for Privacy"
Ekistics, January 1964, **98,** 47–51.

A report of an interview survey made in London to determine how people define privacy. Responses relate to internal privacy, being overlooked, privacy in relationship to neighbors, window location, and design. Conclusions suggest that privacy is more important in times and areas of social change. The article does not draw conclusions related to designs. (SMS)

1966
RAINWATER, LEE
"Fear and the House as Haven in the Lower Class"
Journal of the American Institute of Planners, 1966, **32,** 23–31.

Designers and architects are urged to understand the effect of environmental dangers, real and/or perceived, on the lower class slum and public housing dweller. Since the outside world, both human and nonhuman, presents a constant and all-encompassing threat to the poor, housing design should address itself to the twin tasks of providing "security and order" and at the same time maintaining "self esteem, dignity, and autonomy" for lower class people. (ES)

MONTGOMERY, ROGER
"Comment on Fear and House-as-Haven in the Lower Class"
Journal of the American Institute of Planners, 1966, **32,** 31–37.

This is the architects' viewpoint on designing housing for the poor. He claimed that architects could not take in the sociological aspects of housing because they work on a very limited budget. Another aspect would be that prearranged federal specifications really set the tone for public housing. In addition, a hidden policy of keeping down the poor is ever present. Finally, the architect even if he is interested finds himself seeking the professional status from designing a better home than the lower class can afford. Lastly, high income distribution may be the answer to motivate architects to design better houses for the more affluent poor. (WP)

1968
BROLIN, BRENT C., AND JOHN ZEISEL
"Mass Housing: Social Research and Design"
Architectural Forum, July–August 1968, 66–71.

A report of a study made in Boston using material gathered for the urban villagers which described social behavior of residents. These observations were translated into requirements for the design of mass housing. A formula for translation is to ask: Who is the actor? What is he doing? Who are the significant others in the situation? What is the relation between actor and others architecturally? (SES)

1969
DENNIS, NORMAN
"Mass Housing and the Reformers Myth"
Planning Outlook, June 1969, **6,** 7–13.

This article deals with what the author refers to as the "reformers myth." By this he means to point out the tendency on the part of some advocates to place too much emphasis on the value of a new home for low income groups without due consideration of other values associated with creating a well-rounded and amenable environment for the individual. He believes that the failure of many public housing projects can be traced to this tendency to ignore other social, cultural, religious, and economic values of the people for whom the housing is intended. (LM)

TAIRA, KOJI
"Urban Poverty, Ragpickers, and the Ants' Villa in Tokyo"
Economic Development and Cultural Change, 1969, **17** (2); *Ekistics,* 1969, **166,** 163–167.
Reprinted in Bell, 1972; McQuade, 1971.

To quote from Walter McQuade's introduction: "The setting may sound exotic, but the comparisons are there. Certainly the average American ghetto dweller in all his misfortune has nothing on the despised and impoverished ragpickers of Tokyo. And certainly anyone familiar with the planning profession in America can only be fascinated by the Dostoevskian cast of characters who helped the ragpickers to better their lives. A ruined businessman; a wandering monk; a tubercular young lady of good family; and a somewhat mysterious promoter-intellectual—these four nonprofessionals performed for the ragpickers a function that in this country would probably be called advocacy. The story of their success is instructive and also, in a modest way, heartening."

Certainly there are two important aspects of this essay: the integration of work into family life and child raising within a small neighborhood and also the role of the advocates in finding a living environment within Tokyo—and a modernizing urban setting. (GB)

REYNOLDS, INGRID, AND CHARLES NICHOLSON
"Living Off the Ground"
Architects' Journal, August 20, 1969, **150** (34), 459–470; *Ekistics,* February 1970, **29,** 139–143.

A sample of 1334 housewives and 369 husbands were interviewed in six high-rise housing projects in Britain. Two examples of five kinds of housing were studied—houses, point blocks, internal corridor slab blocks, balcony access blocks, and deck access blocks. Satisfaction was associated with attractiveness and maintenance of the estate as well as the view seen from their own windows. The presence of young children affected satisfaction with living off the ground; in other cases nervousness and loneliness were as serious for those on the ground as those off. The findings are detailed and would seem to have application outside of Britain. (GB)

1970
RAINWATER, LEE
Behind Ghetto Walls: Black Families in a Federal Slum
Chicago: Aldine Publishing Co., 1970.

An important housing study which deals specifically with the Pruitt Igoe housing project in St. Louis but has wider application. It contains a description of the life style of the lower economic apartment dweller and the confinement of their lives. Shows that housing alone cannot break the cycle of poverty or create a good life. The author concludes that the total welfare system needs revising. However, the major findings for this study are the design evaluations of the housing project as it fits the lives of lower-income people. (ER)

1971
YANCEY, WILLIAM L.
"Architecture, Interaction and Social Control"
Environment and Behavior, March 1971, **3** (1), 3–21.

This article examines the relationship between architectural design and the development of the informal social networks frequently found in lower working class neighborhoods. It is noted that residents have isolated themselves in their apartments as a protective device and have established no informal interaction with their neighbors. The informal social networks that would provide social support, protection, and control, never had have a chance to develop. The author maintains that the provision of semi-public spaces and facilities would retard or alleviate the existing atomization of the project residents. (BJ)

1972
HALL, E. T., AND GERDA WEKERLE
"High Rise Living: Can One Design Serve Both Young and Old"
Ekistics, March 1972, **33,** 186–191.

A study of high-rise buildings in central Chicago. It articulates the utilization of the environment by young married and young-single tenants versus older families past the child rearing stage. The slow moving elevator proved to be the sociopetal pivot bringing the young together (which was a reason for moving to these apartments in the first place). The concern of the young was for space for socialization; that of the old was the quality of the dwelling itself. (GB)

205

RAVETZ, ALISON
"Tenancy Patterns and Turnover at Quarry Hill Flats, Leeds"
Urban Studies, October 1971, **8** (3), 181–207.

Quarry Hill was built between 1934 and 1950 and has 924 flats on a 26-acre site, about 35 flats per acre. Complete records were kept of the moves to or from each flat. Thus Ravetz was able to study the changing tenancy over time. While the mean turnover per year is 7.2%, there is variation in years which is related to the total number of new tenants—a "tenant cohort." Large cohort groups had lower leaving rates, but there were people from each cohort still living in the project in 1968. It is suggested that there is a decay rate over time in projects and it would be interesting to have comparative data with other areas of similar size and age. (GB)

Middle Density Housing

This grouping indicates that solutions, other than low and high density, exist and attempts to describe the value of them.

For anyone who has forgotten the early important work of Henry Wright there are two entries to refresh his mind. The 1935 publication of Henry Wright (which still stands as an important statement) and an evaluation of Radburn by his son published in 1971. The Ritter, Berkeley, and Meyerson entries provide complimentary material on self-contained housing groupings.

Ronald Blythe's book, *Akenfield,* in the small neighborhood scale, is included here as well. This impressionistic study, comparable to the work of Robert Coles, provides a valuable look into a traditional village dwelling group and uncovers a lot of surprising material. This study shows that even today fundamental human needs are satisfied within urbanized country villages, which have not been replicated in suburbia.

1935
WRIGHT, HENRY
Rehousing Urban America
New York: Columbia University Press, 1935.

Comprehensive study of group housing, especially of relatively low density group housing. Site plans and floor plans. Related to his development of Radburn.

1960
RITTER, PAUL
"Radburn Planning: A Reassessment"
The Architects' Journal, 1960, **132** (3421), **132** (3423), **133** (3434); *Ekistics,* April 1961, **11** (66); July 1961, **12** (69).

Ritter examines some of the housing areas in Cumbernauld, Eastwick, Philadelphia, and Sennestadt, Germany, and evaluates them as latter day "Radburns." He specifically analyzes the use of the pedestrian paths. This is now quite a dated article but has a good variety of comparable plans. (GB)

1963
MEYERSON, MARTIN, J. TRYWHITT, B. FALK, AND P. SEKLER
Face of the Metropolis
New York: Random House, 1963.

The basic premise of this volume is feedback on examples of design for living and working in the center city. Like Stein's book on new towns it provides a very clear overview of a variety of projects—but from a later vintage, the fifties. (GB)

1969
BERKELEY, ELLEN PERRY
"Westbeth: Artists in Residence"
Forum, October 1970, **133,** 44–49.

Comparable to Le Corbusier unit in size and variety of facilities, Westbeth is a dynamic community for artists in Greenwich Village, New York. The specialized needs of the artists and other residents are met in the studio, commercial, and public gathering places. The concept of creating self-contained communities from rehabilitated structures for individuals who share common specialized need is discussed. The architect conceives of Westbeth as a living building, left unfinished for the residents to complete according to their perceived needs. (AW)

1970

BLYTHE, RONALD

Akenfield: Portrait of an English Village

New York: Delta Book, 1970.

A profile of a contemporary English Village constructed in the words of the inhabitants. This methodology adds a measure of credibility (which scientism seems to require) as it develops a comprehensive statement of some literary distinction. It is a rare view into an industrial farming village and the changes that have taken place in its physical and social structure with the input of technology. Starting with the oldest villagers—who are almost from another world—to the young/ moderns, it uncovers the attitudes regarding place and activities, the village, and the outside world.

1971

WRIGHT, HENRY

"Radburn Revisited"

Forum, July–August 1971; *Ekistics,* March 1972, **33** (196), 196–201.

Henry Wright revisits the ideas of his father and Clarence Stein. He traces their impact and also the points made by their critics. There are site plans and illustrations to substantiate the major points. Although Wright is a trifle too defensive of his father's input, it is an excellent defense of the need for neighborhood in order to provide the amenities for everyday life within the complexity of megalopolis.

1972

SAILE, DAVID G., R. BORRAH, AND M. G. WILLIAMS

"Families in Public Housing: A Study of Three Localities in Rockford, Illinois"

Environmental Design: Research and Practice, EDRA 3/AR 8, Los Angeles, 1972.

Fairly detailed analysis by observation and interview of three public housing projects. Physical characteristics of the buildings and sites were analyzed in terms of their behavioral implications. The research encompassed the orientation of each house, each housing group, and the development of the small neighborhood. While it is interesting, there is still more work to be done here. (JR & GB)

1973
SANOFF, HENRY, AND M. SAWHNEY
"Residential Livability: A Study of User Attitudes toward Their Residential Environment"
Environmental Design: Research and Practice, EDRA 3/AR 8, Los Angeles, 1972.

A questionnaire was administered to low income families in a small southern city to determine preferences for "ideal" neighborhood versus their present one and also for the physical characteristics of dwellings. Results may have been skewed by the nature of the sketches if the illustrations in the report were accurate reproductions of those shown to the subjects during the interviews. (JR)

Children in the Dwelling Group

The entries under this heading have been sorted from the rest to point out the lack of concern for those most confined by the dwelling group. Although the Reynolds and Nicolson study in high-rise evaluation seriously discusses child-rearing in the dwelling group, the needs of the child at this scale are largely ignored.

Menie Gregoire and Margaret Mead deal with the confinement of the urban child. Gregoire is especially concerned with the massive scale of the dwelling groups and how this limits the child's freedom.

The Dennison work is an account of a Block school in a "deprived" neighborhood. His work points out not only the needs of children but an educational scale which has largely been ignored since the demise of the one room rural school house. The dwelling group, especially with the new interest in day care, is a "draw" to be seriously considered.

1969
DENNISON, GEORGE
The Lives of Children
New York: Random House, 1969.

Perhaps the best of many recent educational publications which defines the aims of learning and describes one successful small scale remedial solution—in a school at the scale of the housing group or the small neighborhood. The cost of this versus the traditional public grade school worked out be the same per pupil. Those children who were having severe learning problems previously learned much better and also related to the sense of community spirit which was encouraged. It should be required reading for all school board members, but also gives the concept of an alternative to designers of the urban setting. (ER)

GREGOIRE, MENIE
"Listening to Life as It Is"
Ekistics, October 1969, **167,** 244–245.

The author, a French psychiatrist, discusses the standards of housing which do not reflect the needs of the contemporary family. Her particular concern is for both the rigidity of modern dwellings and their lack of privacy. She also makes some interesting statements to the affect that architecture offers only male symbolism. Fun and insight. (GB)

MEAD, MARGARET
"Childrearing and the Family"
Ekistics, October 1969, **28** (167), 232–233.

She says it best: "The nuclear family is a most precarious unit in economic and social terms, and if both are working it is even more precarious. I think that most people believe that, although societies with extended families are likely to go through a nuclear family phase that cannot be presented, we will return in the future to groups of people who will live together long enough and in close enough proximity so that children can grow up with a range of choice among the adults in their environment . . . we can bring up children with more varied relationships with adults. This means the little boy who is interested in mechanical things will be able to find somebody to teach him, and the little girl whose mother always cooks out of cans, can find someone down the street to teach her how to make a pie."

1970
GREGOIRE, MENIE
"The Child in the High Rise"
Revue Politique, October 1970, **72** (814), 81–86. Freely translated by J. Tyrwhitt
in *Ekistics,* May 1971, **31** (186), 331–333.

Menie Gregoire calls the huge high-rise housing projects that started to spring
up all around Paris in the early 1950's "modern concentration camps" for young
children. She makes specific recommendations for taking into account their needs
in the program for housing projects, particularly the needs of ingress and egress:
"If given the choice of either running about freely or having a bar of chocolate,
the child always chooses his liberty and a piece of dry bread." (GB)

The Dwelling Unit

Disequilibrium of the larger scales funnel to the private pressure point of the
family dwelling. Here the economic and political reality of the work system is
experienced most directly. The inequities of confinement are comprehended at
an early age within the ghetto, especially by those who have migrated from the
farm. Public intervention at this private scale is the most difficult and has been
the least successful because the dwelling unit is the natural framework for everyday
frustrations. Intervention for social reform is seen as an infringement of private
rights both by those who receive public assistance and by the larger public which
does not. Our particular private enterprise system, coupled with fierceness of
the "natural rights" of the family and their basic human need for protective home-
space, has made governmental intervention a denial of the "American dream."

Traditionally, the dwelling unit has existed as a personal refuge and small-scaled
base for daily subsistence. Society has depended on the family to satisfy daily

human needs and transfer culture to the next generations. William Goode in his book, *The Family,* finds that since this unit has become an antidote for the ills of industrial society, both its attraction and its fragility have become magnified. Societal substitution for family functions has been difficult to duplicate.

The friction generated by our competitive system is privately experienced in the family group and success is increasingly measured and determined by residential location. The comforts provided by housing technology are coupled with an expensive trade-off of impermanent residence. There has been a complimentary trade-off between the physical labor and the new strain to expand mental power. The automobile, the product of industrialism, has fractured the diversity of close-knit residential areas. While it has permitted many families to escape the incompatibility of industrial cities and child rearing, this movement has been offset by unforeseen confinement for all young. The price tag for personal mobility has been the massing of sameness.

The thread of the industrial mold is emphasized at the scale of the dwelling unit because technological inventions have effected everyday life in the family home even though it no longer serves any economic function. The removal of work from the home base has altered both urban form and the function of family.

The family has shown an amazing resistance to the industrial society. In response to industrial needs, it has stripped down to the basic conjugal unit. It has relinquished its kin, its major health care activity, and the education of its young, but it has clung to the personal comfort and continuity of the family group and the home base.

Society has traditionally depended on the dwelling unit to satisfy daily human needs and as a small scaled aid in the transfer of culture to the next generation. The dwelling unit has provided a personal refuge, a protective framework, a decentralized ordering and orientation. Over time it has grown more intensely private and increasingly protective. First stripped of its economic home base and recently of community as a place bound phenomenon it can no longer assure cultural continuity to the next generation. It has turned inward and become a substitute for the lack of personal unity with the larger, more artificial, and anonymous society. The function of child rearing has become abnormally intense and elongated by the industrial needs and the hazards of the industrial city.

Child rearing does provide a "live" experience and immediate reward of care and being cared for. In an artificial, uncaring, and anonymous society, this is a reward with a high emotional price for both parent and child. The "live" experience is caring, in the sexual act of comfort, but if not coupled with responsibility this situation can confine the child to the house at the mercy of the private family. Other than personal responsibility, there is little to temper the natural right of the child at birth. For those with little or no satisfaction from society at large, bearing children allows them to gamble for future hope. Too often, there is only added despair, in the present and the future as well.

There has been growing resistance in the young to the nuclear family. The speed of change of technological society, the isolation and intensity of the family experience, and the new pressures for academic achievement have contributed to the generation gap. Evidence includes experimentation in mind expanding drugs, new communal living arrangements, a reluctance to formalize the male–female relationship, and the power of the industrial work system has been questioned.

From the serious students of family life there is support for the family system for child rearing. Most societies which have attempted to replace the family and private home space have returned to it. Even in one generation societal alterations have been possible with substitute child-rearing arrangements, but it has been difficult to duplicate the functions of the family as a carrier of civilization or its small scale service to society.

Any designer dealing with dwelling units at any scale would do well to investigate the findings on his client "the American family," its traditions and directions. Important findings in addition to those listed are William Goode's publication *The Family,* Phillip Aries' *Centuries of Childhood,* Margaret Mead's *New Lives for Old,* Maria Montessori's *The Absorbent Mind* and *The Child and the Family,* Robert Coles' *Wages of Neglect Migrants, Sharecroppers and Mountaineers* and *The South Goes North,* Bruno Bettleheim's *The Children of the Dream,* John Demos' *The Little Commonwealth: Family Life in the Plymouth Colony,* Moshe Safdie's *Beyond Habitat,* Lee Rainwater's *And the Poor Get Children* and *Behind Ghetto Walls,* Elizabeth Janeway's *Man's World–Woman's Place,* Lewis Mumford's *The Culture of Cities,* and Jacques Ellul's *The Technological Society.*

The following information gives a societal view of the dwelling unit. With industrialism and large-scaled living there is an increased emphasis on the "hygiene of housing," which is the first subgrouping. The next two relate to minor alterations of the space by its inhabitants and then the adaption of people to their spaces. The final set addresses the question of total misfit, i.e., the movement of people to find a house to suit them. Three entries are worthy of special note, as they take a holistic approach to the design of the dwelling unit. These are listed first.

213

1953

KENNEDY, ROBERT WOODS
The House and the Act of Its Design
New York: Reinhold, 1953.

Kennedy speaks to the architect designing a single family house for a specific client, but much of what he says can be generalized to producing more satisfactory housing for a mass market than F.H.A. Minimum Property Standards require. The basic organization of a family dwelling should be based on a scale of increasing privacy from the front door, the point of contact with the rest of the world, through living and dining areas where relatives, friends, and neighbors interact with family members to the bathroom and bedroom areas, where intimate and private activities occur. A significant study of the American family, how it behaves, and the design of the physical setting that will best meet its needs. (JR)

1965

CHERMAYEFF, S., AND CHRISTOPHER ALEXANDER
Community and Privacy, Towards a New Architecture of Humanism
Garden City, New York: Anchor Books, 1965.

The authors advocate a science for environmental design based on the premise that every activity must have its own physical zone and that there is a hierarchy of relationships between man and his environment. They define basic requirements for urban dwellings to have a maximum of privacy and still relate to the community and analyze some housing plans and also types of housing in relation to these requirements. I found it very interesting and thought provoking. (NSM)

MATHER, WILLIAM G.
"Attempts to Introduce Human Requirements into Building Requirements"
Man-Environment Systems, March 1972, **2** (2), 117–124.

Mather reports on the progress of the National Bureau of Standards in developing a "performance approach" to housing. In doing this, a simple matrix was developed relating the built elements (eg., walls and lighting) to nine attributes: (1) structural servicability, (2) structural safety, (3) health safety, (4) fire safety, (5) acoustic environment, (6) illuminated environment, (7) atmospheric environment, (8) durability/time reliability (function), (9) spatial characteristics and arrangement. No measurement index was developed and the author finishes his report with a series of ethical questions on the desirability of government regulation of housing. (GB)

Health Maintenance in the Dwelling Unit

The 1950 report of the Committee on the Hygiene of Housing contains a statement of the goals of housing to serve human needs and suggestions for the implementation of these goals. The concern is no longer really with sanitation but the desirable attributes of producing future populations with stable personalities.

As we noted earlier, the house has its greatest influence on the children. Both the studies by Wilner and Walkeley and by Coles find that poor housing conditions contribute to the maladjustment of the lives of children and are generally compounded by economic and social problems of the adult members of the family. This collaborates with the findings of Lee Rainwater.

The work of Coles particularly dwells on inner strength obtained from having roots in place, no matter how bad it is. He finds that the children of those most adversely affected by technology and blocked from future economic satisfactions adjust to their particular reality, grim as it is. This argument should not be used by designers as a cop-out, but as the necessity for providing frameworks for the dwelling units—no matter how densely they are constructed—where the child can put down his home base and venture forth to understand the world.

1950

COMMITTEE ON THE HYGIENE OF HOUSING
Basic Principles of Healthful Housing, 2nd ed. New York: American Public Health Association, 1950.

In this report, the Committee on the Hygiene of Housing formulated basic health needs which housing should serve. The report consists of 30 basic principles with specific requirements and suggested methods of attainment for each. These 30 basic principles are divided under four major headings: physiological needs, psychological needs, protection against contagion, and protection against accidents.

1963

WILNER, DANIEL, AND ROSABELLE PRICE WALKELEY
"Effects of Housing on Health and Performance"
Duhl, L. (Ed.), *The Urban Condition*, New York: Basic Books, 1963.

A review of the results of 40 studies which investigated the relationship between housing types and physical and social pathologies. These studies served as the basis for an in-depth Johns Hopkins study, which is described. Results indicated that poor housing conditions were not exclusive determinants of maladjustment. Material and familial considerations also played a major role. (RB & MT)

1965

NATIONAL INSTITUTE OF CHILD HEALTH AND HUMAN DEVELOPMENT
Patterns of Living and Housing of Middle Aged and Older People
Proceedings of a Research Conference, March 21–24, 1965, Washington, D.C.

A compilation of studies of and articles on older people and housing by noted doctors, psychiatrists, housing specialists and other specialists in the field of housing. Articles approach the problem of housing for the aged from many points of view, including: (1) ego development and milieu therapy, (2) the effects of stress on aging, (3) different housing requirements of the aged, (4) age segregated living, (5) mobility and forced moves, (6) housing preferences of rural people, (7) and the effects of change in residence on old people. The importance and impact of housing and environments is shown in each document. (PM)

1966

BURNS, LELAND
"Cost-Benefit Analysis of Improved Housing: A Case Study"
Ekistics, May 1966, **21** (126), 304–312.

Leland Burns studied improved housing on an Indian reservation. Health benefits were directly computed and related to housing benefits. He came out with a positive ratio of cost–benefit in this case. It is interesting in its methodology of assessment and these techniques could be easily replicated elsewhere. (GB)

1969
FRASER, THOMAS M.
"Relative Habitability of Dwellings: A Conceptual View"
Ekistics, January 1969, **27** (158), 15–18.
Suggests a research model for holistic determination of the criterion for dwelling units. Question whether it is operational. (GB)

Housing Adjustment to People
The recent thrust of these works emphasizes the fine-grained physical arrangements and smaller and smaller human groups in action. This is the historical outgrowth of housing failures, reflected by the accumulation of knowledge and the growth of new specialists. The new material is moving toward specific needs and particular housing solutions to serve these needs.

The wide range of conceptual analysis among these entries makes any generalization difficult. The variation in needs and even the private evaluation of these needs complicate the adjustment of housing for people. Some basic needs of the dwelling are articulated, as well as some of the sources which contribute to the problems of intervention into this private domain.

1969
SINTON, DAVID
"Attitudes, A Source of the Housing Problem"
Urban Housing Issues and Problems, *Connection,* 1969, Harvard Graduate School of Design.

A survey of periodicals was used to examine the image of housing in the United States, the United Kingdom, and France. Image building in the United States and the United Kingdom is found to be reinforcing to the single unit dwelling. In France, periodicals showed no major emphasis on either single or multiple units. Land was intensively used as part of the house in the English ads. American ads projected the house as part of the land. Author believes that the poor could be better housed if land ownership could be discouraged as an American practice in home ownership. Suggests marketing techniques and leadership could alter housing attitudes. (ER)

1971
LERUP, LARS
"Suburban Residential Environment: Analysis, Evaluation and Selection"
Ekistics, February 1971, **31,** 184–200.

An architectural thesis which attempts to build in the social and psychological variables of image: clarity; visual and verbal communication; and public–private outdoor space activities. He also suggests an iterative evaluation and selection mechanism whereby individuals (users) can select alternative trade offs. (GB)

CAPPON, DANIEL
"You're Living in the Wrong House"
Ekistics, September 1971, **32,** 233–235.

A simple article based on the premise that people do not understand their own needs in shelter. It has a good check list. (GB)

ESBER, GEORGE, AND CHARLES ALBANESE
"Apache Proxemics"
Design and Environment, Winter 1971, **2,** 26–27.

The authors report on how anthropologists have worked with Apaches squatting on reservation land to determine their housing needs and "design" dwellings for them. They note the slow anthropological technique of getting into the culture that is significant in the dwelling design. Some of the findings and one plan are also presented. (GB)

1972,
SAUER, LOUIS, AND DAVID MARSHALL
"An Architectural Survey of How Six Families Use Space in Their Existing Houses"
Environmental Design: Research and Practice, EDRA 3/AR 8, Los Angeles, 1972.

Well written report of an architect forced to redesign because of over-budget estimates on an original design. He somehow convinced the public sponsor to permit a limited input into the programming on the part of the potential residents. A survey of the living conditions and evaluation of original plans led to a new design which both cut costs and better satisfied the life style of the tenants. Recommended reading and methodology for designers of housing and their public agency clients. (JR)

SUMMERS, LUIS H.
"The House Design Game"
Environmental Design: Research and Practice, EDRA 3/AR 8, Los Angeles, 1972.

A description of a gaming simulation involving a family in the design of their house through the preplanning, planning, and operational stages. Useful only for architect designed single family house problems. (JR)

HINSHAW, MARK, AND KATHRYN ALLOTT
"Environmental Preferences of Future Housing Consumers"
Journal of the American Institute of Planners, March 1972, **38** (2), 102–107.

This paper reports and analyzes a survey measuring preferences toward housing types (from single family to high rise) and toward the attributes of the neighborhood. They found that the desire for single-family home ownership is ubiquitous and not in the process of radically changing. The most important attribute was that it was a "safe place to live"; other high ranking attributes were "attractiveness, near transit stops, friendly neighbors, near good schools." The lowest ranking two were "near entertainment" and "near place of work." Could be compared with the study by DiAiso *et al.* (GB)

Human Adjustment to Housing

Five entries from four different cultures relate the different adjustments people make to housing. In the chapter on the Dwelling Group there is additional information (especially Rainwater) on human adjustment to apartment living.

The recent work of Constance Perin is worthy of special note. Her contribution is applicable for public policy for the development of more appropriate housing forms, as she finds people to be objective actors in the utilization of housing space. This is in line with the basic human trait of man as an actor who can articulate his needs rather than a simple adapter to be studied only by ethologists. Her work is in consensus with that of Piaget and other work in cognitive studies reflecting the growing sophistication regarding man's spatial requirements. Another example among the entries is the work of Rene Hirschon and Thakurdesai, an anthropologist and architect who studied cultural use of confined habitable spaces. The value of both studies is that they were carried out with the designer in mind, with the hypothesis that if space utilization is understood then it can be designed for.

1969

LEE, DAVID R.
"The Nubian House: Persistence of a Cultural Tradition"
Landscape, Winter 1969, **18,** 36–40.

As a result of the construction of the Aswan Dam, 35,000 Nubians were forced to migrate and take up new housing in unfamiliar villages. This article describes the inventiveness of the Nubians in striving to retain their traditional values in new and different house styles. The new housing differed from the old in materials, construction, and design. The author describes how these differences affected the inhabitants, how they adapted to the new situation, and how their decorative elements survived. (AD)

1970
HIRSCHON, RENEE, AND THAKURDESAI
"Society, Culture and Spatial Organization"
Ekistics, September 1970, **30** (178), 187–196.

The authors investigated a refugee settlement of Turkish Greeks established in 1927 in Athens. They did in-depth surveys of 30 households obtaining detailed house plans, familial relationships, and observations of use of the space. The detailed findings provide a unique, anthropological-architectural case study bringing out the shaping of habitable space by specific cultural norms. (GB)

1971
KURTZ, STEPHEN A.
"And Now a Word from the Users"
Design and Environment, Spring 1971, **2**, 40–49.

A random and limited post-design evaluation of the effect of space on the life style of residents in two apartment towers in New York City (University Towers, I.M. Pei, architect). This article details the inadequacies that two families found in the living arrangements of their dwellings. A persuasive case is made by the author, a design journalist, for more post-design evaluation studies, but they would have to be more extensive and systematic to be really effective. (BJ & ES)

LEE, HYO-JAE
"Life in Urban Korea"
Royal Asiatic Society Transactions, 1971, **46**.

A number of Korean sociologists participated in this study of three urban neighborhoods by living in them and interviewing residents with formal schedules. A traditional inner city neighborhood, an apartment area, and a new suburban area were studied. House plans are presented for each type. Unfortunately the report is rather superficial (and perhaps presumes knowledge of Korean life styles) in covering the topics of level of living, daily life schedules, family and kinship relations, and religion and social values. Although the different environments were compared the specific relationships between environment and social life were not drawn. (GB)

1972
PERIN, CONSTANCE
"Concepts and Methods for Studying Environments in Use"
Environmental Design: Research and Practice, EDRA 3/AR 8, Los Angeles, 1972.

The author hypothesizes that people actively pursue objectives that they are aware of in their utilization of space rather than responding to stimuli in the environment (the hypotheses growing out of research in perception and cognition). To test this idea, the subjects took photographs of their own housing and discussed them. The discussions showed that the behavioral setting theory operates to the extent that living spaces can be adapted to the individual's own preferences. The standard living unit (house or apartment, particularly in public housing) appears to limit satisfaction by preventing cumulative work or play, particularly by children. If "small" houses are inadequate for developing self-esteem, it is suggested, these standards ought to be re-evaluated in terms of the behavioral needs of the people who live in them. (JR)

People's Movement to Get a House

The Rossi work of 1955 on why families move gets at the root of mobility in human need adjustment and housing. Considering the transient nature of the family today it would seem that there would be much more material available on the "press" for housing. The search for housing satisfaction is however pretty much left to family choice and the discretion of the private markets. In the literature on the neighborhood, there is added information on housing selection. Considering educational location as a prime "mover," it is surprising that this new *raison d'être* for housing preference has not produced more studies. Undoubtedly the educational literature has material available on the public cost (socially, emotionally, and economically) of the private preferences or the lack of them.

As a final annotation, we include a whimsical article on the life of "Avioners," the new gypsies, non-child bearing people who live on the road, avoiding property taxes, and enjoying the benefits of industrialized society while drinking in the wonders of perpetual good weather and natural beauty.

1952
RIEMER, SVEND, AND J. J. DEMERATH
"The Role of Social Research in Housing Design"
Land Economics, August 1952, **28,** 230–243.

The authors ask: "What are families' housing preferences in terms of the relative importance assigned to activities competing for consideration in residential design construction?" Several important variables are isolated: (1) social position; (2) daily rhythm of home activity; (3) everyday life and special occasions; (4) weekly rhythm of home activities; (5) seasonal fluctuations; (6) social change; (7) patterns of authority and dominánce; (8) personality trends; (9) family cycle, and (10) special problems. Dated but valuable. (MT)

1955
ROSSI, PETER H.
Why Families Move
Glencoe, Ill.: Free Press of Glencoe, 1955.

This study considered the environmental characteristics which triggered decisions for mobility. The following conclusions were reached:

Mobility is the mechanism by which a family's housing is brought into adjustment to its housing needs. The substantive findings stress space requirements as the most important of the needs generated by life cycle changes. Families in large units and who own their homes, almost regardless of their life cycle position, contribute least to mobility. Large families renting small apartments are the most mobile of all households, especially when they are in the earliest stages of the family cycle.

This is a very substantial research effort which is planning oriented. An "oldie, but a goodie." (GB)

1963
FELLEN, PHILLIP, AND EUGENE LITWAKS
"Neighborhood Cohesion under Conditions of Mobility"
American Sociological Review, June 1963, **28,** 364–376.

The issue of whether groups are structured to deal with mobility or not is examined. If the structure is right, mobility is not disruptive. Aspects which minimize the disruptive effects of mobility are suggested. (EC)

1970
LIFSON, BEN
"Home on the Road"
Design and Environment, Fall 1970, **1,** 32–37; *Ekistics,* March 1971, **31** (184), 224–246.

   Case history of the Avioners, retired couples who travel in caravans, never staying more than two or three days in any one place. Traveling is both a process and an object of quest. Describes the elaborate decoration of Avion trailers as a dwelling unit on the move. (GB)

The Room

As the open space of our cities becomes more costly, more hectic, and even more dangerous, the private space of the room becomes of necessity more important. The satisfactions experienced at this scale, whether in a school, an office, or the home are crucial.

The room is the smallest environmental unit in which human behavior is coordinated. Almost all of the entries in this section deal with the room as a work space. The very emphasis on work, in the material accumulated at this scale, is indicative of the pervasiveness of the work ethic with its emphasis on efficiency. The increased interest in both the climate for learning and the spatial requirements which cultivate it are a response to the needs of our technological society. Only in industry and in offices has there been much concern either psychologically or sociologically with the room.

Planning has yet to seriously dip down into the private space of the room except quantitatively at the macro-scale. Unfortunately private space, or the lack of it, aggravates and affects both behavior and public problems at the larger scales.

Early spatial adaptation complicates later adjustments to the totally urbanizing world. Perhaps nowhere, as much as in the United States, is there such a wide divergence from what is considered ideal in regard to the room. Just as physical mobility and an individualized society have made the house in the center of a plot an ideal dwelling so has the pressure for individual talent spawned the separate room for each family member (except the wife). The increased space requirements may indicate the tensions of the isolation of the nuclear family, but it undoubtedly reflects the press for intellectual development as a response to future work needs. The private bedroom does provide an enclosure to nurture individual academic achievement, much as the monastery in the middle ages provided the quiet and privacy which nurtured the beginning of the knowledge explosion.

The historical trend toward individualism and the development of the need for privacy which accompanied it, expanded spatial requirements for housing in the United States. Status is measured by the scale of the room and its seclusion. This is as true for a bank president as it is for an infant. Early in the 1900's building codes recognized the physiological needs of an urbanized population. Recently, even more accelerated urbanization, public regulations, and expanded costs have denied many of the unskilled access to the "ideal" spatial requirements. For some, denied the physiological and psychological protection provided by minimum density per room requirements, future possibilities of success in the work system is denied. (See the section on density for many relevant studies.)

Of all the entries at the scale of the room, there is not one which investigates the expansion of the spatial requirements for quiet concentration or the social costs of a private bedroom. The manifestations of the scale of the room are too far flung and too important in the web of other scales to be only considered cosmetically by decorators. The room is a human field which is ready for serious investigation beyond the limited approaches which have been used to date.

There are five studies which are exceptions. Any of them might lead into reports synthesizing the role of the room. Two have practical applications and the others are basic readings.

The Ellis and Burnette entries should be of interest to those especially concerned with the child at the Room Scale. Ellis finds that children at play prefer a central location in a room and perhaps more significantly they then tend to build an enclosure for themselves with their toys. This finding should be of special interest to those interested in territorial theory. As children are, in their immaturity, more "natural" human creatures, this study may have uncovered some basic human conservation traits. Piaget in his observations has discovered that the pre-school child explains the world in terms of self. The central choice in space may mirror the development model of the child. The adult preference for the perimeters of rooms, easily observed in the choice of seats in a restaurant, could reflect the decentering process of mature development.

The Burnette article is a discussion of toys, the "tools of the children's trade" which are most suited for various stages of development. Research of this nature, if applied, should protect the child from some of the dangers of forced educational feeding, in order to encourage total development of the child's capacities.

The Fraser volumes are job descriptions by actual workers. He has uncovered some important attitudes to work in industrial society. The major thread running through all the job evaluations is their lack of purpose, even for the professions. Although the workers are English, this study has wider theoretical application and many of the descriptions contain information of the use of space at the room scale, as well as other scales.

More specifically, the Sloan entry is a proxemic study of work space. It has practical application for spatial arrangement to reduce human friction in the work-room.

Perhaps the most basic reading on human activity and the room is the Doxiadis' article. It, more than any of the entries, analyzes the room as a basic unit; the place for "interaction between man's biological necessity, his needs and abilities" and the space in which man has the greatest alternatives. This article promises to be a prelude to a book which will hopefully add new comprehension to the room as a much neglected spatial unit.

1969
FRASER, RONALD (Editor)
Work 1 & 2
Harmondsworth Middlesex, England: Penguin Books, 1969.

A two-volume collection of personal job descriptions and evaluations by actual workers in England. Offers insights into particular job and human needs but more importantly uncovers a general dissatisfaction in workers today. The editor's introduction provides a short evaluation of work activity as the way we make society and the principal way in which people are transformed. The conclusion (by an American professor) is that all work is moving toward a "housewife culture," comfortably supported but with a vague lack of utility. (ER)

1972
BURNETTE, CHARLES H.
"Designing to Reinforce the Mental Image: An Infant Learning Environment"
Environmental Design: Research and Practice, EDRA 3/AR 8, Los Angeles, 1972.

A discussion of the kinds of space and equipment needed to stimulate learning by infants at various stages of their development. He translates the concepts of Werner, Piaget, and Bruner into spatial terms. (JR)

ELLIS, MICHAEL J.
"Play: Theory and Research"
Environmental Design: Research and Practice, EDRA 3/AR 8, Los Angeles, 1972.

Children are observed using play objects. They are found to prefer to be in the center of a space (a room) and then to build with the objects to encapsulate themselves. An interesting article for those designing play equipment or spaces for children. (JR)

SLOAN, SAM A.
"Translating Psycho-Social Criteria into Design Determinants"
Environmental Design: Research and Practice, EDRA 3/AR 8, Los Angeles, 1972.

Sloan applies Ed Hall's theories of proxemics to the analysis of behavioral patterns of people in a working environment in terms of aggressiveness, sociability, and territoriality. The relationship developed in these areas with the physical settings in which they are displayed in a working situation are well documented, informative, and valuable reading for any designer or social-behavioral scientist. (JR)

DOXIADIS, C. A.
"The Formation of the Human Room"
Ekistics, March 1972, **33** (196), 218–229.

This article presents the Greek planner's basic hypothesis and conclusions on the room which will be expanded in the book, *THE FORM OF THE ROOM.* For the author, the evolution of the room is seen as an interaction between man's biological necessity, his needs and abilities at the scale of the room. Man is seen to realize his greatest choice of alternatives. The five basic principles defined for all men's building are: (1) the maximization of potential contacts, (2) minimum effort, energy, time, and cost, (3) optimization of protective space, (4) optimization of relationship with environment, and (5) synthesis of above four principles. The author warns that "we have constantly to distinguish between what is basic and common to all and what is peculiar to a particular individual. We cannot generalize from the latter." (ER)

Adult Work Space

Office work space is the major concern of almost all of the studies included. Although most of the information in the articles has sociological or psychological inferences, three of the entries are specifically sociological in their input. One study deals with the spatial considerations of crowding which has wider application than just keeping the workers happy.

1967
WELLS, BRIAN
"Individual Differences in Environmental Response"
Arena, *Architectural Association Journal*, January 1967, **82** (908), 167-171.

A clerical staff of 2,500 persons were surveyed in a new office building. The questionnaire was designed to cover both a wide range of detail of personal history and environmental experience. While the findings are not conclusive, the study illustrates the importance of such research. (GB & GS)

1969

DUFFY, FRANCIS

"Role and Status in the Office"

Architectural Association Quarterly, October 1969, **1** (4), 4–14.

Settings in offices are compared and differences in built form related systematically to different kinds of role conflict. Good article because role setting is used as analytical unit or socialization unit to determine what affects arrangement of space in terms of (1) characteristics (origin, processes, structure, status, roles), (2) technical subsystems, (3) social subsystems, (4) authority subsystems. (SES)

1971

JOINER, DUNCAN

"Social Ritual and Architectural Space"

Architectural Research and Teaching, April 1971, **1** (3), 11–22.

This paper reports the findings of an investigation into the use and layout of small office space in various types of organizations. The findings suggest that spatial relationships between people are used to sustain and reinforce social relationships, and that spaces and spatial relationships are used to supplement other methods of person-to-person communication, such as speech and gesture. Zone definition and territoriality achieved through personal distance, orientation, and symbolic decoration are seen to be central to this communicative aspect of space organizations. (GS)

1972

BROOKES, MALCOM J.

"Changes in Employee Attitudes and Work Practices in an Office Landscape"

Environmental Design: Research and Practice, EDRA 3/AR 8, Los Angeles, 1972.

A study of work space for office workers from file clerks to a vice-president changing from standard office layout to open landscape. Results will not encourage manufacturers of office landscape equipment but should be read by designers considering such installations. Lack of information about the old and new space and equipment assigned to each employee makes this report difficult to evaluate. (JR)

DAVIS, GERALD
"Using Interview of Present Office Workers in Planning New Offices"
Environmental Design: Research and Practice, EDRA 3/AR 8, Los Angeles, 1972.

A report by the architectural programmers of a project for 4,000 employees in the British Columbia Building in Vancouver, B.C., including functional requirements, interpersonal relationships, and perception. (JR)

MOLESKI, WALTER H., AND R. J. GOODRICH
"The Analysis of Behavioral Requirements in Office Settings"
Environmental Design: Research and Practice, EDRA 3/AR 8, Los Angeles, 1972.

An analysis of a corporation as a complex social organization was developed using an "activity site model as a concept." Interviews, observation, and a questionnaire were utilized. Neither the subject survey nor the method are discussed in enough detail to be useful other than as a basis for formulation of another similar process. (JR)

STOKOLS, DANIEL
"A Social-Psychological Model of Human Crowding Phenomena"
Journal of the American Institute of Planners, March 1972, **38** (2), 72–83.

Stokols differentiates between spatial considerations in terms of the physical conditions of crowding (density) and the psychological experience which is crowding. Although the limitation of space remains as the essential ingredient of crowding the proposed model introduces personal and social variables which have a direct bearing on a person's perception of spatial restrictions as well as on his attempts to cope with the constraint. His experimental hypotheses all relate to relatively small scaled settings. These are: (1) the limitation of space will engender an experience of crowding to the extent that it introduces noxious physical effects or places constraints on personal or social activities; (2) under conditions of spatial limitation: (a) a noisy situation will be perceived as more crowded than a quiet one; (b) a cluttered area will appear more crowded; (c) situations involving social interference will appear more crowded; (d) time will increase a feeling of crowding; (e) persons who are by nature aggressive or impatient will experience stronger crowding sensations. (GB)

CONNOLLY, D. J.
"Social Repercussions of New Cargo Handling Methods in the Port of London"
International Labor Review, Vol. 105, No. 6, June 1972, pp. 543–568.

This is a contemporary study of the interrelations of work patterns on the daily life and dignity of a community of working class people. In making the port more efficient, decision-making was taken from the workers who were degraded into being programmable slaves. In addition, shortening the working hours and the establishment of a second shift disrupted personal, family, and community life. Symptoms include anomie on the job, insomnia and break down of group meal times in the home, and inability to carry out usual functions (as union member or club member) in the community. The author points out the paradox of progress: that economic growth often means social costs which are extremely disruptive during the lifetime of the involved individuals and their families and communities. (GB)

Childhood Learning Space

With all the concern as to why "Johnny can't read," it would seem that the scale of the room and its arrangement would have had many entries. Undoubtedly, in the mountain of educational literature, there is to be found more on this topic. Among the entries, there are two authors (Coles and Montessori) who have made a life work of seriously listening to children for clues to their needs for development, and both have important information as to what constitutes a space for children's learning. The other entries included in this section are narrower in focus, often leaving the reader wondering.

1967
MONTESSORI, MARIA
The Absorbent Mind
New York: Delta Book, Dell Publishing, 1967.

An extremely convincing and compassionate view of the preschool child written by a pioneer educator and champion of all children. Important material on the capabilities of children and the needs that must be met to develop them. Rare insights into the child's adaptation into the adult world. (ER)

1969
COLES, ROBERT, AND MARIA PIERS
Wages of Neglect
Chicago: Quadrangle Books, 1969.

Description of the behavior patterns of children who have been deprived of the early, imperative material relationship. The authors find the city slum the most retarding environment for child development. Major conclusions are that the absence of the mother and absence of play are the greatest causes of stunted development. Suggest society must supplement inadequate mothering. (ER)

1971
EASTMAN, CHARLES, AND JOEL HARPER
"A Study of Proxemic Behavior: Toward a Predictive Model"
Environment and Behavior, December 1971, **3** (4), 418–437.

A study of the use of space in a reference section of a library. Conclusion is that it is dangerous to make assumptions on homogeneity, self-selection, and supports for certain behavior. Two alternatives are spelled out—to maximize behavioral freedom or to channel behavior. The designer has the responsibility to make the aims of his design clear. (ER)

1972
COLES, ROBERT
Migrants, Sharecroppers, Mountaineers
Children in Crisis, Vol. II
Boston: Atlantic Monthly Press, Little, Brown, & Co., 1972.

The second (and the best to date) volume in an important series on the lives of children in various regions of the United States. Although it is a description of rural life, it has urban application, as many of the problems and the strengths of these people are imported to the city. This volume is not only an important statement about post technological society, it is also a high point in literary achievement in attitudinal studies. If you are going to read just one book, on either the poor or the child, read this particular volume. (ER)

BRUNETTI, FRANK A.
"Noise, Distraction and Privacy in Conventional and Open School Environments"
Environmental Design: Research and Practice, EDRA 3/AR 8, Los Angeles, 1972.

An evaluation of the visual and acoustical environment of schools with open space design in terms of distraction and privacy. As a result of the case study improvements have been designed and implemented in both the behavioral and environmental components of the instructional programs. (JR & GB)

DURLACK, JEROME T., B. E. BEARDSLEY, AND J. S. MURRAY
"Observation of User Activity Patterns in Open and Traditional Plan School Environments"
Environmental Design: Research and Practice, EDRA 3/AR 8, Los Angeles, 1972.

Empirical comparison of activity patterns in three styles of schools, ranging from open to traditional. The authors concluded that although it was established that the activity patterns were different, it was not clear whether or not these patterns have differential effects on what the children learn. (JR)

DREW, CLIFFORD
"Research on the Psychological Behavioral Effects of the Physical Environment"
Review of Education Research, 1972, **41** (5), 447–465.

The author is interested in better design of educational settings for learning. He has done a quite thorough review of the literature and is rightfully confused. He specifically puts together some of the implications for educational design, i.e., that complexity and symmetry may well have important practical implications. He also provides a framework for environmental organization. (GB)

AFTERTHOUGHT:
BIBLIOGRAPHIES AND
SETS OF READINGS

This bibliography of bibliographies includes books of hard-to-get readings as well as listings. These cover a wide range of sources which can lead the researchers in tangential directions.

The bibliographies of the Council of Planning Librarians, which now number almost 300, are recommended with caution as there are no quality criteria applied to publication. Only seven are included in the listing below.

1957

HATT, PAUL, AND A. J. REISS, JR.
Cities and Society (Second edition)
Glencoe, Illinois: The Free Press, 1957.

This set of readings touches on some behavioral questions and includes six items in the bibliography. (GB)

1961

THEORDORSON, G.
Studies in Human Ecology
New York: Harper and Row, 1961.

This book of readings reprints articles on ecology in relation to human geography and regional studies. Six articles are appropriate for this bibliography. (GB)

1962

CHAPIN, F., STUART AND WEISS SHIRLEY (Eds.)
Urban Growth Dynamics in a Regional Cluster of Cities
New York: John Wiley & Sons, 1962.

A book of articles on various points relating to a regional cluster in the Carolina area. Two are appropriate to this bibliography. (GB)

1964

ELIAS, C. E., JAMES GILLIES, AND SVEND RIEMER
Metropolis: Values in Conflict
Belmont, California: Wadsworth Publishing Co., 1964.

A problems approach to urban problems with most of its articles now dated or superficial. In the readings, 3 of the 55 are relevant to this bibliography. (GB)

HEYMAN, M.
"Space and Behavior: A Selected Bibliography"
Landscape, 1964, **13,** 4–10.

Thirty-six annotated selections from journals and books. Articles seem to range in scale from research reports to broader analyses such as are found in *The Organization Man* and *The Hidden Dimension;* good and exactly to the point of our inquiries. (SMS)

1966

BESTOR, G. C., AND HOLWAY R. JONES
City Planning: A Basic Bibliography of Sources and Trends
Sacramento: California Council of Civil Engineers and Land Surveyors, 1966.

A helpful annotated bibliography for city and regional planners, researchers, students of urban affairs. Concerns nature, function, processes of city planning along with nature and form of cities, history of cities and city planning, and planning education. Useful for publishers' addresses, and cross-references. Reviews of annotations up to 1961. (AT)

(ED.) WARREN, RONALD LESLIE
Perspectives on the American Community: A Book of Readings
Chicago: Rand McNally & Co., 1966.

This book of readings interrelates sociology and government, including planning. Six of the articles reprinted are considered appropriate for this bibliography. (GB)

WILSON, JAMES Q.
Urban Renewal: The Record and the Controversy
Cambridge: M.I.T. Press, 1966.

This overall book of readings on urban renewal includes issues on the design of projects, effects of environment on people, and potential role of the citizens. Three articles are related to the scope of this bibliography, the other 23 deal more generally from a governmental standpoint. (GB)

1968

GANS, HERBERT J.
People and Plans
New York: Basic Books, 1968.

Gans' book is a collection of essays dealing with the sociological dimensions of American planning. He has organized these into six chapters, each addressing itself to an urgent aspect of theory and urban policy development: (1) behavior and environment, (2) city planning and goal-oriented planning, (3) planning for new towns and suburbs, (4) planning against urban poverty and segregation, (5) the racial crisis, and (6) an approach to sociological analysis and planning. A classic work and highly recommended for its insight and wisdom. (MT)

1969

MONTGOMERY, ROGER
A General Booklist on Urban Design
Council of Planning Librarians *Exchange Bibliography* #84; May 1969.

This is a bibliography of the classics in urban design, covering authors such as Doxiadis, Goodman, Gropius, Le Corbusier, Lynch, Sitte, Weber, etc. The annotations are short (one to three sentences), clear, and designed to locate the works in the stream of design thought rather than to report extensive findings. (GB)

HARRISON, JAMES D.
"An Annotated Bibliography on Environmental Perception with Emphasis on Urban Areas"
Council of Planning Librarians, *Exchange Bibliography* #93, August 1969.

This bibliography is only partially annotated and draws heavily on non-annotated lists provided by George Priddle and Kevin Lynch. It is divided into five sections: (1) space, culture, and personality; (2) decision making and resource management; (3) city planning and the critic; (4) the sensuous form of cities; and (5) personality and perception. (GB)

SHEPARD, PAUL, AND DANIEL MCKINLEY
The Subversive Science: Toward an Ecology of Man
Boston: Houghton Mifflin, 1969.

A book of readings designed to show the oneness of ecology: "There is only one ecology, not a human one on the one hand and another for the subhuman." Only 2 of the 37 essays are appropriate in the context of this bibliography; the others deal predominantly with the relation of man and large populations to the natural world. (GB)

SAARINEN, THOMAS F.
Perception of Environment
Commission of College Geography, Resource Paper 5, 1969.

This monography provides a review of studies and research centered on man's perception of his environment. The review is organized according to scale. The first five sections are relevant to the study of the relationships between behavior and space. They are: (1) personal space and room geography; (2) architectural space; (3) neighborhoods or districts; (4) paths and roads, and (5) the city. (GB)

1970
GUTMAN, ROBERT, AND DAVID POPENOE
Neighborhood, City and Metropolis: An Integrated Reader
New York: Random House, 1970.

This book tries to make the link from sociological theory to sociological action through the planning process. Eleven of the 60 readings are appropriate in this bibliography; the others are more directly sociological or planning theory and action oriented without the environmental framework. (GB)

JAKLE, JOHN A.
The Spatial Dimensions of Social Organization: A Selected Bibliography for Urban Social Geography
Council of Planning Librarians *Exchange Bibliography #118,* 1970.

This bibliography reviews the literature of the spatial arrangement of the physical environment and the study of human spacing and spatial behavior. It brings together the full spectrum of socio-geographical investigation and is limited to urban research and study; focusing on literature produced since World War II. The bibliography is divided into nine areas; of which the literature which relates the most seems to be "territoriality, distance and spacial interaction, neighboring and neighborhood, and perception of place and space." It is not annotated and there are a variety of mistakes. It takes one more completely into geographer's contributions. (BO & GB)

PROSHANSKY, HAROLD M., WILLIAM ITTELSON, AND LEEANN G. RIVLIN
Environmental Psychology: Man and His Physical Setting
New York: Holt, Rinehart and Winston, 1970.

Approximately half of the readings from this book have been included in the bibliography—and many of the others are tangential, on the one hand delving into psychology and peculiarities of hospital design and on the other into some of the basic concepts of urban planning that are not particularly behavioral. The editors have contributed four articles. In the first they enunciate their assumptions on the influence of the physical environment on behavior. In the second they explore the problems of the need for privacy and the individual's freedom of choice—his identity. The third article is a report on their own research regarding behavior in hospital wards. Their final article relates to the mapping of behavior in hospitals. Unfortunately, since hospital behavior is significantly specialized and abnormal, this slant of their research makes the book less useful for those concerned with the larger environment than it might have been. (GB)

1971

HOLLANDER, ARNOLD PETER
High Density Environments: Some Cultural, Physiological and Psychological Considerations—An Annotated Bibliography
Council of Planning Librarians *Exchange Bibliography #221,* September 1971.

In a brief introduction the author comments on the status of findings about density and defines terms often used in density studies. Entries are alphabetic by author, but in addition are typed as studies about: (1) responses to high density, (2) causes of reactions to density, (3) control factors that differentiate the response to density, or (4) background literature. The annotations are clear, evaluative, and unusually personal (subjective). The author often indicates which sections of a work seem of most value. (ES)

GARBRECHT, DIETRICH
Pedestrian Movement: A Bibliography
Council of Planning Librarians, *Exchange Bibliography*, #225, October 1971.

Although the entries are not annotated, they are carefully organized by topic. Sections are: (1) image, subjective map; (2) behavioral characteristics of pedestrian movement; (3) origin–destination; (4) safety; (5) models; (6) counting; (7) design criteria; and (8) example projects. An author index is included. (GB)

MCQUADE, WALTER (Ed.)
Cities Fit to Live in
New York and London: The MacMillan Company, 1971.

This is a very thin little book of readings that starts with the "black" and "violence" 'problems' of the mid-sixties in the U.S., then adds some rather irrelevant 'plans' (with the exception of Alexander's approach), and finally considers advocacy and participation on the issue of the way the future may be achieved. I found it on a department store bookshelf and it is really meant for garden club or informed women's study groups—he has added lots of pictures, especially of black young men—to add spice to the verbiage.

Three of the 17 articles are worthy of this bibliography. (GB)

MANN, LAWRENCE, AND GEORGE HAGEVIK
"The New Environmentalism: Behaviorism and Design"
Journal of the American Institute of Planners, September 1971, **37** (5), 344–347.

A short review article which summarizes the main points of Michelson's book, *Man and His Urban Environment,* the reader of Proshansky, Ittelson, and Rivlin, *Environmental Psychology,* in relation to the natural environmentalism esposed by McHarg in *Design with Nature.* The authors conclude that planning must include the concept of "behavioral environmentalism." The authors include articles and books on natural environmentalism in their bibliography which are not included in this reference. (GB)

1972
WELLMAN, BARRY, AND WHITAKER, MARILYN
Community-Network-Communication: An Annotated Bibliography
Council of Planning Librarians *Exchange Bibliography* #282–283, May 1972.

This bibliography documents "the impact of communications on networks of primary relationships and their organization into communities" (p. 3). The annotations are fairly long, but clear and succinct and generally include the major findings of each study along with some evaluative comments. Major sections follow the concepts making up the title of the bibliography, and a subsection of each is devoted to studies on the future of communities, networks, and communications. Cross references are listed at the end of each section. (GB)

GRANT, DONALD P.
Systematic Methods in Environmental Designs: An Introductory Bibliography
School of Architecture and Environmental Design, California State Polytechnic University, San Luis Obispo, 1972.

A brief introduction describes the field of design methods and its development. References from the field and from related areas are then listed in an outline of the field, followed by an alphabetical, annotated reference list of bibliographic data containing the items listed in the outline of the field. The appearance of a literature in this field is a recent phenomenon—of the approximately 300 items referred to in this bibliography, more than half are dated 1970 or later, and even then the bulk of the "related fields" literature is in the pre-1970 group, placing the great bulk of the literature of the field itself in the last two and one-half years. (GB)

BELL, GWEN, AND JAQUELINE TYRWHITT
Human Identity in the Urbanized Environment
London and New York: Penguin Books, 1972.

This reader covers the six ekistic elements. Three are approached from the viewpoint of behavior as evidenced in the problems of maintaining human identity. The other three—nature, networks, and synthesis—are primarily concerned with the urbanized environment itself. (GB)

Guide to Periodicals

Fourteen periodicals have been found to frequently cover the material related in this bibliography. These should be included in any research or educational center which is concerned with the environmental fit.

Of these fourteen, four are those that address design professionals; four planning professionals; one sociologists; and the other five seek to look at the interface of design and behavior.

Forty-three other journals were also utilized; sometimes there was only one relevant article from them, or one special issue.

The best of the articles are often available from several different sources, either reprinted in a second journal or in one of the sets of readers listed in this section.

Key Periodicals

American Journal of Sociology, University of Chicago Press, 5750 Ellis Avenue, Chicago, Illinois 60637.

Architectural Association Quarterly, Pergamon Press Inc., Maxwell House, Fairview Park, Elmsford, New York 10523. Quarterly, 60s.

Architectural Design, 26 Bloomsbury Way, London, WCI, England. Monthly, $14.40.

Architectural Forum (Forum), Urban America Inc., 111 West 57th Street, New York, New York 10019. 10 per year, $10.

Design and Environment, RC Publications, 6400 Goldsboro Road, Washington, D.C. 20034. Quarterly, $11.00.

Ekistics, P.O. Box 471, Athens 136, Greece. Monthly, $24 per year.

Environment and Behavior, Sage Publications, 275 South Beverly Drive, Beverly Hills, California 90212. 8 issues, $10.

Environment and Planning, Pion Ltd., 207 Brondesbury Park, London NW 2, 5 JN England. Quarterly, $27

Environmental Design Research Association, Proceedings. Various Publishers. Yearly.

Journal of the American Institute of Planners, 917 15th Street, NW, Washington, D.C. 20005. Bi-monthly, $8.

Journal of the (Royal) Town Planning Institute, 26 Portland Place, London, W 1, England. 10 issues a year, 63s.

Landscape, Box 7177, Landscape Station, Berkeley, California, 94707.

Town and Country Planning, The Planning Center, 28 King Street, London WC2, England. Monthly, 37s6d.

Town Planning Review, Liverpool University Press, 123 Grove Street, Liverpool L7, England. Quarterly, 42s. ($6)

Other Journals Utilized (Country of origin included if not the U.S.A.)
American Behavioral Scientist
American Sociological Review
Annals of the American Association of Political and Social Scientists
The Architect
The Architects' Journal (UK)
Behavioral Science
City
Connection
Culture and Leisure (Czechoslovakia)
Daedalus
Design Methods Group Newsletter
The Developing Economies (Japan)
Economic Development and Cultural Change
Fortune
The Geographical Review
Hospitals and Community Psychiatry
Housing Review
Human Organization
Human Relations
International Journal of Environmental Studies (UK)
International Labour Review (Switzerland)
Journal of the American Institute of Architects
Journal of Architectural Research and Teaching
Journal of Developing Areas
Journal of Housing
Journal of Leisure Research
Journal of Social Psychology
Land Economics
Landscape Architecture Quarterly
Marriage and Family Living
Official Architecture and Planning (UK)
Planning Outlook (UK)
Progressive Architecture
Psychological Review
Regional Science Association Papers

Review of Educational Research
Revue Politique (France)
Royal Architectural Institute of Canada Journal (Canada)
Royal Asiatic Society Transactions (Korea)
Science
Social Forces
Social Problems
Society and Leisure
Socio-Economic Planning Sciences (UK)
Transactions of the Bartlett Society (UK)
Urban Studies

Index of Annotations

Abernathy, W. D. "The Importance of Play," 182

Adams, F. J., S. Riemer, R. Isaacs, and R. B. Mitchell "The Neighborhood Concept in Theory and Application," 162

Alexander, Christopher "Changes in Form," 86

"The City as a Mechanism for Sustaining Human Contact," 109

"A City is Not a Tree," 67

"Major Changes in Environment Form Required by Social and Psychological Demands," 85

Notes on the Synthesis of Form, 67–68

Alexander, Christopher, Sanford Hirshen, Sara Ishikawa, Christie Coffin, and Shlomo Angel *Houses Generated by Patterns*, 85

Andrews, Frank M., and George W. Phillips "The Squatters of Lima: Who They Are and What They Want," 171

Appleyard, Donald, and Mark Lintell "The Environmental Quality of City Streets: The Residents' Viewpoint," 191

Appleyard, Donald, Kevin Lynch, and J. R. Meyer *The View from the Road*, 16

Andrew, Paul, Malcolm Cristie and Richard Martin "Squatter Manifesto," 44

Argyle, Michael *The Scientific Study of Human Behavior*, 115–116

Athens Center of Ekistics "Participation of Residents in Local Community; Use of Common Facilities," 171

Babcock, Richard F., and Fred P. Bosselman "C. P.: A Suburban Suggestion for the Central City," 45–46

Beck, Kurt W. *Slums, Projects, and People*, 188–189

Bakema, J. B. "Some Thoughts about Relationships between Buildings and Cities," 77

Bangs, Herbert P., Jr., and Stuart Mahler "Users of Local Parks," 185

Bardet, Gaston "Social Topography, An Analytical-Synthetic Understanding of the Urban Texture," 166–167

Barker, Roger G. *Ecological Psychology, Concepts and Methods for Studying the Environment of Human Behavior,* 96
"Ecology and Motivation," 95

Barker, Roger G., and Louise S. Barker "The Psychological Ecology of Old People in Midwest, Kansas, and Yoredale, Yorkshire," 95–96

Batchelor, Peter "Residential Space Systems: Generic and Specific Concepts of Urban Structural Analysis," 127

Bauer, Catherine "Good Neighborhoods," 173
Modern Housing, 201

Bechtel, Robert B. "A Behavioral Comparison of Urban and Small Town Environments," 98
"The Public Housing Environment: A Few Surprises," 198

Beck, Robert "Spatial Meaning and the Property of the Environment," 17

Bell, Gwen, and Jacqueline Tyrwhitt *Human Identity in the Urbanized Environment,* 242

Bell, G., and Margrit Kennedy "Age Group Needs and their Satisfaction: A Case Study of the East Liberty Renewal Area, Pittsburgh," 145

Berkeley, Ellen Perry "Environmental Education from Kindergarten On Up," 48
"Urban Renewal Need Not Be a Dirty Word," 190
"Westbeth: Artists in Residence," 207
"Woodlawn Gardens," 43–44

Bestor, G. C., and R. Holway Jones *City Planning: A Basic Bibliography of Sources and Trends,* 237

Bettleheim, Bruno *The Children of the Dream,* 182–183

Bird, Caroline *The Crowding Syndrome: Learning to Live with Too Much and Too Many,* 55

Bishop, Robert L., G. L. Peterson, and R. M. Michaels "Measurements of Children's Preferences for the Play Environment," 186

Blasdel, Hugo G. "Multidimensional Scaling for Architectural Environments," 32

Blecher, Earl M. *Advocacy Planning for Urban Development,* 42

Blumenfeld, Hans " 'Neighborhood' Concept is Submitted to Questioning," 165–166

Blumenfeld, Hans, M. Bogdanov, G Burgel, A. Christakis, P. A. Emery, R. L. Meier, B. E. Newling, G. A. Papageorgiou, J. G. Papaioannou, and P. Pappas "Population Densities in Human Settlements," 56

Blythe, Ronald *Akenfield: Portrait of an English Village,* 156–157, 208

Boeschenstein, Warren "Design of Socially Mixed Housing," 120

Bolt, Beranek, and Newman, Inc. *Noise in Urban and Suburban Areas: Results of Field Studies,* 19

Bott, Elizabeth *Family and Social Network,* 115

Brill, William H. "Innovation in the Design and Management of Public Housing: A Case Study of Applied Research," 199

Broady, Maurice "The Sociology of the Urban Environment," 148

Broady, M. *et al.* "The Design and Use of Central Area Dwellings," 188

Brodey, Warren "The Other Than Visual World of the Blind," 20
"Sound and Space," 19

Brolin, Brent C., and John Zeisel "Mass Housing: Social Research and Design," 203

Brookes, Malcom J. "Changes in Employee Attitudes and Work Practices in an Office Landscape," 230

Brunetti, Frank A. "Noise Distraction and Privacy in Conventional and Open School Environments," 234

Brunhes, Jean *Human Geography,* 89

Bull, C. Neil "Prediction of Future Daily Behaviors: An Empirical Measure of Leisure," 125

Burnette, Charles H. "Designing to Reinforce the Mental Image: An Infant Learning Environment," 228

Burns, Leland "Cost-Benefit Analysis of Improved Housing: A Case Study," 216

Burns, Mary "Planning for People," 38

Burton, Thomas L. "Identification of Recreation Types through Cluster Analysis," 130

Butman, Robert "Site Planning and Social Behavior," 102–103

Buttimer, Anne "Social Space in Interdisciplinary Perspective," 93
"Sociology and Planning," 93–94

Byers, Paul "Still Photography in the Systematic Recording and Analysis of Behavioral Data," 30

Calhoun, John B. "The Role of Space in Animal Sociology," 54

Canter, David V. "The Place of Architectural Psychology: A Consideration of Some Findings," 83

Canter, David, and Sandra Canter "Close Together in Tokyo," 54

Caplow, T., and R. Foreman "Neighborhood Interaction in a Homogeneous Community," 113

Cappon, Daniel R. "Mental Health in the Hi-Rise," 195
"You're Living in the Wrong House," 218

Carlson, Eric "Evaluation of Housing Projects and Programmes: A Case Report from Venezuela," 196–197
"High-Rise Management: Design Problems as Found in Caracas," 196

Carr, Stephen "The City of the Mind," 68

Chapin, F. Stuart "Activity Systems and Urban Structure: A Working Scheme," 127
"The Study of Urban Activity Patterns," 126

Chapin, F. Stuart, and Richard K. Brail "Human Activity Systems in the Metropolitan United States," 124

Chapin, F. Stuart, and Henry Hightower "Household Activity Patterns and Land Use," 126–127

Chapin, F. Stuart, and Shirley Weiss, eds. *Urban Growth Dynamics in a Regional Cluster of Cities,* 236

Chapin, F. Stuart, Jr. "Free Time Activities and Quality of Urban Life," 131

Chein, Isidor "The Environment as a Determinant of Behavior," 76

Chermayeff, S., and Christopher Alexander *Community and Privacy, Towards a New Architecture of Humanism,* 67, 214

Chombart de Lauwe, Paul Henry *Des Hommes et des Villes,* 92

Churchill, Henry S., and Roslyn Ittleson *Neighborhood Design and Control,* 159

Clark, W. A. V., and G. Rushton "A Method of Analyzing the Relationship of a Population to Distributed Facilities," 172

Clavel, Pierre "Planners and Citizen Boards: Some Applications of Social Theory to the Problem of Plan Implementation," 46

Clinard, Marshall B. *Slums and Community Development,* 49

Coates, Gary "Residential Behavior Patterns," 103–104

Coates, Gary, and H. Sanoff "Behavioral Mapping: The Ecology of Child Behavior in a Planned Residential Setting," 186

Cobb, Edith "The Ecology of Imagination in Childhood," 180

Coles, Robert *Children of Crisis: A Study in Courage and Fear,* 5
Migrants, Sharecroppers, Mountaineers, 233–234
The South Goes North, 178–179

Coles, Robert, and Maria Piers *Wages of Neglect,* 233

Committee on the Hygiene of Housing *Basic Principles of Healthful Housing,* 215
Housing for Health, 8

Connolly, D. J. "Social Repercussions of New Cargo Handling Methods in the Port of London," 232

Cooper, Clare *The Adventure Playground: Creative Play in an Urban Setting,* 184

Cummins, Jane *Planning for Play,* 185

Dahir, James "Neighborhood Planning is a 'Three-in-One' Job," 161

Dahir, James *The Neighborhood Unit Plan: Its Spread and Acceptance,* 160

Dart, Francis E., and Panna Lal Pradhan "Cross Cultural Teaching of Science," 24

Davidoff, Paul "Advocacy and Pluralism in Planning," 41

Davies, J. Clarence *Neighborhood Groups and Urban Renewal,* 37

Davis, Gerald "Using Interview of Present Office Workers in Planning New Offices," 231

Dee, Norbert, and Jon C. Liebman "A Statistical Study of Children at Urban Playgrounds," 184–185

De Jouvenal, Bertrand "Utopia for Practical Purposes," 5

Dennis, Norman "Mass Housing and the Reformers Myth," 203–204

Dennison, George *The Lives of Children,* 210

Dewey, Richard "The Neighborhood, Urban Ecology and City Planners," 162

DiAiso, R., D. M. Friedman, L. Mitchell, and E. Schweitzer *Perception of the Housing Environment,* 27

Dixon, John Morris "Planning Workbook for the Community," 44

Dobush, Peter, John C. Parkin, and C. E. Praff "Report of the Committee of Inquiry into the Design of Residential Environment of the Royal Architectural Institute of Canada, 1960," 65–66

Downs, Roger B. "The Cognitive Structure of an Urban Shopping Center," 144–145

Doxiadis, C. A. "Densities of Human Settlements," 56
"The Formation of the Human Room," 228–229
"Man's Movement and His Settlements," 110

Drew, Clifford "Research on the Psychological Behavioral Effects of the Physical Environment," 234

Dubos, René "Man and His Environment: Adaptation and Interaction," 6

Duffy, Francis "Role and Status in the Office," 230

Duoskin, Stephen "The Disabled's Encounter with the Environment," 34

Durlack, Jerome T, B. E. Beardsley, and J. S. Murray "Observation of User Activity Patterns in Open and Traditional Plan School Environments," 234

Eastman, Charles, and Joel Harper "A Study of Proxemic Behavior: Toward a Predictive Model," 233

EDITORS, Progressive Architecture "Advocacy Planning—What It Is, How It Works," 43

Elias, C. E., James Gillies, and Svend Riemer *Metropolis: Values in Conflict,* 236

Ellis, Michael J. "Play: Theory and Research," 228

Ellis, William R., Jr. "Planning Design and Black Community Style: The Problem of Occasion-Adequate Space," 98–99

Esber, George, and Charles Albanese "Apage Proxemics," 218–219

Estes, Mark D. "Data Management Techniques Applied to People/Activity Relationships within the Built Environment," 32

Fava, Sylvia Fleis "Contrasts in Neighboring: New York City and a Suburban Community," 116

Fellen, Phillip, and Eugene Litwaks "Neighborhood Cohesion under Conditions of Mobility," 223

Fellman, Gordon, and Barbara Brandt "Working Class Protest against an Urban Highway," 47

Festinger, Leon "Architecture and Group Membership," 113–114

Festinger, Leon, and Daniel Katz "Observation of Group Behavior," 114

Festinger, Leon, Stanley Schacter, and Kurt Back *Social Pressures in Informal Groups: A Study of Human Factors in Housing,* 113

Firey, Walter *Land Use in Central Boston,* 91
"Sentiment and Symbolism as Ecological Variables," 187

Fiske, Donald W., and Salvatore R. Maddi *Functions of Varied Experience,* 76–77

Fitch, James Marston "Experiential Bases for Aesthetic Decision," 79

Foa, Uriel G. "Interpersonal and Economic Resources," 7

Foley, Donald L. "Urban Daytime Population: A Field for Demographic-Econological Analysis," 123

Fox, David J. "Patterns of Morbidity and Mortality in Mexico City," 11

Frankenberg, Ronald *Communities in Britain: Social Life in Town and Country,* 156

Fraser, J. M. "Choi Hung Housing Estate, Hong Kong," 197–198

Fraser, Ronald, ed. *Work 1 & 2,* 227–228

Fraser, Thomas M. "Relative Habitability of Dwellings: A Conceptual View," 217

Fricker, L. J. "A Pedestrian's Experience of the Landscape of Cumbernauld," 181

Fried, Marc "Grieving for a Lost Home," 189

Fried, Marc, and Peggy Gleicher "Some Sources of Residential Satisfaction in an Urban Slum," 188

Friedberg, Paul M., and Ellen Perry Berkeley *Play and Interplay,* 184

Frieden, Elaine "Social Differences and their Consequences for Housing and Aged," 33

Fromm, Erich "Humanistic Planning," 6

Fruin, John J. *Pedestrian Planning and Design,* 150–151

Galle, Omer R., Walter R. Gove, and J. Miller McPherson "Population Density and Pathology: What Are the Relations for Man?," 55

Gans, Herbert J. "The Balanced Community, Homogeneity or Heterogeneity in Residential Areas," 174
People and Plans, 237
"Planning for People not Buildings," 82
"Planning and Social Life, Friendship and Neighbor Relations in Suburban Communities," 117
The Urban Villagers, 178

Garbrecht, Dietrich *Pedestrian Movement: A Bibliography,* 240
"Pedestrian Paths through a Uniform Environment," 151

Gardiner, Stephen "Cruel Aesthetics," 84

Index of Annotations

Geddes, Patrick *Cities in Evolution,* 75

Gilbert, Neil, and Joseph W. Eaton "Who Speaks for the Poor," 46–47

Glass, Ruth *The Social Background of a Plan: A Study of Middleborough,* 160

Godschalk, David R., and William E. Mills "A Collaborative Approach to Planning through Urban Activities," 123

Goldsteen, Joel "Group Composition in Urban Planning," 72

Golledge, Reginald, and Georgia Zannaras "The Perception of Urban Structure: An Experimental Approach," 31

Goodman, Robert *After the Planners,* 71

Goss, Anthony "Neighborhood Units in British New Towns," 170

Gottlieb, David "The Neighborhood Tavern and the Cocktail Lounge," 170

Gottman, Jean "Urban Centrality and the Interweaving of Quaternary Activities," 110

Grant, Donald P. *Systematic Methods in Environmental Designs: An Introductory Bibliography,* 241–242

Gregoire, Menie "The Child in the High Rise," 211

"Listening to Life as It is," 210

Group for Environmental Education, Inc. *Our Man-Made Environment Book Seven,* 48

Gulick, John, C. E. Bowerman, and Kurt Back "Newcomer Enculteration in the City: Attitudes and Participation," 118

Gump, Paul V. "Milieu, Environment, and Behavor," 98

Gutheim, Frederick "Urban Space and Urban Design," 78

Gutman, Robert "Site Planning and Social Behavior," 79–80

Gutman, Robert, and David Popenue *Neighborhood, City and Metropolis: An Integrated Reader,* 239

Hall, Edward, T. *The Hidden Dimension,* 61

"Human Needs and Inhuman Cities," 6

"Proxemics and Design," 62

Hall, E. T., and Gerda Wekerle "High Rise Living: Can One Design Serve Both Young and Old," 205

Halprin, Lawrence *The RSVP Cycle–Creative Processes in the Human Environment,* 70

Hannerz, Ulf *Soulside: Inquiries into Ghetto Culture and Community,* 178

Hare, A. Paul *Small Group Research,* 117–118

Harrison, James D. "An Annotated Bibliography on Environmental Perception with Emphasis on Urban Areas," 238

Hartman, C. W. "Social Values and Housing Orientation," 189

Harvey, David "Social Process and Spatial Form: An Analysis of the Conceptual Problems of Urban Planning," 93

Harvey, W. Lawrence, *et al.* "The Square: Descriptive Modeling of Central Courthouse Square Towns of the South Central U.S.," 143

Hassan, Riaz "Social Status and Bureaucratic Relationships among Public Housing Tenants in Singapore," 199

Hatch, Richard C. "Some Thoughts on Advocacy Planning," 42

Hatt, Paul, and A. J. Reiss, Jr. *Cities and Society,* 236

Hawley, Amos H. *Human Ecology: A Theory of Community Structure,* 91, 155

Haythorn, William H. "A Needs by Sources of Satisfaction Analysis of Environmental Habitability," 7

Hemmens, George C. "Analysis and Simulation of Urban Activity Patterns," 127–128

Hendricks, Francis, and Malcolm McNair

"Concepts of Environmental Quality Standards Based on Life Styles," 175

Hershberger, Robert G. "Toward a Set of Semantic Scales to Measure the Meaning of Architectural Environments," 32

Heyman, M. "Space and Behavior: A Selected Bibliography," 236

Higasa, Tadashi "A Study of the Planning Unit and the Organization of Facilities of the Residential Unit," 167

Hinshaw, Mark, and Kathryn Allott "Environmental Preferences of Future Housing Consumers," 219

Hirschon, Renee, and Thakurdesai "Society, Culture and Spatial Organization," 221

Hitchcock, John R. "Daily Activity Patterns: An Exploratory Pattern," 124

Hoinville, G. "Evaluating Community Preference," 31

Hole, Vere "Social Effects of Planned Rehousing," 116

Hole, V., and A. Miller "Children's Play on Housing Estates," 181

Hollander, Arnold Peter *High Density Environments: Some Cultural, Physiological and Psychological Considerations–An Annotated Bibliography,* 240

Hollingshead, A. B., and L. H. Rogler "Attitudes toward Slums and Public Housing in Puerto Rico," 197

Honikman, Basil "An Investigation of the Relationship between Construing of the Environment and its Physical Form," 27

Howard, Ebenezer *Garden Cities of Tomorrow,* 158

Howard, Roger B., F. Gernan Mlynarski, and G. C. Sauer, Jr. "A Comparative Analysis of Affective Responses to Real and Represented Environments," 29

Hutt, S. M., and Corine Hutt *Direct Observation and Measurement of Behavior,* 135

Hyman, Herbert H. "Planning with Citizens: Two Styles," 38

Isaacs, Reginald "Are Urban Neighborhoods Possible?," 161
"The Neighborhood Theory," 160

Izumi, Kiyoshi "Psychological Phenomena and Building Design," 79

Jacobs, Jane *The Death and Life of Great American Cities,* 156

Jakle, John A. *The Spatial Dimensions of Social Organization: A Selected Bibliography for Urban Social Geography,* 239

Janisova, Helena "Leisure Time of City Residents in the Light of Urban Living Conditions and Environment," 130–131

Joiner, Duncan "Social Ritual and Architectural Space," 230

Jones, Emrys "A Note on Some Aspects of Location and Network Activities," 142

Jorgensen, Lisa "New York's Squatters: Vanguard of Community Control?," 40

Kaplan, Stephen, and John S. Wendt "Preference and the Visual Environment: Complexity and Some Alternatives," 28

Kasmer, J. "Development of a Usable Lexicon of Environmental Descriptors," 97–98

Kates, Robert W. "Stimulus and Symbol, the View from the Bridge," 80

Katz, Robert D. "Intensity of Development and Livability of Multi-Family Housing Projects," 202

Kaufman, Edgar, Jr. "2001 B.C. to 2001 Centre Avenue," 44

Kaufman, Harold "Toward an Interactional Conception of Community," 37

Keller, Suzanne "Human Communication and Social Networks at the Micro Scale," 120
"Neighborhood Concepts in Sociological Perspective," 164
The Urban Neighborhood, 164

Index of Annotations

Kennedy, Donald "Indoor Territoriality: An Anthropological Perspective," 62

Kennedy, Robert Woods *The House and the Act of Its Design,* 214

Kepes, György *The New Landscape in Art and Science,* 76
"Notes on Expression in the Cityscape," 66

Kerr, Madeleine *The People of Ship Street,* 177

Kilbridge, Maurice, Robert O'Block, and Paul Teplitz "Population Density Concepts and Measures," 57

Kranz, Peter "What Do People Do All Day?," 124

Kriesburgh, Louis "Neighborhood Setting and the Isolation of Public Housing Tenants," 119–120

Kunze, Donald "Observation of Residential Behavior Settings," 97

Kuper, Leo *Living in Towns: Selected Research Papers,* 146
"Social Science Research and the Planning of Urban Neighborhoods," 163

Kurtz, Stephen A. "And Now a Word from the Users," 221

Lamanna, Richard "Value Consensus among Urban Residents," 146

Lansing, John B., and Robert W. Marans *Planned Residential Environments,* 147–148

Lazarfeld, P. F., ed. *Language of Social Research,* 133

Lee, David R. "The Nubian House: Persistence of a Cultural Tradition," 220

Lee, Hyo-Jae "Life in Urban Korea," 221

Lee, Terence "The Effect of the Built Environment on Human Behavior," 83–84
"The Psychology of Spatial Orientation," 82–83
"Urban Neighborhood as a Socio-Spatial Schema," 168

Lerup, Lars "Suburban Residential Environment: Analysis, Evaluation and Selection," 218

Lifson, Ben "Home on the Road," 224

Linn, Karl "Neighborhood Commons," 182

Loring, William C. "Housing Characteristics and Social Disorganization," 52–53

Lowenthal, David "Methodological Problems in Environmental Perception and Behavior Research," 135

MacMurray, Trevor "Aspects of Time and the Study of Activity Patterns," 128

Maki, Fumihiko, and Jerry Goldberg "Linkage in Collective Form," 77

Maltby, James, Cecily Martin, Dimitri Philippedes, and Bjorn Roe "Ilisses, A Village Community in Athens," 49

Mann, Lawrence D. "The Internal Hierarchy of Sub-Areas in Urban Settlements," 167

Mann, Lawrence, and George Hagevik "The New Environmentalism: Behaviorism and Design," 241

Mann Peter H. "The Concept of Neighborliness," 115
"The Neighborhood," 163
"The Socially Balanced Neighbourhood Unit," 173–174

Marans, A. E. "Towards Preparing Man for a Changed Environment," 182

Marans, Robert W., and John B. Lansing "Evaluation of Neighborhood Quality," 46

Marcuse, Peter "Black Housing; A New Approach for Planners," 174

Markman, Robert "Sensation-Seeking and Environmental Preference," 27

Markus, Thomas A. "A Doughnut Model of the Environment and Its Design," 72

Marshall, Nancy J. "Environmental Components of Orientations toward Privacy," 58

Martin, A. E. "Environment, Housing and Health," 9

Martin, Ann "The Pedestrian in the City: A Bibliography," 150

Martineau, Thomas R. "The Urban Activity Model," 125

Maslow, A. H. "A Theory of Human Motivation," 4–5

Mather, William G. "Attempts to Introduce Human Requirements into Building Requirements," 214

Maw, Ray "Construction of a Leisure Model," 130, 171

McCue, Gerald M., William R. Ewald, Jr., and The Midwest Research Institute *Creating the Human Environment,* 70–71

McKay, Henry "The Neighborhood and Child Conduct," 180

McKechnie, George "Measuring Environmental Dispositions with the Environmental Response Inventory," 31

McKenzie, R. D. "The Scope of Human Ecology," 89–90, 153

McKie, Robert "Peterborough Amenities and Social Change," 147

McQuade, Walter, ed. *Cities Fit to Live in,* 240–241

Mead, Margaret "Childbearing and the Family," 210

"Neighborhoods and Human Needs," 181

"Research with Human Beings: A Model Derived from Anthropological Field Practice," 134

Meier, R. L. *A Communicatons Theory of Urban Growth,* 108

"Human Time Allocation: A Basis for Social Accounts," 123

"The Metropolis as a Transaction-Maximizing System," 110

Meyerson, Martin, J. Tyrwhitt, B. Falk, and P. Sekler *Face of the Metropolis,* 207

Michelson, William "An Empirical Analysis of Urban Environmental Preferences," 103

Michelson, William *Man and His Urban Environment: A Sociological Approach,* 103

"Urban Sociology as an Aid to Urban Physical Development: Some Research Strategies," 134

Value Orientation and Urban Form, 102

Miller, J. M. "Residential Density: Relating People to Space Rather than to Ground Area," 53

Milne, Murray A. "The Beginnings of a Theory of Environmental Control," 84

Mogey, J. M. "Changes in Family Life Experienced by English Workers Moving from Slums to Housing Estates," 201

Family and Neighborhood, 187

Moleski, Walter H., and R. J. Goodrich "The Analysis of Behavioral Requirements in Office Settings," 231

Moller, Clifford B. *Architectural Environment and Our Mental Health,* 10

Montessori, Maria *The Absorbent Mind,* 233

Montgomery, Roger "Comment on Fear and House-as-Haven in the Lower Class," 203

A General Booklist on Urban Design, 238

"Pattern Language," 86

Morris, Robert, and S. B. Zisman "The Pedestrian, Downtown, and the Planner," 149

Mumford, Lewis *The Culture of Cities,* 75–76

"The Neighborhood and the Neighborhood Unit," 163

Nakanishi, Naomichi "Changes in Living Patterns Brought about by Television," 130

National Institute of Child Health and Human Development *Patterns of Living and*

Housing of Middle Aged and Older People, 216

New, Peter Kong-Ming, Richard M. Hessler, and Luis S. Kemnitzer "Community Research, Research Commune?," 135

New, Peter Kong-Ming, and J. Thomas May "Alienation and Communication among Urban Renovators," 45

Olson, Leonard, Jr. "Optimization of Choice in a Semi-Structured Physical Environment: A Model of Environmental Design," 99

Osgood, Charles S., George J. Suci, and Percy H. Tannenbaum *The Measurement of Meaning,* 133–134

Packard, Vance *A Nation of Strangers,* 111

Pande, Shashi K. "From Hurried Habitability to Heightened Habitability," 7

Pappas, P. "Trip Lengths in Relation to Facilities," 172

Park, Robert Ezra *Human Communities: The City and Human Ecology,* 89, 154
"Human Ecology," 90, 154

Parr, A. E. "The Child in the City," 142
"Environmental Design and Psychology," 78
"Problems of Reason, Feeling and Habitat," 83
"Psychological Aspects of Urbanology," 80

Parsons, Sir John Herbert *An Introduction to the Theory of Perception,* 15

Pearson, Norman "Planning a Social Unit," 167

Peattie, Lisa R. "Reflections on Advocacy Planning," 41–42

Perin, Constance "Concepts and Methods for Studying Environments in Use," 222
With Man in Mind, 104

Perraton, Jean K. "Community Planning: An Analysis of Certain Social Aims," 119

Perry, Clarence *Housing for the Machine Age,* 159
"The Unit," 159

Peterson, George "Measuring Visual Preferences of Residential Neighborhoods," 26

Pioro, Zygmunt "An Ecological Interpretation of Settlement Systems," 164–165
"The Social Environment of Two Housing Estates in Lublin, Poland," 201–202

Pitt, Gillian M. "Leisure in a New Town: A Survey of the Leisure Habits of Tenants in Crawley," 129
"The Problem of Loneliness," 118

Planning Research Unit, University of Edinburgh *Planning for Disabled in the Urban Environment,* 34

Plant, James S. "The Personality and an Urban Area," 180

Pollowy, Anne-Marie, and Michel Bezman "Design-Oriented Approach to Developmental Needs: An Operational Framework Relating Activity Patterns to Environmental Requirements through the Performance Approach," 72, 128

Porteous, J. Douglas "Design with People: The Quality of the Urban Environment," 71

Preiser, Wolfgang F. E. "The Use of Ethological Methods in Environmental Analysis," 99

Pritchard, Norman "Planned Social Provision in New Towns," 146

Proshansky, Harold M., William Ittelson, and LeeAnn G. Rivlin *Environmental Psychology: Man and His Physical Setting,* 239–240

Rainwater, Lee *Behind Ghetto Walls: Black Families in a Federal Slum,* 205
"Fear and the House as Haven in the Lower Class," 202–203

Rand, George "Pre-Copernican Views of the City," 24

Randall, Edwina *The Crisis of the Child and the Crisis of the City: The Same Crisis,* 185

Rappoport, Amos "Australian Aborigines and the Definition of Place," 63

Rappoport, Amos, and Robert Kantor "Complexity and Ambiguity in Environmental Design," 81

Ravetz, Alison "Tenancy Patterns and Turnover at Quarry Hill Flats, Leeds," 206
"The Use of Surveys in the Assessment of Residential Design," 104

Ravitz, Mel J. "Use of the Attitude Survey in Neighborhood Planning," 170

Reichek, Jesse "Additional Remarks on the Design of Our Cities," 81–82

Reynolds, Ingrid, and Charles Nicholson "Living Off the Ground," 204

Reynolds, Josephine P. "Public Participation in Planning," 38–39

Richards, Cara E. "City Taverns," 170–171

Richardson, N. H. "Participatory Democracy and Planning," 39

Riemer, Svend "Hidden Dimensions of Neighborhood Planning," 162

Riemer, Svend, and J. J. Demerath "The Role of Social Research in Housing Design," 223

Ritter, Paul "Radburn Planning: A Reassessment," 207

Rosenberg, Gerhardt "High Population Density in Relation to Social Behavior," 54
"The Landscape of Youth," 183

Rosow, I. "The Social Effects of the Physical Environment," 101

Rossi, Peter H. *Why Families Move,* 223

Rothblatt, Donald N. "Housing and Human Needs," 195

Rozelle, Richard M., and James C. Bazer "Meaning and Value in Conceptualizing the City," 25

Rudofsky, Bernard *Streets for People,* 150

Rusch, Charles W. "On the Relation of Form to Behavior," 97

Saarinen, Thomas F. *Perception of Environment,* 238–239

Saile, David, R. Borrah, and M. G. Williams "Families in Public Housing: A Study of Three Localities in Rockford, Illinois," 208

Sanoff, Henry "Social Perception of the Ecological Neighborhood," 168–169
Techniques of Evaluation for Designers, 30
Visual Attributes of the Physical Environment, 26

Sanoff, Henry, and M. Sawhney "Residential Livability: A Study of User Attitudes toward Their Residential Environment," 209

Sauer, Louis, and David Marshall "An Architectural Survey of How Six Families Use Space in Their Existing Houses," 219

Schmitt, Robert C. "Density, Health, and Social Disorganization," 54
"Implications of Density in Hong Kong," 53

Schorr, Alvin L. "Housing and Its Effects," 102, 197

Scott, James "Testing a Housing Design Reference: A Pilot Study," 30

Seaton, R. W., and J. B. Collins *Validity and Reliability of Ratings of Simulated Buildings,* 29

Segall, Marshall H., Donald T. Campbell, and Melville J. Jeskovits *The Influence of Culture on Visual Perception,* 23

Shepard, Paul, and Daniel McKinley *The Subversive Science: Toward an Ecology of Man,* 238

Sieverts, Thomas *Architectural Association Quarterly,* 43

257

Simmie, J. M. "Public Participation: A Case Study from Oxfordshire," 39–40

Sinton, David "Attitudes, A Source of the Housing Problem," 24, 218

Sitte, Camillo *The Art of Building Cities,* 140

Skinner, B. F. *Beyond Freedom and Dignity,* 8

Slayton, William L., and R. Dewey "Urban Redevelopment and the Urbanite," 36

Sloan, Sam A. "Translating Psycho-Social Criteria into Design Determinants," 228

Smith, Richard Alan "Crowding in the City: The Japanese Solution," 59

Smithson, Allison, and Peter Smithson *Urban Structuring,* 69

Soen, Dan "Neighborly Relations and Ethnic Problems in Israel," 120

Solow, Anatole, Clifford Ham, and E. Owen Donnelly *The Concept of the Neighborhood Unit,* 164

Sommer, Robert "Can Behavior Studies Be Useful as Well as Ornamental?," 61, 69
"Man's Proximate Environment," 61
"The New Evaluator Cookbook," 63
Personal Space, the Behavoral Basis of Design, 62

Sonnenfeld, Joseph "Monadic and Dryadic Approaches to the Study of Behavior in Environment," 104
"Variable Values in Space and Landscape. An Inquiry into the Nature of Environmental Necessity," 81

Sorokin, Petirim, and Clarence Berger *Time-Budgets of Human Behavior,* 122

Southworth, Michael "The Sonic Environment of Cities," 20

Spencer, Paul "Towards a Measure of Social Investment in Communities," 191

Spiegel, Hans B. C. *Neighborhood Power and Control: Implications for Urban Planning,* 41

Spivack, Mayer "The Political Collapse of a Playground," 183
"Sensory Distortions in Tunnels and Corridors," 17

Stea, David "Territoriality, the Interior Aspect: Space, Territory, and Human Movement," 60

Stea, David, and Roger W. Downs "From the Outside Looking in at the Inside Looking Out," 26

Stein, Clarence *Towards New Towns for America,* 162

Stein, Maurice R. *The Eclipse of Community,* 155

Steinetz, Carl "Meaning and Congruence of Urban Form and Activity," 82

Stevens, P. H. M. "Densities in Housing Areas," 56

Still, Henry *In Quest of Quiet,* 20

Stokols, Daniel "A Social-Psychological Model of Human Crowding Phenomena," 63, 231

Stone, G. "City Shoppers and Urban Identification; Observations on the Psychology of City Life," 144

Stuart, Darwin G. "Planning for Pedestrians," 150

Studer, Raymond G. "Behavior Manipulation," 96
"The Dynamics of Behavior-Contingent Physical Systems," 97

Studer, Raymond G., and David Stea "Architectural Programming, Environmental Design, and Human Behavior," 96

Summers, Luis H. "The House Design Game," 219

Szalai, A. "Trends in Comparative Time Budget Research," 123

Taira, Koji "Urban Poverty, Ragpickers, and the Ants' Villa in Tokyo," 50, 190, 204

Tannebaum, Judith "The Neighborhood: A Socio-Psychological Analysis," 161

Taylor, G. Brooke "Telford's Social Relations Department," 147

Team 10 "Team 10 Primer," 66–67

Terence, Lee "Perceived Distance as a Function of Direction in the City," 22

Thiel, Philip "Notes on the Description, Scaling, Notation and Scoring on Some Perceptual and Cognitive Attributes of the Physical Environment," 77

"Professional Architecture," 17

Theodorson, G. *Studies in Human Ecology,* 236

Thomas, William L., Jr. *Man's Role in Changing the Face of the Earth,* 92

Tiger, Lionel *Men in Groups,* 10

Tomeh, Aida K. "Informal Group Participation and Residential Patterns," 119

Turner, John "Architecture That Works," 70

Turner, John F. C. "Housing Issues and the Standard Problem," 199–200

Tyrwhitt, Jaqueline "The Size and Spacing of Urban Communities," 166

Useem, Ruth Hill, and Duane L. Gibson "The Function of Neighboring for the Middle Class Male," 117

Vapnarsky, C. A. "An Approach to the Sociology of Housing," 102

Varming, Michael "The Planning of Motorroads in the Landscape," 17

Vash, Carolyn L. "Discrimination by Design: Mobility Barriers," 34

Vigier, Françoise "Experimental Approach to Urban Design," 78

Walker, Geoffrey, and Alan G. Rigby "Public Participation in the Rhonda Valleys," 39

Wallace, A. *Housing and Social Structure,* 194

Wallin, Paul "A Guttman Scale for Measuring Women's Neighborliness," 115

Warren, Ronald Leslie, ed. *Perspectives on the American Community: A Book of Readings,* 237

Webber, Melvin M. "Order in Diversity: Community without Propinquity," 109

"The Urban Place and the Nonplace Realm," 109

Webber, Melvin M., and Carolyn C. Webber "Culture, Territoriality and the Elastic Mile," 92

Weil, Simone *The Need for Roots,* 5

Wellman, Barry, and Marilyn Whitaker *Community–Network–Communication: An Annotated Bibliography,* 241

Wells, Brian "Individual Differences in Environmental Response," 229

Whyte, William H., Jr. "How the New Suburbia Socializes," 114

Wicker, Allan W. "Mediating Behavior-Environment Congruence," 99

Willis, Margaret "Designing for Privacy," 58, 202

"Sociological Aspects of Urban Structure," 147

Willmott, Peter "Housing Density and Town Design," 58

Willmott, Peter, and Michael Young *Family and Class in a London Suburb,* 116–117

Wilner, Daniel, and Rosabelle Price Walkeley "Effects of Housing on Health and Performance," 216

Wilson, James Q. "Planning and Politics: Citizen Participation in Urban Renewal," 37

Urban Renewal: The Record and the Controversy, 237

Wirth, Louis "Human Ecology," 91

"Urbanism as a Way of Life," 90

Wober, Mallory "Styles of Home Life and Personality Among Nigerian Workers," 189–190

Wolff, Sula *Children and Stress,* 183–184

Wood, Elizabeth "Social Aspects of Housing and Urban Development," 198

Wright, Henry *Rehousing Urban America,*
208

Wright, Henry, Jr. "Radburn Revisited,"
208

Wylie, Laurence *Village in the Vaucluse,*
155

Yancey, William L. "Architecture, Interaction and Social Control," 205

Zehner, Robert B. "Neighborhood and Community Satisfaction in New Towns and Less Planned Suburbs," 148

Subject Index

Abernathy, W. D., 182
Activity studies, 125–8, 231, 234
Adams, F. J., 162
Advocacy planning, 40–3, 64, 240
Aesthetics, 3–5, 77, 79, 84, 134
Aged people, 7, 33–4, 95–6, 116, 138, 144
    184, 216
Air pollution, 10
Albanese, Charles, 218–19
Alexander, Christopher, 34, 65, 67–8, 84–6,
    108–9, 157, 214
Allott, Kathryn, 219
American Public Health Association, 8, 164
    215
Andrew, Paul, 44
Andrews, Frank M., 171
Apaches, 218–19
Apartment buildings, 193–95, 221
Appalachia, 177
Appleyard, Donald, 16, 191
Architectural determinism, 73–4, 80, 83

Architectual psychology, 75, 79–80, 83
Ardrey, Robert, 60
Argyle, Michael, 115–16
Aries, Philip, 213
Asia, 24
Aswan Dam, 220
Athens Center of Ekistics, 56, 171
Auditory perception, 18–21, 79
Australia, 63, 129
Automobile, 15–18, 141–2, 163, 198, 202,
    212

Babcock, Richard F., 45–6
Back, Kurt, 111–13, 118, 188–9
Bakema, J. B., 77
Baltimore, Md., 156, 184–5
Bangs, Herbert P., Jr., 185
Bardet, Gaston, 166–7
Barker, Louise S., 95–6
Barker, Roger G., 73, 94–6
Barriada, 70, 171

Batchelor, Peter, 127
Bauer, Catherine, 172, 173, 200, 201
Bazer, James C., 25
Beardsley, B. E., 234
Bechtel, Robert B., 98, 198
Beck, Robert, 17
Behavioral settings, 68, 94–9
Bell, Gwen, 145, 165, 242
Berger, Clarence, 122
Berkeley, Ellen Perry, 43–4, 48, 184, 190, 206, 207
Bestor, G. C., 237
Bettleheim, Bruno, 182–3, 213
Bezmen, Michael, 72, 128
Bird, Caroline, 55
Bishop, Robert L., 186
Blasdel, Hugo G., 32
Blecher, Earl M., 40, 42
Blumenfeld, Hans, 56, 165–6
Blythe, Ronald, 156–7, 206, 208
Boeschenstein, Warren, 120
Bogdanou, M., 56
Bolt, Beranek & Newman, Inc., 18–19
Borrah, R., 208
Bosselman, Fred P., 45–6
Boston, Mass., 20–1, 35, 38, 52–3, 91, 113, 120, 151, 156, 176, 178, 183, 186–9, 203
Bott, Elizabeth, 112, 115
Bowerman, C. E., 118
Brail, Richard K., 124
Brandt, Barbara, 47
Brill, William H., 199
Broady, Maurice, 145, 148, 187, 188, 200
Brodey, Warren, 19, 20
Brolin, Brent C., 203
Brookes, Malcom J., 230
Bruner, Jerome, 228
Brunetti, Frank A., 234
Brunhes, Jean, 88–9
Bull, C. Neil, 125
Burgel, G., 56
Burnette, Charles H., 226, 227, 228

Burns, Leland, 216
Burns, Mary, 38
Burton, Thomas L., 130
Buttimer, Anne, 93–4
Byers, Paul, 30

Calhoun, John B., 51, 54–5
Campbell, Donald T., 23
Canada, 39, 65
Canter, David, 54, 83
Caplow, T., 113
Cappon, Daniel R., 194, 195, 218
Caracas, Venezuela, 196–7
Carlson, Eric, 196
Carr, Stephen, 68
Center for Environmental Structure, 86
Central place theory, 141
Chapin, F. Stuart, 8, 124, 125, 126, 127, 131 236
Chein, Isador, 74, 76
Chermayeff, S., 67, 214
Chicago, Ill., 43, 55, 144, 156, 205
Child
    behavior, 135, 186
    civil rights movement, 5
    environmental education, 48, 193, 228
    family size, 166
    housing, 204, 209–11, 215
    in Kibbutz, 182–3
    learning space, 232–4
    mobility, 141–2, 192
    needs, 111, 147, 172, 176–85, 209
    play, 89, 105, 154, 179–81, 226–7
    raising, 50, 190, 212–13
    socialization, 183–4
    territory of, 138, 157, 191
    visual perception, 24
Chombart de Lauwe, Paul Henry, 92–3, 167
Christakis, A., 56
Churchill, Henry S., 159
Cincinnati, Ohio, 151
City planners, 9, 36, 42, 45, 93–4, 140

Clark, W. A. V., 172
Clavel, Pierre, 46
Clinard, Marshall B., 49
Cluster analysis, 130
Coates, Gary, 103–4, 186
Cobb, Edith, 180
Coles, Robert, 5, 177–9, 206, 213, 215, 232–4
Collins, J. B., 28–9
Committee on the Hygiene of Housing, 215
Communication, 61, 66, 69, 80, 105, 107–8, 120, 134, 141, 155, 241
Community facilities, 169–72
Community studies, 152–7
Computor simulation, 127–8, 172
Connolly, D. J., 232
Construction, 18
Cooper, Clare, 184
Council of Planning Librarians, 235
Crime, 52 (see also Youth, juvenile delinquency)
Cristie, Malcolm, 44
Culture
  and built environment, 74, 109
  and housing design, 220
  and human behavior, 76
  and human needs, 6, 59–60, 212
Cummins, Jane, 185

Dahir, James, 160, 161
Dart, Francis, 24
Darwin, Charles, 6
Data collection methods, 30
Davidoff, Paul, 40–1
Davies, J. Clarence, 37–8
Davis, Gerald, 231
Dee, Norbert, 184
De Jouvenal, Bertrand, 5
Demerath, J. J., 223
Demos, John, 213
Dennis, Norman, 203–4
Dennison, George, 210
Density, 8, 10, 45, 51–63, 66, 147, 159, 170, 191, 202, 206, 226, 240 (see also Overcrowding)
Design methodology, 132, 241
Design Methods Group, 100
Designers, 137, 218
Detroit, Mich., 119, 170
Dewey, Richard, 52, 162
Diaiso, R., 27
Disabled (see Handicapped)
Disease, 3, 8, 11
Dixon, John Morris, 44
Dobush, Peter, 65–6
Donnelly, E. Owen, 164, 165
Downs, Roger B., 26, 144
Doxiadis, C. A., 7, 56, 108, 110, 137, 167, 227, 228–9
Drew, Clifford, 234
Dubos, René, 6
Duffy, Francis, 230
Duhl, Leonard, 8–9, 197
Duoskin, Stephen, 34
Durkheim, Emile, 93
Durlack, Jerome T., 234
Dwelling group, 138, 192–211
Dwelling unit, 211–17

Eastman, Charles, 233
Eaton, Joseph W., 46–7
Ecology (see Human ecology)
Ecological psychology, 94, 96
Education, 4, 6, 44, 47–8, 95, 110, 134, 160, 190, 209–10, 237 (see also Child)
Ekistics, 137–8, 242
Elias, C. E., 236
Eliot, T. S., 3
Ellis, Michael J., 226, 228
Ellis, William R., Jr., 98–9
Ellul, Jacques, 213
Emery, P. A., 56
Employment (see Work)
England (see United Kingdom)
Environmental design, 67–8, 78, 80, 96, 99

Environmental Design Research Association, 100
Environmental determinism, 89
Environmental psychology, 94, 239
Erikson, Erik, 85
Esber, George, 218–19
Estes, Mark D., 32
Europe, 4, 74, 201
Ewald, William R., 70

Falk, B., 207
Family
  housing, 9, 102, 190, 193, 201, 210
  neighborhood, 159, 165, 166, 187
  nuclear, 210
  organization, 195
  private space, 57
  social interaction, 105, 112
  system, 7, 115–17, 211, 212
  work, 50, 190
  (see also Child)
Fava, Sylvia Fleis, 116
Fellen, Philip, 223
Fellman, Gordon, 47
Festinger, Leon, 107, 111–14
Firey, Walter, 91, 187
Fiske, Donald W., 76–7
Fitch, James Marston, 79
Foa, Uriel G., 7
Foley, Donald L., 123
Foreman, R., 113
Fox, David J., 11
France, 3, 5, 24–5, 88, 92–3, 155, 211, 218
Frankenberg, Ronald, 153, 156
Fraser, J. M., 197–8
Fraser, Ronald, 227–8
Fraser, Thomas M., 217
Fricker, L. J., 181
Fried, Marc, 35, 169, 186, 188
Friedenberg, Paul M., 184
Frieden, Elaine, 33
Friedman, D. M., 27

Friendship formation, 111, 113 (see also Neighboring)
Fromm, Erich, 6
Fruin, John J., 150–1

Galle, Omer R., 51, 55
Gans, Herbert, 35, 82, 92, 100, 101, 107, 112, 117, 172, 173, 174, 176, 178, 186, 188, 237
Garbrecht, Dietrich, 151, 240
Garden city, 140, 158, 166
Gardiner, Stephen, 84
Geddes, Patrick, 74–5
Germany, 43, 207
Ghetto culture, 178
Gibson, Duane, 117
Gibson, James J., 14, 16
Gilbert, Neil, 46–7
Gillies, James, 236
Glass, Ruth, 160
Gleicher, Peggy, 188
Godschalk, David R., 122, 123
Goldberg, Jerry, 74, 77
Goldsteen, Joel, 72
Golledge, Reginald, 31
Goode, William, 212–13
Goodman, Robert, 64, 71
Goodrich, R. J., 231
Goss, Anthony, 170
Gottlieb, David, 170
Gottman, Jean, 107, 110
Gove, Walter R., 51, 55
Grant, Donald P., 241–2
Greece, 48, 49, 56, 171, 172, 221
Greensboro, N.C., 146
Gregoire, Menie, 209, 210, 211
Group for Environmental Education, Inc., 48
Gulick, John, 118
Gump, Paul V., 98
Gutheim, Frederick, 78
Gutman, Robert, 79–80, 102–3, 239
Guttman scale, 115

Habitability, 7
Hagevik, George, 241
Hall, Edward T., 6, 59, 61, 62, 200, 205, 228
Halprin, Lawrence, 70
Ham, Clifford, 164 165
Handicapped people, 33–4
Hannerz, Ulf, 176, 178
Hare, A. Paul, 117–8
Harper, Joel, 233
Harrison, James D., 238
Hartford, Conn., 190
Hartman, Chester W., 35, 186, 189
Harvey, David, 93
Harvey, W. Lawrence, 141, 143
Hassan, Riaz, 199
Hatch, Richard C., 40, 42
Hatt, Paul, 236
Hawaii, 24, 54
Hawley, Amos H., 91, 152, 155
Haythorn, William H., 7
Health
  community health indices, 10
  density, 10, 54, 56
  environmental, 9, 10
  health centers, 9
  housing, 8, 9, 202
  maintenance of, 215–17
  mortality, 11, 55
  services, 160
  (see also Diseases, Mental health)
Hemmens, George C., 127–8
Hendricks, Frank, 172, 173, 175
Hershberger, Robert G., 32
Hessler, Richard M., 135
Heyman, M., 236
Higasa, Tadashi, 167
Hightower, Henry, 126–7
Highways, 16–18
Hinshaw, Mark, 219
Hirschon, Rene, 220, 221
Hitchcock, John R., 122, 124
Hoinville, G., 31

Hole, Vere, 116, 181
Hollander, Arnold Peter, 240
Hollingshead, A. B., 197
Hong Kong, 52, 53
Honikman, Basil, 27
Housing
  and health, 8, 9, 11, 55, 101, 215–17
  building requirements, 214
  condominiums, 196
  confinement and anonymity, 193
  co-operatives, 196
  cultural needs, 6
  design, 11, 30, 65–6, 210, 214, 223
  deterioration, 51, 52
  high density, 195, 196, 200
  high rise, 193–206, 221
  human adjustment, 220–22
  low cost, 85, 178
  low density, 207
  low income, 43, 119–20
  management, 195–6
  middle density, 206–9
  modular, 59
  participation, 34–5, 45–6, 198
  preferences, 189, 222–4
  public, 105, 119–20, 194–8, 200, 202–3, 208
  racial preferences, 27
  safety, 202–3
  (see also Density, Self help housing)
Houston, Texas, 25
Howard, Ebenezer, 140, 145, 158, 164, 172
Howard, Roger B., 29
Human activity systems, 124
Human ecology, 89–91, 153–55, 162, 236, 238
Human needs
  affection and belonging, 3, 195
  community fulfillment of, 125
  cultural patterns, 86
  culturally conditioned, 6
  housing, 195, 206, 215, 222
  private space, 192

roots, 2, 4–5, 7, 89, 155, 176–7
security, 200
(see also Child, Aged, and Family)
Hutt, Corine, 135
Hutt, S. M., 135
Hyman, Herbert H., 38

India, 48, 49, 74
Indian reservation; 216, 218
Industry, 4, 70, 76, 139–40, 212
Information theory, 108
Isaacs, Reginald, 160, 161, 162, 172
Israel, 120, 173
Italy, 129, 149
Ittelson, William, 239–40, 241
Ittleson, Roslyn, 159
Izumi, Kiyoshi, 79

Jacobs, Jane, 52, 69, 153, 156
Jakle, John A., 239
Janeway, Elizabeth, 213
Janisova, Helena, 130–1
Japan, 48, 50, 54, 59, 130, 190, 197, 204
Jeskovits, Melville J., 23
Johns Hopkins University, 216
Joiner, Duncan, 230
Jones, Emrys, 141–2
Jones, Holway R., 237
Jorgenson, Lisa, 40

Kantor, Amos, 81
Kaplan, Stephen, 28
Kasmar, J., 97–8
Kates, Robert W., 80
Katz, Daniel, 114
Katz, Robert D., 202
Kaufman, Edgar, Jr., 44
Kaufman, Harold, 37
Keller, Suzanne, 100, 112, 120, 152, 161, 164
Kemnitzer, Luis S., 135
Kennedy, Donald, 62
Kennedy, Margrit, 145

Kennedy, Robert Woods, 214
Kepes, Georgy, 66, 75–6
Kerr, Madeleine, 176, 177, 187
Kibbutz, 182–3
Kilbridge, Maurice, 57
Korea, 221
Krantz, Peter, 124
Kriesburgh, Louis, 119–20
Kunze, Donald, 97
Kuper, Leo, 145–6, 163
Kurtz, Stephen A., 221

Lamanna, Richard, 146
Land use, 55, 57, 91, 125–8
Lansing, John B., 46, 145, 147–8
Laslett, Peter, 139–40
Lazarfeld, P. F., 133
Learning space (see Education)
Le Corbusier, 164, 207
Lee, David R., 220
Lee, Hyo-Jae, 221
Lee, Terence, 22, 74, 82–4, 168
Leisure time (see Recreation)
Lerup, Lars, 218
Lieberman, James E., 9
Liebman, Jon, C., 184
Lifson, Ben, 224
Lima, Peru, 171
Linn, Karl, 182
Lintell, Mark, 191
Litwaks, Eugene, 223
London, England, 30, 58, 116–18, 130 151, 171, 202, 232
Loring, William C., 51–3
Los Angeles, Calif., 82
Lowenthal, David, 135
Lynch, Kevin, 16, 21, 22, 23, 81, 151, 168

MacMurray, Trevor, 128
MacNair, Malcolm, 173, 175
Maddi, Salvatore R., 76–7
Mahler, Stuart, 185
Maki, Fumihiko, 74, 77
Maltby, James, 49

Mann, Lawrence D., 100, 167, 241
Mann, Peter H., 115, 163, 172, 173–4
Marans, A. E., 182
Marans, Robert W., 46, 147–8
Marcuse, Peter, 172, 174
Markman, Robert, 27
Markus, Thomas A., 72
Marshall, David, 219
Marshall, Nancy J., 57, 58
Martin, Ann, 150
Martin, Cecily, 49
Martin, Richard, 44
Martineau, Thomas R., 125
Maslow, A. H., 3, 4, 7, 8, 85
Massachusetts Institute of Technology, 111, 113
Mather, William G., 214
Maw, Ray, 126, 130, 169, 171
May, J. Thomas, 45
McCue, Gerald, 70
McKay, Henry, 180
McKechnie, George, 31
McKenzie, R. D., 89–90, 152, 153
McKie, Robert, 145, 147
McKinley, Daniel, 238
McPherson, J. Miller, 51, 55
McQuade, Walter, 240–1
Mead, Margaret, 132, 134, 181, 209, 210, 213
Meier, R. L., 56, 107, 108, 110, 122, 213
Men, 10, 11
Mental health, 8–10, 55, 61, 66, 78, 90, 101, 109, 111, 189, 194–5, 215–17
Mexico City, 11
Meyer, J. R., 16
Meyerson, Martin, 206, 207
Michaels, R. M., 186
Michelson, William, 93, 100, 102–3, 133–4, 163
Midwest Research Institute, 70
Migration, 4
Miller, A., 181
Miller, J. M., 52, 53
Mills, William E., 122, 123

Milne, Murray A., 75, 84
Mitchell, R. B., 162
Mlynarski, F. Gernan, 29
Mogey, J. M., 187, 200, 201
Moleski, Walter H., 231
Moller, Clifford B., 10
Montessori, Maria, 213, 232, 233
Montgomery, Roger, 86, 200, 203, 238
Morris, Robert, 149
Mumford, Lewis, 75–6, 139, 163, 165, 213
Murray, J. S., 234

Nakanishi, Naomichi, 130
National Institute of Child Health and Human Development, 216
Neighborhood, 39, 46, 61, 107, 109, 111, 113, 120, 138, 152, 159–91, 205, 239
Neighboring, 111–20, 147, 164, 173
Netherlands, 195
New, Peter Kong Ming, 45, 132, 135
New towns, 105, 118, 129, 138, 145–8, 162, 170
New York City, 37, 40, 51–2, 116, 156, 171, 221
Newark, N.J., 180
Newling, B. E., 56
Nicholson, Charles, 200, 204, 209
Nigeria, 189
North Carolina, 97, 236
North Carolina State University, 27
Norway, 142
Nubians, 220

O'Block, Robert, 57
Olson, Leonard, Jr., 99
Osgood, Charles, 132–4
Overcrowding, 52–5, 63, 180, 231
Owen, Robert, 140

Packard, Vance, 111
Pande, Shashi K., 7
Papageorgiou, G. A., 56
Papaioannou, J. G., 56

Pappas, P., 56, 172
Park, Robert Ezra, 73, 89, 90, 94, 95, 152, 154–5
Park, Forest, Ill., 114
Parkin John C., 65
Parr, A. E., 74–5, 78, 80–1, 83, 141–2
Parsons, Sir John H., 14–15
Participation, 34–48, 71, 85, 95, 104, 122, 123, 132, 134, 240
Pattern language, 65, 84–6
Pearson, Norman, 167
Peattie, Lisa R., 40, 41
Pedestrian
  paths, 77, 151, 207
  perception, 15, 17, 149–51, 181
  planning for, 150, 163, 240
  shopping centers, 143, 147
Pei, I. M., 221
Perception
  cultural conditioning, 59
  design for, 77–8, 80, 231
  distance, 22–3
  environmental quality, 46, 238
  neighborhood, 157, 168–9
  sensory experience, 76, 79, 93
  space, 92, 149–51, 222, 239
  structure of cities, 31, 68, 71
  (see also Visual perception, Auditory perception)
Perin, Constance, 100, 101, 104, 220, 222
Perraton, Jean K., 119
Perry, Clarence, 158–9, 162–5, 167
Personal space, 59–63, 71, 188, 218, 225–6, 228, 230, 233, 239
Peru, 85
Peterson, George, 26, 81, 186
Philadelphia, Pa., 194, 207
Philippedes, Dimitri, 49
Phillips, George W., 171
Photography, 25–30, 222
Piaget, Jean, 220, 226, 228
Piers, Maria, 233
Pioro, Zygmunt, 164–5, 201–2
Pitt, Gillian M., 118, 129

Pittsburgh, Pa., 44, 145
Planning Research Unit, University of Edinburgh, 34
Plant, James S., 180
Poland, 201
Pollowy, Anne-Marie, 72, 128
Pollution - Noise, 18, 191, 234
Popenoe, David, 239
Population, 172–5
Porteous, J. Douglas, 71
Pradhan, Panna Lal, 24
Praff, C. E., 65
Prague, Czechoslovakia, 130
Preiser, Wolfgang E., 99
Pritchard, Norman, 145, 146
Privacy
  acoustic, 18, 19, 21, 147, 234
  concept of, 76
  density, 51, 54, 56, 200
  family, 57–9, 183, 214
  housing, 26, 67, 202, 210
  human need, 181, 192, 226
  visual, 84
Proshansky, Harold M., 239–40, 241
Proxemics (see Personal space)
Pruitt Igoe, St. Louis, 196, 200, 205
Psychiatrist, 7, 210, 216
Psychoanalysis, 6, 155
Psycholinguistics, 134
Psychology, 134
Puerto Rico, 188, 197

Quarry Hill Flats, UK, 104, 206

Radburn, 206, 207, 208
Rainwater, Lee, 200, 202, 205, 213, 215, 220
Rand, George, 23, 24
Randall, Edwina, 185
Rappoport, Amos, 63, 81
Ravetz, Alison, 104, 206
Ravitz, Mel J., 170
Recreation, 5, 110, 124–5, 128–31, 143, 147, 170–1, 173, 184, 201

Reichek, Jesse, 81–2
Reiss, A. J., Jr., 236
Relocation, 188 (see also Human needs, roots)
Research techniques, 28–32
Retirement colonies, 106
Reynolds, Ingrid, 200, 204, 209
Reynolds, Josephine P., 38–9
Richards, Cara E., 169, 170–1
Richardson, N. H., 39
Reimer, Svend H., 8, 162, 223, 236
Rigby, Alan G., 39
Ritter, Paul, 206, 207
Rivlin, Leeann G., 239–40, 241
Rockford, Ill., 207
Roe, Bjorn, 49
Rogler, L. H., 197
Role identification, 109, 230
Room, 4, 137, 138, 225–9 (see also Personal space)
Rosenberg, Gerhardt, 52, 54, 183
Rosow, I., 101
Rossi, Peter H., 222, 223
Rothblatt, Donald N., 195
Rozelle, Richard M., 25
Rudofsky, Bernard, 150
Rusch, Charles W., 97
Rushton, G., 172
Russia, 167

Saarinen, Thomas F., 238–9
Safdie, Moshe, 213
Safety
  automobile, 15, 16
  human needs, 3, 4, 7
  neighborhood, 26, 107, 202
  pedestrian, 240
Saille, David G., 208
Sanitation, 2, 3, 8
Sanoff, Henry, 26, 30, 168–9, 186, 209
Sauer, G. C., Jr., 29
Sauer, Louis, 219
Sawhney, M., 209
Shacter, Stanley, 111, 112, 113

Schmitt, Robert C., 52, 53, 54
School, 5, 11, 17, 234 (see also Education)
Schorr, Alvin L., 102, 197
Schweitzer, E., 27
Scott, James, 30
Seaton, R. W., 28, 29
Segall, Marshall H., 23
Sekler, P., 207
Self-help, housing, 48–50, 70, 198
Semantic differential, 27, 32, 132, 133
Sensory perception (see Perception)
Shepard, Paul, 238
Shopping centers, 129, 143–5
Sieverts, Thomas, 43
Simmie, J. M., 39–40
Singapore, 199
Sinton, David, 24, 218
Site planning, 79–80, 102, 117
Sitte, Camillo, 140
Skinner, B. F., 8
Slayton, William, 35, 36
Sloan, Sam A., 227, 228
Slums, 49–50, 101, 105, 176, 178, 188, 190, 197, 200–1, 202, 205, 233
Smith, Richard Alan, 59
Smithson, Allison and Peter, 68, 69
Social anthropologist, 189
Social class, 3, 37, 40–2, 91–2, 117, 120, 155, 159, 172, 173, 178–9, 182, 189, 192, 197, 200, 232
Social disorganization, 52, 54, 161
Social ecology, 88, 152, 156
Social psychology, 5, 7, 114, 115
Social science, 132–5, 137, 163
Sociologists, 92, 93, 95, 134, 152–3, 157, 221
Soen, Dan, 120, 173
Solow, Anatole, 164, 165
Sommer, Robert, 60–3, 69
Sonnenfeld, Joseph, 81, 104
Sorokin, Pitirim, 121–2
Southworth, Michael, 19, 20
Spencer, Paul, 191

Spiegel, Hans B. C., 41
Spivack, Mayer, 17, 183
Squares, 141, 143
Squatters, 40, 44, 171, 196, 199, 218
Stea, David, 26, 60, 96
Stein, Clarence, 162, 165, 167, 207, 208
Stein, Maurice, 153, 155
Steinetz, Carl, 74, 82
Stephens, P. H. M., 56
Still, Henry, 19, 20
Stokols, Daniel, 60, 63, 231
Stone, G., 144
Stuart, Darwin G., 150
Studer, Raymond G., 96, 97
Suci, George J., 133–4
Summers, Luis H., 219
Syracuse, N.Y., 119
Szalai, A., 122, 123

Taira, Koji, 50, 190–1, 204
Tannebaum, Judith, 161
Tannenbaum, Percy H., 133–4
Taylor, G. Brooke, 145, 147
Team 10, 65, 66
Teenagers (see Youth)
Television, 130
Teplitz, Paul, 57
Territoriality (see Personal space)
Thakurdesai, 220, 221
Theil, Philip, 17, 74, 77
Theordorson, G., 236
Thomas, William L., Jr., 92
Tiger, Lionel, 10, 11
Time budget, 121–25, 128, 130, 171
Tomeh, Aida K., 119
Traffic density, 191
Transportation, 66, 69, 147, 162–3, 171, 192 (see also Automobile, Pedestrian)
Turner, John F. C., 70, 196, 199–200
Tyrwhitt, Jaqueline, 165, 166, 207, 242

United Kingdom, 129, 142, 144, 160, 168, 177, 188, 201, 206

behavior settings, 95
children, 181
community studies, 153, 156, 176
consumer behavior, 144
family, 115
housing, 24, 25, 30, 116, 187, 204, 218
pre-industrial England, 140
public participation, 38–40
workers, 227–8
Urban design, 2, 41, 48–9, 61, 69, 71, 73, 78, 82, 102, 144, 238
Urban ecology (see Human ecology)
Urban form (see Urban design)
Urban renewal, 4, 35–9, 41, 45, 145, 156, 186, 190, 237
Urban sprawl, 69, 159
Urban structures, 2, 127
Urban sub-center, 137–40
Urbanization, 7, 75, 91, 139–40, 155, 161, 192, 226
Useem, Ruth Hill, 117
Utopia, 5, 140, 167

Vacation (see Recreation)
Vancouver, B.C., 231
Vapnarsky, C. A., 102
Varming, Michael, 17–18
Vash, Carolyn L., 34
Vigier, Francoise, 73, 78
Violence, 10
Visual perception, 15–18, 21–28, 79 (see also Perception)

Walkeley, Rosabelle Price, 9, 215, 216
Walker, Geoffrey, 39
Wallace, A., 194
Wallin, Paul, 115
Warner, Lloyd, 155
Warren, Ronald Leslie, 237
Washington, D.C., 131, 178
Webber, Carolyn C., 92
Webber, Melvin M., 92, 107, 109
Weil, Simone, 3–5

Weiss, Shirley, 236
Welfare system, 200, 205
Wendt, John S., 28
Wekerle, Gerda, 205
Wellman, Barry, 241
Wells, Brian, 229
Whitaker, Marilyn, 241
Whyte, William H., Jr., 107, 114, 155
Wicker, Allan W., 99
Williams, M. G., 208
Willis, Margaret, 58, 145, 147, 200, 202
Willmott, Peter, 58, 116–17
Wilner, Daniel, 9, 215, 216
Wilson, James Q., 36–7, 237
Wirth, Louis, 90–1, 152
Wober, Mallory, 189–90
Wolff, Sula, 183–4
Women, 33, 115, 117–18, 144, 168, 177, 226
Wood, Elizabeth, 198
Woods Hole, Mass., 106

Worcester, Mass., 24
Work, 4, 50, 60, 125, 190, 226
Work space, 227–32
Wright, Henry, 206, 207
Wright, Henry, Jr., 208
Wylie, Laurence, 155

Yancey, William L., 205
Young, Michae., 116–17
Youth
    facilities for, 182, 184, 198
    family system, 7
    juvenile delinquency, 55, 78, 89, 141, 154, 184, 198
    shopping, 144

Zambia, 44
Zannaras, Georgia, 31
Zehner, Robert B., 145, 148
Zeisel, John, 203
Zisman, S. B., 149

Lewis and Clark College - Watzek Library

Z5942 .B35   wmain
Bell, Gwen/Urban environments and human

3 5209 00408 6068